PKZIP, LHARC & Co.

The Ultimate Data Compression Book

by Istok Kespret

A Data Becker Book

Copyright © 1995   Abacus
                         5370 52nd Street SE
                         Grand Rapids, MI 49512

Copyright © 1993   Data Becker, GmbH
                         Merowingerstrasse 30
                         4000 Duesseldorf, Germany

Managing Editor: Scott Slaughter
Editor: Louise Benzer
Technical Editor: Gene Traas, George Miller
Book Design: Scott Slaughter
Cover Art: Abby Grinnell, John Plummer

This book is copyrighted. No part of this book may be reproduced, stored in a retrieval system, or transmitted in any form or by any means, electronic, mechanical, photocopying, recording or otherwise without the prior written permission of Abacus Software or Data Becker, GmbH.

Every effort has been made to ensure complete and accurate information concerning the material presented in this book. However, Abacus Software can neither guarantee nor be held legally responsible for any mistakes in printing or faulty instructions contained in this book. The authors always appreciate receiving notice of any errors or misprints.

This book contains trade names and trademarks of several companies. Any mention of these names or trademarks in this book are not intended to either convey endorsement or other associations with this book.

Printed in the U.S.A.

ISBN 1-55755-203-7

10 9 8 7 6 5 4

Contents

1 Data Compression 1

Uses for data compression programs 1
About this book 2
Why Compress Data? 2
Advantages of data compression programs 3
Overview of Data Compression 4
Types of compression 4
Reducing text files 7
Data Compression In Detail 10
How does this method work? 10
Huffman method 11
Structure of the new codes 12
How space is saved 14
Comparing Compression Programs 16
How we tested the compression programs 16
Results of the tests 17
What do the results mean? 19
Using a cache program 21

2 Data Compression Elements 23

Data Compression Command Line Structure 23
Data compression components 24
Archive Files 25
Structure of archives 26
Self-extracting Archives 27
Structure of an SFX archive 28

EXE Compression Programs	29
Making programs smaller	29
New programs	29
Data Compression Shells	**29**
How data compression shells work	30
Data Compression Terms	**31**

3 Using Compression Programs 35

Compressing Individual Files 35
- From drive to archive 36
- Update 37
- Freshen 38
- Move 40
- Changing the way Move works 40
- Listing archive contents 43
- File lists 45
- Excluding files from an archive 47

Compressing Directories 48
- Recursive search 48
- Using LHA 49
- Using PKZIP 51
- Using ARJ 54
- Empty directories 55

Editing Archives 56
- Examining the archive 57
- PKPAK 58
- LHA and LH-ICE 59
- Temporary directories 60
- PKZIP 62
- ARJ 63
- ZOO 65

Using Batch Files to Compress Data 66

4 Decompressing Data 71

Integrated or diversified 71

Contents

Decompressing Archives 72
- Selecting working directories 74
- Creating directories 74
- Preventing prompts 77
- Protecting existing files 77
- Switching off safety prompts 79
- ARJ 79
- LHA and ICE 80
- PAK 82
- ZOO 83
- PKUNZIP 83
- PKUNPAK 84

Decompressing Directories 85
- Relative and absolute paths 86
- Restoring directory structures 86
- PKUNZIP 87
- LHA and ICE 88
- ARJ 90

Damaged Archives 91

5 Self-Extracting Archives 97

Structure of SFX archives 97
Using Self-Extracting Archives 98
- SFX archives and ARJ 99
- ARJSFX features 100
- ARJ's mini mini-module 103
- SFX archives and LHA 103
- LHA's SFX modules 104
- Functions of the LHA SFX module 105
- Automatic batch files 105
- SFX archives and PKZIP 106
- PKSFX archive options 107
- SFX archives and PAK 108
- Combining SFX archives 109

Identifying SFX Archives 111
Tips On Self-Extracting Archives 117
- Root directories 117

Contents

6 Advanced Data Compression Features .. 119

Password Protection **119**
    Scrambling and garbling 120
    Entering the password 121
    Accessing protected archives 122
    Protecting SFX archives 123
    Password protection limitations 124

Comments **125**
    Using comments in PKZIP 126
    Comments in ZOO 127
    Comments in ARJ 128

Time Stamps **131**
    ARJ and time stamps 133

Using Attributes to Select Files **135**
    Attribute masking 139

Data Compression Methods **139**
    ARJ: Six methods 139
    PKZIP is flexible 142
    Compatibility of compression methods 143

Using ARJ As a Multi-packer **145**
    Creating a simple multi-volume archive 145
    Optimizing memory space 148
    Combining commands 150
    Using batch files to check files 152
    Extracting multi-volume archives 154
    Listing multi-volume archives 155

7 EXE Compressors 157

    How EXE Compressors Work 157
    COM and EXE file structures 158
    Limitations of program compressors 158
    Using EXE compressors 159

LZEXE **159**
    Windows programs and LZEXE 161
    Compressing COM files 161

Contents

PKLite 162
- Compressing programs 162
- Overlays 164
- Decompressing programs 165
- Options 165

DIET 166
- Compressing files 166
- DIET *.COM 168
- Managing files 169
- Compressing problem files 170
- Decompressing files 173
- Memory-resident DIET 174
- Temporary directory 175
- Deactivating DIET 175
- Example 177

8 Command Summary And Switches 181
- Errorlevel basics 181

ARJ 2.30 182
- Syntax 182
- Restrictions 182
- Memory requirements 183
- Commands 183
- Switches 193
- Extended switches 204

LHA 2.13 212
- Syntax 212
- Commands 212
- Options 215
- ERRORLEVELS 221

PKZIP/PKUNZIP 222
- PKZIP - Syntax 222
- PKUNZIP - Syntax 222
- Commands 222
- ERRORLEVELs in PKZIP 231
- ERRORLEVELs in PKUNZIP 232

Contents

ZOO 233
    Syntax 233
    Commands 233
        ERRORLEVELS 236

Appendix 237

Index 239

Data Compression

Even if you're not aware of it, you've probably already used some type of data compression. Fax machines have been compressing data for years. Also, Microsoft, Borland, Lotus, Novell, and most other major software publishers use data compression for distributing the programs included in their software packages. If you've ever used CompuServe, Prodigy, America Online, or other online services, then you've used data compression to download files to your PC.

If the term "data compression" is new, you may have heard some of the other terms used for data compression. Maybe you've heard it called packing, squeezing, squashing, crunching, etc.

Data compression lowers the cost of passing data from one medium to another. So you can send and receive information more economically. Data compression is also useful when you back up your hard drive because fewer tapes or diskettes are needed.

Although the concept of data compression was originally developed to make data communication more cost effective, it has become extremely useful for both software developers and users.

Now there are several data compression programs. Many of these programs first appeared as shareware. These programs are usually well worth their low price, especially since most software companies distribute their programs in compressed form. Often, these companies use some variation of these shareware programs as part of their installation procedure. This is one reason why data compression programs are so popular.

Uses for data compression programs

Like most users, you probably think that the data on your PC takes up too much disk space. Data compression programs make it possible to reduce the amount of disk space needed by your data. For some types of data, a typical data compression program can decrease the required amount of disk space by 50% to 90%.

If you connect to one of the many bulletin boards using a modem, you can decrease telephone charges by compressing files. Also, a compressed file can be transferred more quickly than an uncompressed file. So, bulletin board systems have also

1. Data Compression

played a major role in the spread of data compression programs. Most of the popular data compression programs are available directly from the bulletin board.

It's relatively easy to compress and decompress data. Recently the number of data compression programs has dramatically increased. Also, the range of functions in these programs has increased.

Today, some data compression programs can be used as backup systems, can write one archive to several diskettes, and can process directory trees node by node. You can even find data compression programs that use 80386 or 80486 processors and special types of memory.

Obviously, when features are added, the program becomes more complex. Most of the features are specified by adding parameters or switches to the commands. Since this process can be confusing, it's difficult to utilize the hidden power of these data compression programs.

About this book

In this book, we'll discuss data compression in general. We won't focus on a particular program. Instead, we'll explain how and what to compress and how to retrieve your data. You'll also find information about the advanced features of data compression programs. This information will help you get the most from your compression program.

We've also included information on all the parameters and options of the data compression programs discussed in this book. Since you probably aren't familiar with all the programs introduced in this book, you'll have a chance to see what these programs have to offer. For example, you may find that another program works faster or is easier to run.

Why Compress Data?

Eventually, most computer users discover that they don't have enough hard drive space for all their data and programs. One way to solve this problem is to buy a second hard drive. However, it seems that the more hard drive space you have, the more you need. Another solution is to back up (temporarily store) data you're not using on diskettes. Unfortunately, doing this can be time-consuming.

As we mentioned, users who send data over telephone lines with a modem were the first ones to use data compression programs. Since each minute saved during data transfer saved money, data compression became very important for these users.

1. Data Compression

Now other computer users are looking for ways to minimize the amount of data transferred not only over telephone lines, but also to external media, such as floppy diskettes. Backing up the data even on a modest sized hard drive can require dozens of floppy diskettes. However, a program that compresses data can significantly reduce the number of floppy diskettes needed.

There are also ways to reduce the amount of space for data on the hard drive. Modern hard drives use a storage method that yields a higher capacity in the same amount of space than hard drives that use other coding methods. Although the hardware already codes and optimizes the data, there are transparent data compression programs, such as Stacker™ or DoubleSpace™, that achieve an even higher increase in storage capacity.

Advantages of data compression programs

Therefore, many programs devoted exclusively to data compression and decompression have been created. Compared to their hardware counterparts, in which special chips in the PC perform data compression, software data compression programs have obvious advantages:

> ➢ Flexibility: Since it's software, a data compression program can be quickly adapted as new developments and improvements in data compression algorithms become available.

> ➢ Low Cost: As you know, hardware is expensive. Because the majority of data compression programs are available as public domain software or shareware, they are more affordable than purchasing new hardware.

Within a short time period, dozens of data compression programs have appeared. Some of the most popular ones are PKZIP, LHARC, ARJ, and LZEXE. Also, many data compression programs are continuously being improved.

Many data compression programs are distributed as shareware. The authors request payment of a specific fee in return for granting you the right to use the program. If you benefit from any shareware programs, register with the author of the program and send him/her the fee they deserve. It's worth your time because the programmer will be motivated to improve and polish his or her product.

> The programs ICE, LHARC, and LHA are from the same developer and follow one another in chronological order. LHARC is one of the classic data compression programs. In this book, we'll base our discussion on the newest version, LHA 2.13. The differences between this version and the older versions mainly involve the enhanced options.

1. Data Compression

Overview of Data Compression

Because this book doesn't contain a lot of technical information, we won't discuss the latest modifications of compression algorithms. Instead, this book is written for the average computer user who wants to know more about data compression.

We'll begin with a brief overview of data compression. This should help you understand the basics of this process.

Types of compression

The type of data compression you use mainly depends on the type of file you want to compress. If a file contains various types of information, it's more difficult to compress the file. For example, let's look at the following file, which shows only the following information when we display it at the DOS prompt using the DIR command:

```
DIR BIG.DAT
```

```
Volume in drive E: is:  It's true!
Directory of E:\WORD\PACKER

BIG.DAT        1180      12-14-92     8:30p
    1 File(s)                    1188 bytes
            10420224 bytes free
```

In this example, we have a file named BIG.DAT, which is 1188 characters in size. This isn't a large file considering that this hard drive has 104 Meg free. If we display the file, by entering

```
TYPE BIG.DAT
```

the following appears on the screen:

1. Data Compression

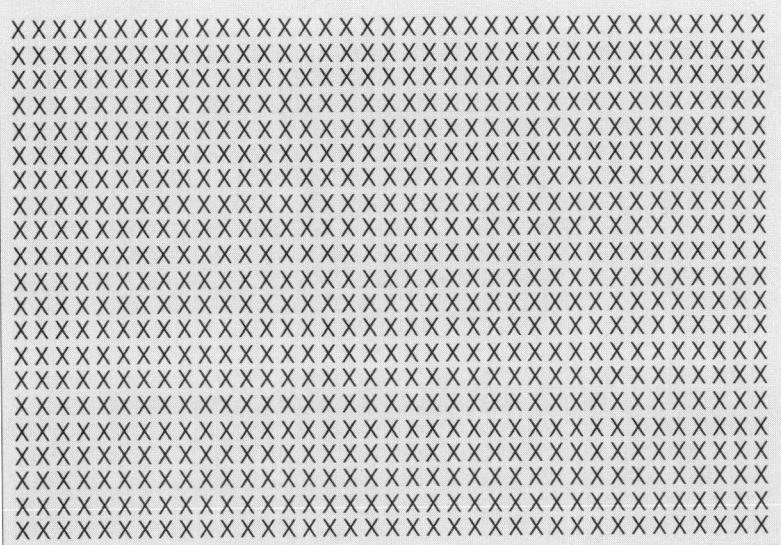

As you can see, this file is simply a sequence of 1,188 "x"s. Instead of wasting all this space by storing all the "x"s separately, we can simply store the number of "x"s. By doing this, we can reduce the file information to a compact form:

```
TYPE SMALL.DAT
x1188
```

Only 5 bytes are needed to save BIG.DAT in a compressed form. This results in a compression ratio of more than 1% of the original size of the file.

According to this method, a file is arranged according to the frequency of specific characters. A table records how often a specific character appears in the file. So, the principle of "X1188" is simply taken one step further.

You may think that you couldn't use this method to compress any of your files. Even if there were any such files, they would probably be nonsensical like our example. Obviously, there aren't very many words with long enough sequences of the same letter. For example, using this method, we could reduce the nonsensical word "Millleader" to the following:

```
MI3LEADER
```

As you can see, we saved only one character. This example also clearly shows this compression method isn't suitable for text files. However, this method is suitable for another type of file: Graphic files. PCs must process an enormous amount of graphic data. Some very complex algorithms are used to reduce the gigantic flow of data in graphic files. A popular format for storing graphics is called the PCX format. For example, the Windows Paintbrush program uses PCX files.

1. Data Compression

The DOS screen as a PCX file

As you can see in the above figure, a program made a "snapshot" of the DOS screen and then converted it into PCX graphics format. Much of the graphics information in the figure appears more than once. Therefore, it would be a waste of memory space if each dot on the screen were assigned a corresponding 1:1 information ratio in the file.

With a resolution of 2,000 characters on a normal text screen and a VGA resolution of 9 x 16 dots per character, 288,000 dots of information must be stored in black and white. If the graphic is in color, then various color mixtures per dot are added, and the information requirements are significantly increased. However, if you look at the actual size of the file, you'll see that it isn't very large:

As you can see, the size of the file has been drastically reduced. We used the method we just discussed to do this. We'll show you a small portion of this FIGURE.PCX file and explain it to you. For example, three byte combinations occur frequently:

1. Data Compression

How a PCX entry is encoded

The FF 00 entry is compressed. The secret lies in the top two bits (bits 6 and 7) of the first byte. If both of these bits are set, then the remaining 6 bits are a repetition factor. Since all the remaining bits are set, the factor is 63.

The color information of the next byte (00, or black) is repeated 63 times as a dot of the graphic. If the first two bits weren't 11, the rest of the byte would have to be interpreted as direct color code of a single graphic dot.

Reducing text files

As we've explained, a simple method of repetition counting won't work when the data is thoroughly mixed, as in text files, for example. To determine an appropriate compression method for these types of files, first you must understand how files and data are stored.

In the PC world, ASCII (American Standard Code for Information Interchange) is the standard code for data. ASCII specifies that all existing characters in the PC are assigned a specific code. This standardization makes it possible for information to be exchanged between different data processing systems. The ASCII code specifies a manageable length of a byte. Since a byte can take on 256 different combinations, there are 256 possible characters.

Perhaps you think 256 characters sounds like too many, considering that there are only 26 letters in the alphabet. However, these characters also include the 10 numerals, punctuation marks, and foreign characters. Graphic symbols, which create borders and lines on the screen in windows and dialog boxes, are also included. ASCII also includes the invisible characters that tell the printer to print

1. Data Compression

in bold, italics, etc.; these characters are called printer control codes. All of these codes come under the category of ASCII characters. There are three groups of character codes:

ASCII Code	Code group
0-31	Control characters
32-173	Text characters
174-255	Graphic characters

Basically, every file is an ASCII file because all the codes stored in the file are stored according to the ASCII standard (although there are some exceptions). In the narrowest definition of ASCII, an ASCII file is a text file. This type of file contains only information that can be read.

Now let's try to compress an ASCII file. Let's assume that a text file should use only codes 32 to 127. Now, if all the characters use a code that is less than 128, you can do without bit 8 of the ASCII code.

This is possible because one character or byte consists of 8 bits. A bit can take on one of two values: Either the value 1 or the value 0.

```
0000 0000  = 0   (all bits are 0)
0000 0001  = 1
0000 0010  = 2
...
...
0111 1111  = 127 (only bit 8 is 0)
...
1111 1110  = 254
1111 1111  = 255 (all bits are 1)
```

So, only 7 bits are needed to represent 128 different combinations. This is sufficient for all of the codes of text files. The leftmost digit of the byte, bit 8, is always 0 for text codes.

It's possible to create a method for converting or encoding the 7-bit code into 8-bit bytes. This would be another method of data compression.

1. Data Compression

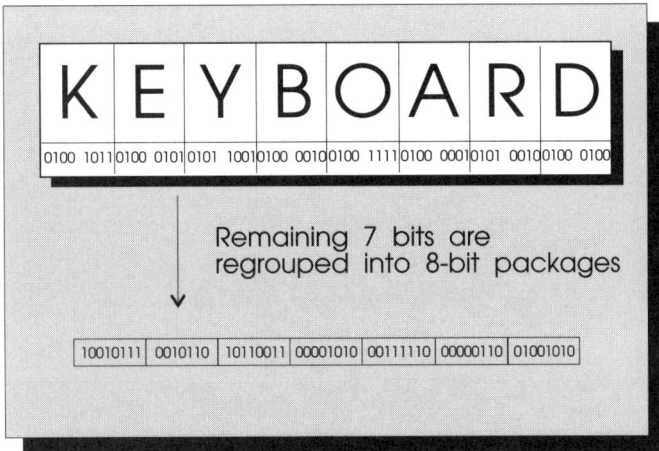

The word "KEYBOARD" being compressed

The above figure illustrates the idea behind this compression method. First, each letter of the word is assigned the corresponding ASCII code. To better represent the compression process, the code is represented as a binary number instead of a decimal number (i.e., the code consists of the appropriate combination of ones and zeros).

Next, the data is compressed. To do this, we ignore the eighth (leftmost) bit of all the characters (since it is always zero). The remaining seven bits give us a chain of 56 ones and zeros (8 letters x 7 bits), which are now regrouped into 8-bit packages and stored.

The file is now reduced to one eighth of the original size. As a result, we've encoded the original file. Using an ASCII table, you can determine which characters replace the word "Keyboard" in the file.

To restore such a file to its original state, simply extract seven bits at a time until the file is restored. To restore the original character, insert a 0 at the leftmost position of each group of seven bits (bit 8).

1. Data Compression

Decompression is compression in reverse

Data Compression In Detail

As you've seen in the previous section, it's possible to make files smaller. However, you're probably not impressed by a compression method that saves only 12.5% (an eighth) of your disk space.

We used text (ASCII) files as an example in the last section because the method won't work on program files. Unlike text files, with program files you cannot assume that the eighth bit of the data bytes will always be 0. So, for non-text files, you must use a completely different method.

How does this method work?

Remember that a byte consists of eight bits. So, each byte can represent one of 256 different values and, therefore, up to 256 characters.

Now we must determine how to compress a file that contains all 256 characters. All eight bits are needed to store the character as an ASCII code. If one bit is missing, the character cannot be reconstructed.

One solution is to assign a short code to the frequently-used characters and assign a longer code to the characters that are rarely used. This doesn't necessarily involve counting letters and using statistical data to change the ASCII codes yourself. Actually, although you won't change the ASCII code, you can create other bit combinations to recode various characters.

1. Data Compression

Huffman method

This is exactly what the Huffman method of data compression does. By assigning short bit patterns to the most frequently-used characters and long bit patterns to the less frequently-used characters, you can decrease the length of the characters below the default length of eight bits.

This method isn't a recent development. Instead, it's a mathematically-based analysis from the 1950s. This method is so safe that all fax devices use a variation based on the Huffman algorithm to compress and transmit information.

Most data compression programs are derived from a (usually modified) Huffman algorithm. Such methods are usually referred to as "squeezing." With this method, the type of code, whether its from the entire ASCII spectrum or whether the characters are even ASCII characters, isn't relevant.

Instead, you must determine the frequency of the characters being encoded. From the results of these frequency tests, the new bit patterns are formed. So, there are two steps in the Huffman algorithm:

1. Determining the number of times (frequency) each character appears in a file.

2. Creating an encoding scheme based on the frequency of each character.

We'll use an example to devise an encoding scheme to compress a file using the Huffman method.

To demonstrate this method, we can use a file of any size with any contents. For this example, we'll use a file called TEST.DAT. We could have also used a large executable file (a spreadsheet program with more than 600,000 bytes) or a large name and address file with hundreds of thousands of entries.

The following appears when we display the directory on our hard drive for this file:

TEST.DAT is 160 bytes long. This is large enough for our example, but the file could also be any other size.

The contents of the file are more important than the size of the file for the Huffman algorithm. First, we must count all the different characters contained in the file. The results are as follows:

1. Data Compression

Counting characters in TEST.DAT

Although we don't know the purpose of the file, we do know that the file contains only the letters T, W, X, C, B, O, and A.

The sequence of the characters in the file isn't important for the compression method. The way the letters in the figure are arranged isn't important either. The table is arranged like this only to make it easier to see the codes in the figures.

Structure of the new codes

Remember our rule for encoding characters: The most frequently used characters have short codes, while the least frequently used characters have long codes.

First, we'll choose the two characters that appear least frequently in the file. From the above figure, you can see that these characters are "X", which appears 3 times, and "W", which appears 12 times. Both characters are "combined" to form a node. The contents of this node are the sum of both frequencies, 3 + 12 = 15.

The first node

At this point, we're no longer concerned with the two original values, 12 and 3. Instead, we'll include the contents of this node as we search for the next pair of characters with the lowest frequencies. This time we find the letter "C", which appears 18 times, and the node made up of W and X appears 15 times. As a result, we have a new node made up of this node pair with a combined value of 33.

1. Data Compression

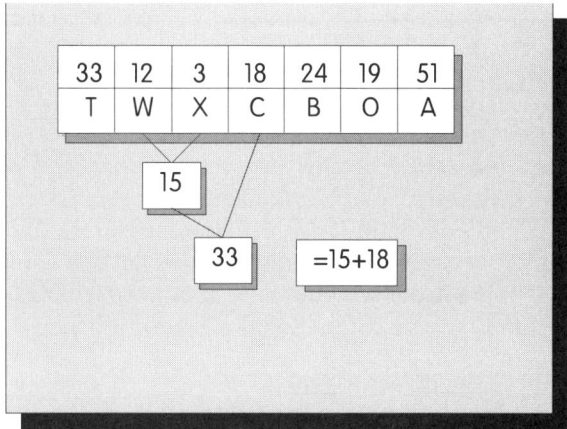

Finding the second node

As you can see, this procedure is actually rather simple. Notice that the value 33 appears twice. However, this isn't a problem.

Continue this method of finding the least frequently used node. When there are no more pairs left to compare, you've reached the bottom (or first) node. This is called the root or anchor, because it's only possible to enter this tree-like structure through the root.

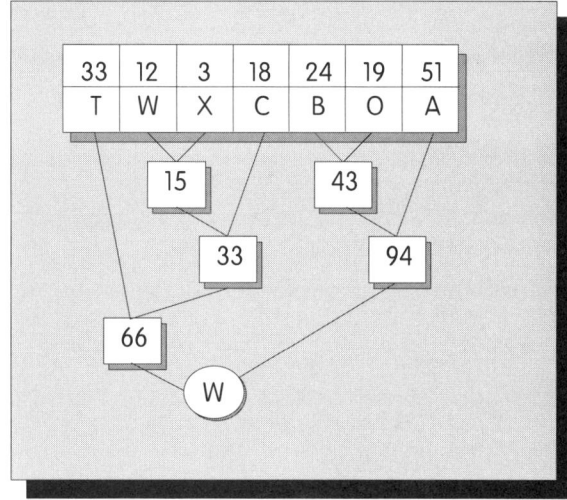

The completed binary tree

1. Data Compression

The tree structure created by repeatedly searching for the smallest value pairs is important to the computer world. This structure is also called a binary tree, because there are a maximum of two branching options from each node.

Now we must determine how to use this binary tree to create an encoding scheme to compress our data. As you can see, there are only two ways to leave a node. Also remember that a bit can have only two values (zero or one). The next step is to start at the root, and at each node decide whether you should move in the direction of the left or right character. If you move to the left of the node, then you will encode a zero; if you move to the right of the node, you'll encode a one. When you reach the top branch, you've completed the encoding scheme for the file.

The following steps are needed for the letter "T":

- ➢ Start at the root
- ➢ **Left(0)** to node 66
- ➢ **Left(0)** to "T"
- ➢ New code ---> **00**

Use the same procedure for the long path to the "X":

- ➢ Start at the root
- ➢ **Left(0)** to node 66
- ➢ **Right(1)** to node 33
- ➢ **Left(0)** to node 15
- ➢ **Right(1)** to target "X"
- ➢ New code is **0101**

The figure on the following page displays the new codes and provides an overview of all the paths from the root to the target letter.

How space is saved

As you can see in the previous figure, characters that occur frequently, such as "A" or "T", receive short 2 bit codes, while characters that don't occur frequently (W or X) have longer 4 bit codes.

You can easily determine the compression ratio.

The original file, TEST.DAT, consists of 160 characters.

- ➢ 160 characters x 8 bits = 1,280 bits

1. Data Compression

Determining the new codes

The calculation for the new file, called TEST.CMP, look as follows:

Character	Number	Code	Total
T	33	2 bits	66 bits
W	12	4 bits	48 bits
X	3	4 bits	12 bits
C	18	3 bits	54 bits
B	24	3 bits	72 bits
O	19	3 bits	57 bits
A	51	2 bits	102 bits
Total	160		411 bits

From the original 1,290 bits, we now have 411. With this method, the file was compressed to 32% of its original size.

After determining the codes, the program must run through the entire file a second time. This time, the program reads every character and replaces it with its shortened code. It's also important to save the code tree in the file. The only way to decompress the compressed file is to use this tree. However, this decreases the compression ratio, because the tree also requires disk space.

1. Data Compression

As you can see, you must be very careful when you compress and decompress files. If even the smallest bit in the file is lost or set incorrectly (0 instead 1), then the file will probably be worthless.

Comparing Compression Programs

Now that you know the theory behind compression methods, we'll discuss which programs are best suited for compressing certain files.

How we tested the compression programs

To determine which compression program should be used with specific files, we performed some experiments using the following hardware:

- 486-33
- 170 HD hard drive
- 8 Meg of RAM

> You should be able to reproduce our results on your computer system. However, remember that as the quality of the hardware increases, so does the speed of the data compression program.

The first time we ran our tests, we didn't use a software cache program. The second time we ran the tests, we used a cache program called Norton Cache 6.0 and reserved two Meg of expanded memory. The differences between the two test runs are significant.

After compressing a file and recording the results, we deleted the files to save hard drive space. This prevented the system from slowing down when accessing data. We tried to use the same starting conditions for each compression program.

We used Version 6.0 of the Norton Control Center as our timekeeper. A small batch file controlled the stopwatch, starting it when the program began compressing and stopping when the program finished. The few hundredths of a second that elapsed between the time the watch started and the program began compressing occurred while all the programs were running.

The following is the batch file we used to record the compression times. If you have Norton's Control Center, you can run your own tests.

1. Data Compression

```
@ECHO OFF

NCC /START /C:"Starting PKZIP">PKZIP.DAT
PKZIP TEST *.BAK

NCC /STOP /C:"Stopping PKZIP">>PKZIP.DAT
ECHO.
TYPE PKZIP.DAT
```

For example, this batch file is suitable for running a test with PKZIP, which compresses all the BAK files of the current directory. Before the program starts, Control Center records the current time in the PKZIP.DAT file and starts the stopwatch. After PKZIP finishes, the current time is stored in PKZIP.DAT. The start and stop times are saved in this file and can be checked. A test run might look as follows:

```
C:\>test.bat

PKZIP (R)   FAST!   Create/Update Utility   Version 2.04g   02-01-93
Copr. 1989-1993 PKWARE Inc.  All Rights Reserved.  Shareware Version
PKZIP Reg. U.S. Pat. and Tm. Off.   Patent No. 5,051,745

■ 80486 CPU detected.
■ XMS version 3.00 detected.
■ Novell Netware version 3.11 detected.
■ Using Normal Compression.

Updating ZIP: TEST.ZIP
Updating: CONFIG.BAK     Deflating (29%), done.
Updating: AUTOEXEC.BAK   Deflating (28%), done.
Updating: START.BAK      Deflating (12%), done.
Updating: TEST1.BAK      Deflating (58%), done.

                         Starting PKZIP 5:55 pm, Monday, October 25, 1993
                         Stopping PKZIP 5:55 pm, Monday, October 25, 1993

                                                             1 second
:\>
```

TEST.BAT timing PKZIP

Results of the tests

The following tables show which compression programs work best with which files. We tested the following programs:

- ARJ 2.30
- LHA 2.13
- PKZIP 1.10
- ZOO 2.01

We used the latest versions of the compression programs for the tests. You'll find more detailed descriptions of the programs we tested later.

1. Data Compression

It's interesting to study the compression ratios achieved by compression programs with different types of files. As you may have realized when we introduced the data compression algorithms, the type of file plays an important role in which compression method is used.

The following are the most frequently used and important file types:

File type	Amount of data (bytes)
Text files	2,298,642
dBase databases	2,126,962
DOS programs	1,182,267
Windows programs	2,487,152
PCX graphic files	2,328,683
TIF graphic files	845,077

"Amount of data" indicates the size of all the files that the programs archived together.

Type	ARJ	LHA	PKZIP	ZOO
Text files	9.7	10.1	11.4	15.3
Databases	9.5	9.7	10.9	14.7
DOS programs	61.9	62.1	65.0	81.6
Windows programs	53.7	54.2	55.8	67.9
PCX graphics	17.5	17.9	20.4	47.4
TIF graphic	65.7	66.4	72.0	77.4

The file size after compression is specified in percentages. ARJ had the best data compression with 9.7%. We chose the default settings for all the programs.

The compression times are almost as important as the compression ratios. The following figures were achieved by data compression programs running without a cache program:

1. Data Compression

Type	ARJ	LHA	PKZIP	ZOO
Text files	0:54	0:52	0:54	0:31
Databases	0:50	0:47	0:50	0:26
DOS programs	1:45	0:54	0:23	1:03
Windows programs	3:08	1:34	1:01	1:36
PCX graphics	1:36	1:11	0:31	1:26
TIF graphic	1:05	0:33	0:21	0:36

PKZIP and ARJ have switches that let you control the kind of compression as well as the time. However, a better compression ratio always slows down compression time (and vice versa). For more information on these settings, refer to Chapter 6.

What do the results mean?

Now we must determine what all these values mean. The following column chart, which contains the information from the table, may help you understand the results.

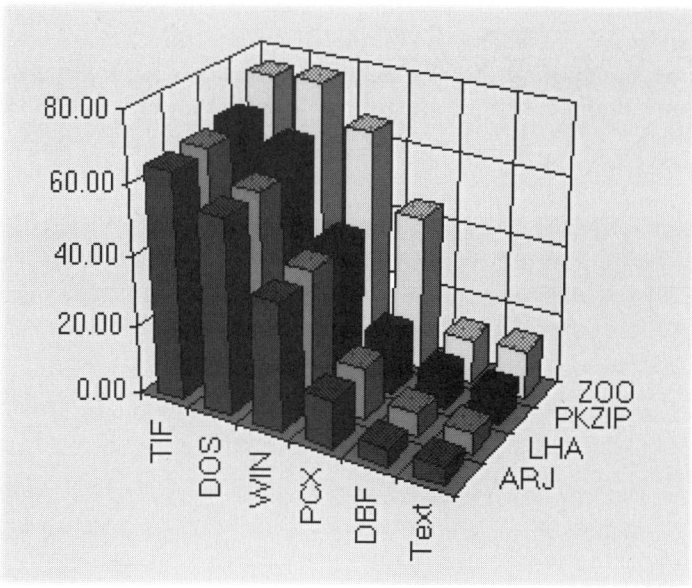

Overview of compression ratios

1. Data Compression

As you've probably already realized, text files (or text-like files) can be compressed the most. The compression programs PKZIP, LHA, and ARJ can compress text files to about 10% of their original size. Although the ZOO program cannot compress files by this much, it is has a faster compression time.

Compressing binary files results in very different compression ratios. DOS programs compress to about half their original size, while Windows programs compress to a little less than half. This is strange, considering the compression times. Despite search times for Windows programs that are much longer, the compression ratio for Windows programs is lower than the compression ratio for DOS programs.

This indicates that Windows programs are structured differently than normal DOS programs. We'll discuss this in more detail later in Chapter 7, "EXE Compressors". Windows programs are structured so differently that these special compression programs (EXE compression programs) refuse to work.

We were surprised by ARJ's compression time. This program took 3 minutes and 8 seconds to compress the same data that LHA compressed in half that time. PKZIP took less than one third the time. Although you may think that ARJ takes longer because it's so thorough and produces the best compression, this isn't the case. We'll explain this in more detail later.

Certain files, for example TIF and GIF graphic files, are more difficult to compress than other files. While you can reduce TIF files to 70% of their original size, it's not unusual to see compression ratios ranging from 90 to 100% for GIF files.

```
C:\TEST>arj a test
ARJ 2.30 Copyright (c) 1990-92 Robert K Jung. Jan 19 1992
NOT REGISTERED for business, commercial, or government use.

Creating archive  : TEST.ARJ
Adding     SAMPLE.GIF     100.0%
Adding     WINOPT.EXE      25.9%
Adding     NC.EXE          56.4%
    3 file(s)

C:\TEST>
```

Poor compression ratios

1. Data Compression

Even ARJ, which is usually so thorough, provides only mediocre results. This occurs because some files, such as GIF graphic files, are already compressed. The image information is compressed very cleverly to keep memory requirements within limits. The other two files, START.EXE and NEW.EXE, are already compressed ARJ files.

Therefore, continually compressing a file to reduce it to the ideal size of one byte simply doesn't work. Even repeating the compression procedure once on a compressed file is useless because the contents of the file are already optimized.

You're probably wondering why a file that's already compressed and (presumably) optimized still produces a compression ratio of 1%. This occurs because every archive file also needs uncompressed data, such as file and pathnames, the coding tree (explained earlier in this chapter), and some other statistical data. Although it's possible to compress some of this data, later the program will create another coding tree, which creates more statistical data, etc.

Also, repeatedly compressing data is dangerous. The more often you compress a file, the more alienated the contents become. Although this isn't dangerous by itself, compressed data is prone to defects. One error in a file that has been compressed once isn't too bad. In this case, usually one defective file of the archive will be lost. However, if you have a file that has been compressed more than once, one error will probably damage the entire archive.

Using a cache program

To increase compression times, use a cache program. This type of program monitors the data traffic between the hard drive and PC and temporarily stores data in RAM. The next time the data is accessed, you won't use the hard drive. Instead, you'll get the data from RAM, which is much faster.

Many people use a cache programs without even knowing it. For example, if you use Windows, you probably have a program called SMARTDRV.EXE in one of your system files (CONFIG.SYS or AUTOEXEC.BAT). PC-Tools has a program called PC-Cache and Norton Utilities has NCACHE.EXE.

Look at both your AUTOEXEC.BAT and CONFIG.SYS files. Many computer users don't know what is in these files. As a result, sometimes these users have all three of these programs running on their computers. Unfortunately, this doesn't mean that their computers run three times as fast. Actually the opposite is true. Therefore, it's important that you choose only one cache program.

When you use a cache program, the compression times for the same data decrease significantly.

1. Data Compression

Type	ARJ	LHA	PKZIP	ZOO
Text files	0:29	0:41	0:50	0:17
Databases	0:28	0:38	0:47	0:15
DOS programs	0:22	0:23	0:18	0:20
Windows programs	0:54	0:52	0:54	0:42
PCX graphics	0:32	0:41	0:26	0:28
TIF graphic	0:18	0:16	0:13	0:13

Obviously, all compression programs benefit from working with cache programs, but the increase in speed isn't the same for all the programs. When using a cache program, the most time is saved with ARJ. More than two minutes is saved when you compress Windows programs. This is a tremendous difference and reveals something about ARJ compression programs. ARJ accesses the hard drive much more frequently than the other compression programs. That's why you get such good results when you combine it with a cache program. The next figure illustrates this:

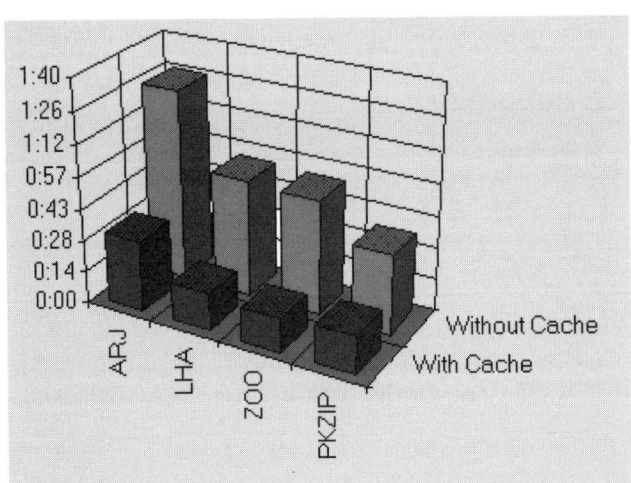

Better compression times using caches

PKZIP doesn't benefit very much, because it's already fast without the cache. ZOO also benefits from using a cache program. However, since cache programs don't influence compression ratios, ZOO is still at the bottom of the scale.

Data Compression Elements

In Chapter 1, we talked about data compression theory. In this chapter, we'll discuss data compression programs in detail. At first, it may seem like compression programs are easy to use. However, it's difficult to use the advanced features of these programs. Although compression programs usually include instructions in a text file, these files confuse users because they don't provide enough information about the commands and switches. So, even after reading the instructions, you still may not understand the options included with the program.

Unfortunately, because of this, most users don't understand how to use compression programs and what the terminology means. In this chapter, we'll explain the technical aspects of compression programs.

Data Compression Command Line Structure

One reason why users don't fully use the capabilities of compression programs is because of the complicated syntax, or the form in which commands are entered. The following command line is a good example of this awkward syntax:

```
LHA <command> [/option[-+012|WDIR]] <archive[.LZH]> [DIR\] [filenames]
```

As you can see, it's difficult to understand this command line. However, when you become more familiar with these command lines, you'll be able to ignore the brackets and slashes. Then you can concentrate on the essentials and discover that compression programs have similar structures.

The structure of a command isn't quite as clear as the example shown in the following figure. However, this is what constitutes inputting a command. If you disregard the names of the compression programs, there are actually only four components that make up the command line of a compression program. Some of these components aren't needed in order to run the program.

2. Data Compression Elements

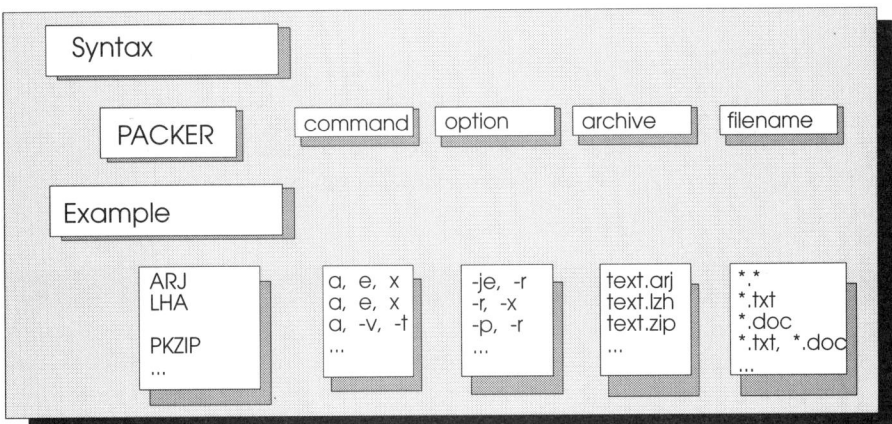

Structure of a command line for data compression

If you want to get the most out of your compression program, you must use the powerful options that are included with it. With some patience and experience, you'll be able to do this easily.

Data compression components

The following table is an overview of the data compression components.

Command (Required)	When you type the command, you're specifying the kind of task the compressor is supposed to perform. For example, simple commands, such as Add or Update, are frequently used, while commands such as Delete or Rename aren't used as often.
Switch (Optional)	Use switches to control the execution of the command and specify deviations from the standard procedure. For example, you would add a switch to the command to specify that subdirectories should be included when you compress a directory. In this book, we use the terms option, switch, and parameter interchangeably, depending on the specific program.
Archive name (Required)	The archive name must appear in the command. Usually specifying the file extension (e.g., ARC, ZIP, etc.) isn't necessary because the compression program assigns the extension automatically.
Files (Optional)	At the end of the command line, specify the files you want processed. You can specify names and wildcards (?, *) with most data compression programs. Depending on the command being processed, the filename you select refers to files in the archive or on the drive. If you don't specify a filename, the program assumes it should process all files (*.*).

2. Data Compression Elements

The following table contains example command lines for various compression programs:

Program	Command	Switch	Archive	Files
ARJ	l		TEST	
ARJ	u	-WC:\	TEST	*.TXT *.DOC
LHA	a	-r-x	ARCHIVE	*.*
PKZIP	-a	-r	TABLE	*.XL?
PAK	a	/Gxyz	SECRET	Packer

If the command line structure is still confusing to you, access the help functions. To do this, use the switch "/?" to display information about the most important commands.

```
ARJ   Enter          (simple overview)
ARJ /? Enter         (complete overview)
LHA   Enter
PKZIP Enter
```

Each compression program provides a different amount of commands and switches. For example, ARJ provides numerous switches. If you activate the help functions, you'll see four screens containing various combinations of commands and switches. All these functions and switches are part of one program.

There are also different options for controlling program functions. For example, some compressors differentiate between the packing module and the unpacking module. PKZIP and its counterpart PKUNZIP make this distinction. Other independent program modules analyze archives or convert archives into self-extracting archives.

Archive Files

The file extensions LHA, LZH, ARC, ZIP, and ARJ identify archive files. Whenever you compress or decompress data, you'll encounter archives. An archive is simply the PC version of a physical archive (i.e., a place where important documents are stored).

When you compress files, they are packed into a separate area. They cannot be processed until you retrieve them again with a data uncompression program.

2. Data Compression Elements

Structure of archives

In order to locate archives, the compression program stores various information with each archived file. There is also different information for the archive itself. Let's look at the schematic structure of a typical PC archive:

The structure of an archive

Every archive is a network consisting of the data from each archived file, the local data, and the information about the total archive.

The local data (i.e., the data that belongs to the individually archived files) is divided into the local header and the compressed data. The header contains important information that is needed for decompressing the file. Actually, without this information it would be impossible to decompress the file. It would even be conceivable to manage all the statistical data in one place, along with the header data of the central header. However, this would be dangerous.

If an error occurs somewhere in an archive, most likely the entire archive isn't useless. Since the archive is divided into individual archived files, the damage is usually limited to only the file containing the error.

2. Data Compression Elements

Every archive also has a global header, sometimes called an archive header. This global header contains statistical data that isn't important to the individual files, but is crucial to the total structure of the archive.

The following is a short section from the header information of a PKZIP archive; it should give you an idea of the complexity of data compression:

- Central header signature
- Packer version
- Required version for unpacking
- General information
- Date of last change
- Time of last change
- 32 bit CRC code
- Compressed size and normal size

Remember, this is only a small section. The entire list of information is much larger. If you add the local headers, you'll understand why the pure compression ratios are drastically different from the final size, especially for smaller files.

The local headers make it possible to make changes to archives. All the important information about the individual files is stored in the headers. To update the files in the archive, simply compare the local header, which can be quickly found in the archive. You can also change the names of archived files just as quickly. To do this, simply make a minor change to the header.

You can determine the contents of an archive quickly by having the data compression program go from header to header and collect the statistical data stored in each one.

Self-extracting Archives

Sometimes it's difficult to unpack archives if a new version of the compression program is being used. Because of this problem, developers created self-extracting archives. With these archives, a small program is added to the archive that handles unpacking. This turns a passive archive into an active program that unpacks itself on demand.

The biggest advantage of a self-extracting archive is that you no longer need the data compression program to access the compressed data. Another advantage is that beginners can access compressed data, even if they've never seen a data compression program or the complicated commands. So, instead of typing

```
LHA x TRANSFER
```

you only need to type

```
TRANSFER
```

Structure of an SFX archive

The term "self-extracting archive" is abbreviated as an "SFX" archive. The only difference in the structure of a normal archive and an SFX archive is that an SFX archive contains additional bytes. These bytes are the commands of the program that automatically unpack the archived files.

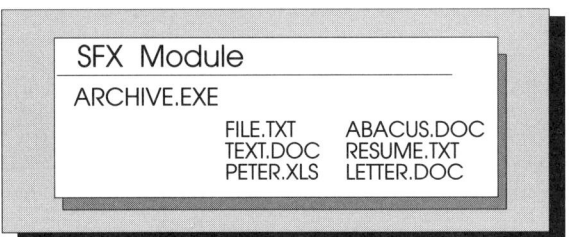

Structure of an SFX archive

The above figure shows a decompression module that is added to the archive. The archive is no longer named ARCHIV.ZIP or .ARJ or .LZH but ARCHIV.EXE. because the archive now includes a program for decompressing the archived files.

The size of this module varies, depending on the compressor. The module could be 1,000 bytes or, in an ARJ archive, it could be more than 15K. Obviously, this is a lot to send via modem. The varying sizes of the module are based on its capacity. ARJ provides numerous commands that you can use with the archive without ARJ. Other SFX modules are only able to decompress.

When you're working with a data compression program, you can handle SFX archives like normal archives. For example, the same command is used to delete all the TXT files in the TRANS archive of a normal archive or of an SFX archive. For a normal archive, enter the following

```
LHA d TRANS *.TXT
```

and for an SFX archive, enter:

```
LHA d TRANS.EXE *.TXT
```

2. Data Compression Elements

EXE Compression Programs

The files located in archives must be decompressed before you can access them. Although this procedure is also necessary for SFX archives, it is faster and more efficient than the one used for normal archive files.

A program from France developed by Fabrice Bellard was the first to approach this problem from a different perspective. His idea was to archive programs in order to decompress and execute them in RAM.

Making programs smaller

You can use this method to reduce programs without limiting their functions. This method reduces the local requirements to about half the original program size. Since you no longer need to decompress the programs before running them, this is a genuine, effective gain of disk space.

Unfortunately, there are disadvantages to this method. What you gain in disk space, you lose in time. You cannot immediately load and run compressed programs when you start the PC. Instead, you must decompress them first. This procedure requires a certain amount of time. The slower your hard drive and PC, the more you'll notice how long this takes. However, if you have a 386 or 486, you shouldn't really notice a slow down.

This method of compression doesn't solve all disk space problems. Some programs cannot be made smaller (for example, Windows programs). Larger DOS programs that work with overlay files (program segments called into memory when needed) can also cause problems. Older COM programs can also be difficult. However, COM programs are smaller than EXE programs, so normally you won't have to worry about compressing them.

New programs

LZEXE is no longer the only EXE program. Other programs, such as PKLITE and DIET are very successful. DIET is special because you can use this program to compress files as well as programs, without having to decompress them before using them. For more information about these programs, refer to Chapter 7.

Data Compression Shells

The various options, commands with the same meanings, and other inconsistencies among the different compression programs can be very confusing. As a result, a new type of compression program has been created. These programs don't

2. Data Compression Elements

actually change how compression programs operate. Instead, they are interfaces that change the way you work with compression programs. These interfaces are often designed according to the Windows standard, so you can communicate with the compression programs by using windows and dialog boxes.

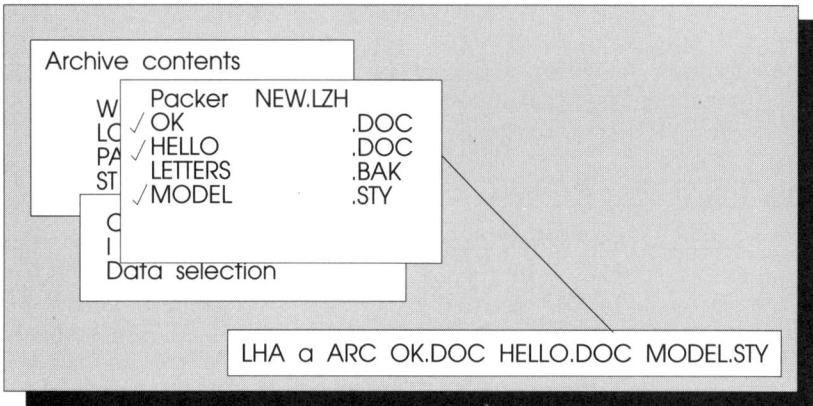

Using windows instead of the command line

These programs are called shells. So, data compression programs have data compression shells.

> The term "shell" refers to a method of accessing a command-driven operating system, like DOS or UNIX, by using a menu-driven or icon-oriented user interface acting as a bridge between you and the computer.

How data compression shells work

The way a data compression shell operates is determined by the function of the compression program. Basically, the program is supposed to place files in an archive so the user can easily work with these files.

Obviously these programs are more complicated than this. The program must manage the archives, and update, delete, rename, or search for files. Shells can do all of this. With a shell, you can process the files of an archive as though you were still at the DOS command prompt.

Also, good shells provide the option of managing archives with the most popular data compression programs. So it doesn't matter whether an archive is called TOTAL.ARJ, TOTAL.LZH, or TOTAL.ZIP. If the command is "delete PETER.TXT from the archive", then this command should be executed, regardless of how. The shell recognizes which compression program was used to create the compressed files.

2. Data Compression Elements

However, to work with data compression shells, the appropriate compression programs must be installed on your computer. Usually data compression shells don't come with the programs for data compression. However, this shouldn't really be a problem, since you need to use a shell only when you're working with several data compression programs and cannot keep track of the various commands and options. If you use only one data compression program, you should be able to keep track of the commands and options.

Several shells are currently available.

Data Compression Terms

Most data compression programs don't include a glossary defining the most important terms. So, in this section, we'll define several terms used in data compression.

Algorithms

Algorithms are instructions to the computer, telling it to solve a problem in a specific, predetermined manner. In data compression programs, algorithms determine how data is compressed. Many data compression programs use the well-known Huffman algorithm.

ANSI

American National Standards Institute. Standard for interpreting codes and characters.

Archive

An archive is a file created by a data compression program. It's used for storing other files. An archive can contain several files which can be compressed.

Archive bit

This bit is one of the attributes that every file has. The archive bit indicates whether a file has been changed since the last time it was saved. Data compression programs can check this bit to determine whether the file must be backed up. Other file attributes are hidden, system, or read-only.

ASCII

Standard that assigns characters different codes from 0 to 255. ASCII is an abbreviation for American Standard Code for Information Interchange.

2. Data Compression Elements

Bit

    The smallest unit of information on a computer. A bit can only be 0 or 1 in value.

Cache program

    A program that places data in temporary storage. This speeds up access to this data. Software cache programs that go back and forth from the hard drive to RAM are very common. When RAM accesses the hard drive, the cache program can often provide the data from temporary storage, which is much faster than accessing the data from the hard drive.

CRC-Code

    Abbreviation for Cyclic Redundancy Check. As a safety precaution, after a program archives files, these files receive a code calculated from the compressed data. During a test or decompression, the code is recalculated. If there are any differences between the current calculation and the old CRC code, it means the file is damaged and cannot be decompressed.

Downwardly compatible

    Programs that are able to process data from earlier program versions. Some compression programs have switches for choosing compatible methods in data compression.

File attributes

    File attributes are information about the status of a file. The following attributes are possible: Hidden, System, Archive, and Read-only.

Garble

    Technical term for archiving with a password.

Header

    File header with important information about a file. Archives have an archive header and local headers, which contain information about the individual archived files.

Hidden

    File attribute. When this attribute is set, the file cannot be displayed at the DOS prompt with the DIR command.

Huffman

    Developed the Huffman algorithm for compressing files.

2. Data Compression Elements

IBM graphic character set

All characters with ASCII codes 128 to 255 are referred to as IBM graphic characters, or the extended graphic character set. The IBM graphic character set includes foreign characters.

Command line

Another word for the DOS prompt. If you aren't running Windows, you enter all your commands and run programs from this line.

Critical error messages

Errors that usually cause the PC system to crash. The following is a typical critical error message:

LZW

Abbreviation for the developers of a data compression algorithm: Lempel, Ziv, and Welch.

Manual

The file containing the manual for your data compression program.

Masking

A process for determining whether a specific bit is set.

Module

A module is a part of a program or program system. If you make an SFX archive from a normal program, then you add a module to the archive that is in charge of decompressing the actual archive.

Multiple-Volume

An archive that's located on more than one diskette.

Options

An option is an alternative that modifies a command in a specific manner. In this book, this term is used interchangeably with parameter or switch.

Parameter

See Options.

2. Data Compression Elements

Progress Bar

A progress bar indicates how much of a job is already completed.

Ratio

The relationship of the original size and the compressed size of a file. Different compression programs treat the ratio differently. Some indicate the percentage by which the compressed file is smaller than the original size, while others indicate the percentage the file has been reduced to.

Switch

See Options.

SFX

Abbreviation for self-extracting archive. This is an archive with a program module that decompresses the data of the archive. A separate compression program is no longer necessary to restore the data.

System file

A system file is a file whose System attribute is set.

Text file

A file containing only readable information.

Time Stamps

Every file has a date and time on which it was created or last changed. This is referred to as a time stamp.

Verbose List

Data compression term for a detailed list of the contents of an archive.

Volume

Refers to a diskette or hard drive.

Volume Label

Name of a diskette or hard drive (Volume).

Using Compression Programs

In this chapter, we'll discuss the basic compression commands and provide examples that illustrate how to use these commands. You'll find all the information you need for compressing your data, from individual files to entire directories and their subdirectories. We'll discuss all the available compression programs, so you should find information for the program you're using.

Compressing Individual Files

As you've probably discovered while using your PC, files can quickly accumulate on your hard drive and take up valuable storage space. Eventually, your hard drive can become overloaded with all of these files. As a result, your hard drive slows down. Although you may use these files only occasionally, they may be too valuable to delete.

In this case, you can improve your hard drive's performance by using a data compression program to compress these files and then delete the original uncompressed file from the hard drive. For example, suppose these files are located in a directory called "TEXTS." In this case, you would do the following:

1. Change to the TEXTS directory.
2. Create a compressed archive.
3. Delete the files that were archived.

First enter the following to change to the TEXTS directory:

`CD\TEXTS`

Now you can compress the files.

> We used the ARJ program in each example to keep them easy to understand. However, these procedures should apply to the other programs we discuss. You'll find a command reference for each program in Chapter 8.

3. Using Compression Programs

If you aren't familiar with the compression command, activate the program's help function. To do this, simply enter the name of the program to see a list of the commands and switches:

ARJ [Enter]

```
ARJ 2.30 Copyright (c) 1990-92 Robert K Jung. Jan 19 1992
NOT REGISTERED for business, commercial, or government use.

All Rights Reserved.  ARJ file compression archiver utility.
List of frequently used commands and switches.  Type ARJ -? for more help.

Usage:     ARJ <command> [-<sw> [-<sw>...]] <archive_name> [<file_names>...]
Examples:  ARJ a -r -wtemp software , ARJ l software , ARJ e software readme

<Commands>
    a: Add files to archive          m: Move files to archive
    d: Delete files from archive     t: Test integrity of archive
    e: Extract files from archive    u: Update files to archive
    f: Freshen files in archive      v: Verbosely list contents of archive
    l: List contents of archive      x: eXtract files with full pathname
<Switches>
    c: skip time-stamp Check         n: only New files (not exist)
    d: with Delete (move)            r: Recurse subdirectories
    e: Exclude paths from names      u: Update files (new and newer)
    f: Freshen existing files        v: enable multiple Volumes
    g: Garble with password          w: assign Work directory
    i: with no progress Indicator    x: eXclude selected files
    m: with Method 0, 1, 2, 3, 4     y: assume Yes on all queries

C:\ARCHIVE>
```

ARJ Help screen

A list of optional switches appears in the lower portion of the Help screen. You must type the appropriate command or switch to create the archive.

From drive to archive

There are four ways to compress files. The most commonly used method involves adding files to an existing archive (**Add files to archive** command). If the archive doesn't exist, the compression program automatically creates it. The other compression methods provide a broader range of options. For example, the original files can be deleted automatically after they are compressed or only recently modified files can be included.

3. Using Compression Programs

Command		Description
A	Add files to archive	Adds the indicated files to the archive. Previously archived files with the same name are overwritten.
M	Move files to archive	Similar to Add, but deletes the original files after the hard drive is compressed.
U	Update files to archive	Adds the indicated files to the archive, if they aren't already there or the archived version is older. This command ensures that your archive will always contain the most recent version of your files.
F	Freshen files in archive	The compression program refreshes the archive by looking for the most recent version of files on the hard drive. If it encounters a version of the file that was modified after a certain date, the newer version is added to the archive. It's impossible to create a new archive with Freshen.

All four commands can be used to add files in an existing archive. Now we'll explain how this process works. The command can either add individual files to an archive:

```
ARJ and ARCHIVE OBJECTS.TXT
```

or the command can add a group of files to an archive:

```
ARJ and ARCHIVE *.TXT
```

Update

There is only a minor difference between **Add** and **Update**. Both commands can create new archives if they don't exist yet and both commands compress files.

Unlike **Update**, **Add** archives a file regardless of whether it has already been archived. So, you may accidentally overwrite a recent version of a file, even though the contents of the file being added are much older. **Update**, however, accepts only new and relatively recent files into the archive. If the archive isn't available when you use **Update**, it's created immediately.

```
ARJ and TEXTS *.TXT
```

The above command adds a new document to the TEXTS archive only if it's either not in the archive already or if an older version of the file is in the archive.

The **Update** command is included in all the compression programs described in this book. The following table shows the proper way to use this command in the different compression programs:

3. Using Compression Programs

Update Command	
Compression Program	Update Command Example
ARJ	ARJ u ARCHIVE (File)
LHA	LHA u ARCHIVE (File)
PKZIP	PKZIP -u ARCHIVE (File)
PKPAK	PKPAK -u ARCHIVE (File)
PAK	PAK u ARCHIVE (File)
ZOO	ZOO -add ARCHIVE (File)

> Always use the **Update** command carefully. If the most recent version of the file is corrupt, and you update an archive containing an older, non-corrupt file, you will overwrite the older file.
>
> To find out how to solve this problem refer to Chapter 6.

Freshen

You can also use the **Freshen** command to update an archive. Based on the file date and timestamp, Freshen replaces files in an archive that are more recent. Unlike **Update**, only the files that are more recent than the ones already in the archive are accepted. Therefore, new files aren't archived. The **Freshen** command can also create a new archive.

The date and time the file was last saved determines whether the version of the file on the hard drive is more recent than the version in the archive. If you look at a listing of the archive contents, you'll see that the date and time is listed for each file. The compression program compares the date and time of the archived file with the current file when compressing and accepts the newer one.

Use the **Freshen** command when you want to keep your archive up-to-date and organized, but don't want to worry about what else the program may be adding to the archive.

We'll use an example to illustrate this. Suppose that you have an archive that contains only files of a certain type. This archive is called "PRESENT" and contains the files for a business presentation.

3. Using Compression Programs

Now suppose that you make daily backups of the files for this project on the archive. By updating with **Freshen**, the compression program guarantees that only files already in the archive will be replaced by the new and current versions. The other files that were updated, but aren't related to your project, aren't placed in the archive. Therefore, **Freshen** is extremely useful for filtering specific files.

> Since the **Freshen** command works "automatically", you don't have to pay close attention to it. Only the files that are already in the archive are updated.

If you use the **Freshen** command to update the archived files in TEXTS, use this command:

```
ARJ f TEXTS
```

"*.TXT" can be omitted (if you want to update the entire archive) because new files won't be added to the archive. However, a file specification can be added to the end of the command, especially when only specific files must be updated.

```
ARJ f TEXTS MEMO*.TXT
```

With the above command, all archived text files that have names starting with "MEMO" must be updated. All the other files in the archive aren't affected. New MEMO documents, which were written in the meantime, aren't archived with **Freshen**. In this case, you should use the **Update** command:

```
ARJ u TEXTS MEMO*.TXT
```

The following table shows how various data compression programs use the **Freshen** command:

3. Using Compression Programs

Freshen Command	
Compression Program	Freshen Command Example
ARJ	ARJ f ARCHIVE (File)
LHA	LHA f ARCHIVE (File)
	LHA f -c ARCHIVE (File)
PKZIP	PKZIP -f ARCHIVE (File)
PKPAK	PKPAK -f ARCHIVE (File)
PAK	PAK f ARCHIVE (File)

LHA has the "-c" option which makes it possible to switch off the checking of the time marker. **Freshen** then works like **Add**, except that only files already in the archive are archived again.

Move

Move is a very useful command. However, use this command carefully because the original files are deleted after they are compressed. In ARJ, the **Move** command looks as follows:

```
ARJ m TEXTS *.TXT
```

With the other compression programs, the **Move** command looks as follows:

```
LHA m TEXTS *.TXT
PKZIP -m TEXTS *.TXT
PKPAK -m TEXTS *.TXT
PAK m TEXTS *.TXT
```

To understand the above command lines, you must read them from the end of the line to the beginning. All the text files of the current directory are compressed in the TEXTS archive and then immediately deleted.

Changing the way Move works

In principle, **Move** works like **Add**. Files are archived even if the version in the archive is more current. However, it's possible to change this process. For example, suppose that you want to combine **Update** or **Freshen** with the deletion features of **Move**. You may want to check the archive before certain files are deleted. To change the way **Move** operates, you must add more options in the command line.

3. Using Compression Programs

In ARJ, you can use the "-jt" parameter, which is a safety feature. If the compression operation was successful, all the archived text documents will be deleted only after an additional check is made. You should use the "-jt" option to protect your data.

```
ARJ m -jt WORDTXT *.TXT
```

If you want ARJ to prompt you for confirmation before deleting files, use the "-d" option. However, "-d" is used with **Add** instead of **Move**.

```
ARJ a -d TEXTS *.TXT
```

Now you know three ways you can "Move" files into an archive with ARJ:

```
ARJ m TEXTS *.TXT     (simple)
ARJ m -jt TEXTS *.TXT      (test first)
ARJ a -d TEXTS *.TXT(test query)
```

As we mentioned, **Move** works like the **Add** command. In other words, all the files are overwritten regardless of whether they're an older version of the file. However, this may not always be desirable and can be changed in many data compression programs.

You can easily do this in PKZIP and PKPAK. If you want to use the **Move** command with **Update** or **Freshen**, enter the first letter of the corresponding command after the "-m" command:

```
PKZIP(PKPAK) -mu TEXTS *.TXT      (Update + Delete)
PKZIP(PKPAK) -mf TEXTS *.TXT      (Freshen + Delete )
```

Additional ARJ switches

ARJ cannot use these particular commands. However, ARJ has three switches that make this change even easier:

Switch	Purpose
-n	Only new files which have not yet been archived are accepted into the archive.
-f	Only recent files are archived. Corresponds to Freshen + Move.
-u	Only recent or new files are archived. Corresponds to Update + Move.

3. Using Compression Programs

Instead of **Move**, it's also possible to use a combination of **Add** and "-d"-**Delete**. Therefore, you can use both

```
ARJ m -n TEXTS *.TXT
```

and

```
ARJ a -dn TEXTS *.TXT
```

to create a Move command that affects only text files that haven't been compressed. LHA uses **Move** differently than the other compression programs. LHA automatically checks the file age and archives only recent and new files. So, LHA has a built-in Update feature, which you can switch off.

```
LHA m -c TEXTS *.TXT (Age isn't checked)
```

The "-c" option, which is also used with **Freshen**, ensures that the archive is renewed regardless of the age of the files.

The ZOO program offers two variations of the **Move** command, which are useful for both beginners and experienced users. The following is the simple version of the command:

```
ZOO -move TEXTS *.TXT
```

This version is the same as the one used by the other compression programs. The more advanced version produces the same result but with increased compression.

```
ZOO aMP TEXTS *.TXT
```

The "a" represents the **Add** command. The additional command "M" (**Move**) deletes the original file and "P" (**Pack**) removes unnecessary (garbage) data. (Remember that the ZOO program is case-sensitive.)

If you also add the "u" or "n" parameter to the above command, it's possible to use this method with **Freshen** and **Update**.

Additional parameters in ZOO

Switch	Purpose
n	Only new files, which have not yet been archived, are accepted into the archive.
u	Only recent or new files are archived. Corresponds to Update + Move.

The following table shows how **Move** can be used with the different compression programs:

3. Using Compression Programs

Move Command		
Program	Command Line	Result
ARJ	ARJ m WORDDOC *.TXT	Default
	ARJ m -jt ...	Move with supplementary test
	ARJ a -d ...	Move with query
	ARJ m -u ...	Move + Update
	ARJ m -f ...	Move + Freshen
	ARJ m -n ...	Move + Only-New-Files
LHA	LHA m WORDDOC *.TXT	Default with age comparison
	LHA m -c ...	Move without file age
PKZIP PKPAK	PKxxx -m WORDDOC *.TXT	Standard
	PKxxx -mu WORDDOC *.TXT	Move + Update
	PKxxx -mf WORDDOC *.TXT	Move + Freshen
PAK	PAK m WORDDOC *.TXT	Default with query
	PAK m /WO ...	Move with age comparison (Update)
	PAK m /WA ...	Move without comparison
ZOO	ZOO -more WORDDOC *.TXT	Default simple
	ZOO -aMP ...	Default complicated
	ZOO -auMP ...	Move + Update
	ZOO -anMP ...	Move + Only-New-Files

> You must use the PAK program carefully. Even if files aren't "moved" into the archive, PAK still deletes them from the hard drive.

Listing archive contents

After compressing files, you should display the archive. You can quickly find the **List** command (command switch "L") in the ARJ Help file.

```
ARJ l SAMPLE
```

A list containing information about the files archived in SAMPLE appears:

3. Using Compression Programs

```
ARJ 2.30 Copyright (c) 1990-92 Robert K Jung. Jan 19 1992
NOT REGISTERED for business, commercial, or government use.

Processing archive: SAMPLE.ARJ
Archive date    : 1993-10-01 12:47:04
Filename        Original Compressed Ratio DateTime modified CRC-32   AttrBTPMGVXx
------------    -------- ---------- ----- ----------------- --------
SAMPLE.GIF         8935       8935 1.000 93-10-01 11:45:24 544B2212 A--W B 0
README.TXT          599        320 0.534 93-09-09 14:49:04 FD704230 ---W B 1
STARS.TXT         36397      16576 0.455 93-09-09 14:13:08 6BE76E31 ---W B 1
LINES.TXT          8774       2672 0.305 93-03-08 14:42:46 0E4DA344 ---W B 1
ASSOC.TXT          4322       1758 0.407 93-02-26 11:49:00 63D730BE ---W B 1
BYTE.TXT         113485      28060 0.247 93-08-19 08:43:56 F02A11D0 ---W B 1
BYTE901.TXT       49900      12715 0.255 93-09-01 16:44:30 BBB3345B ---W B 1
BYTECON.TXT        2541        324 0.128 93-07-13 13:22:54 A8C43728 ---W B 1
BYTEDESC.TXT       2662        326 0.122 93-06-16 09:22:58 5FC4DF7B ---W B 1
JCI.TXT            9080       4773 0.526 93-09-01 16:47:48 96DD78A4 ---W B 1
JCI816.TXT        18813       8019 0.426 93-08-17 09:48:20 ABEFAE64 ---W B 1
JCI901.TXT        44541      13950 0.313 93-09-01 16:43:08 5C596E8D ---W B 1
MAIL819.TXT      190519      73646 0.387 93-08-19 08:49:44 B515F05C ---W B 1
MJCI.TXT          59860      18226 0.304 93-08-17 09:14:04 9CE945AA ---W B 1
------------    -------- ---------- -----
    14 files    550428     190300 0.346

C:\TEST>
```

The contents of the documents archive

The most interesting thing in this list is probably the compression ratio, which is listed for each file. The overall ratio for all the archived files results from the average of the individual rates.

With an average compression ratio of as much as 31% of the original size, ARJ is one of the most effective data compression programs currently available. Remember, the compression ratio always depends on the file type.

Even larger compression ratios are possible, which proves how much compression programs can help you create space on your hard drive. The **List** commands for the other compression programs are located in the following table:

List Commands	
Compression Program	Command line
ARJ	ARJ l ARCHIVE (File)
ICE	ICE l ARCHIVE (File)
LHA	LHA l ARCHIVE (File)
PAK	PAK l ARCHIVE (File)
PKPAK	PKPAK -V ARCHIVE (File)
PKZIP	PKZIP -V ARCHIVE (File)
ZOO	ZOO -List ARCHIVE (File)

3. Using Compression Programs

As you can see, it's easy to create and display archives. The commands of these file compression programs are very similar. Since PKZIP and PKPAK use the "V" parameter for list, you may get confused and accidentally type the "L" parameter. However, if this happens, don't worry. This parameter just displays the license information for your data compression program.

If you want to save the contents of an archive or print the contents, you can redirect the output to a file or to the printer instead of to the screen. To do this, enter the ">" sign after the command for listing an archive, followed by a filename or the printer interface (usually LPT1):

```
ARJ l ARCHIVE > FILE
```

or

```
ARJ l ARCHIVE > LPT1
```

The first command sends the output to a text file, which you'll be able to process like a normal text. The second command sends the archive contents to the printer.

File lists

To specify the files to be compressed, type either their complete filenames or use wildcards (* or ?). Entering these commands can be time-consuming, especially if you can't use wildcards. In this case, you must type the same command several times:

```
LHA a PRESENT LAST.TXT
LHA a PRESENT LETTER.BAK
LHA a PRESENT DATA.DBF
LHA a PRESENT TABLE.XLS
LHA a PRESENT START.XLM
LHA a PRESENT GRAPH.CHT
...
```

However, there is an easier way to do this. You can simply pass an entire list of files to the compression programs in a single command as in:

```
LHA a PRESENT LAST.TXT LETTER.BAK DATA.DBF TABLE.XLS START.XLM
GRAPH.CHT
```

This command line can also be combined with the other commands, such as "L" for **List**.

The following is an archive from ZOO:

3. Using Compression Programs

ARCHIVE WORDDOC.ZOO						
Length	CF	Size	Date	Time	Now	
64512	64 %	23404	8 Apr 92	15:53:36	1e05	last.txt
3584	49 %	1837	25 Jul 89	12:00:00	f9b6	letter.bak
37584	57 %	16312	25 Jul 89	12:00:00	68ff	data.dbf
3072	41 %	1800	22 Aug 91	16:05:14	da60	table.xls
10121	48 %	4858	22 Aug 91	16:05:14	a88b	start.xlm
8972	55 %	4934	22 Aug 91	16:05:14	5f90	graph.cht
127845	60 %	53145				6 files

You can also prepare a file list in advance. You can generate the file list with any text editor, even with the DOS editors EDIT or EDLIN. For a small file, even the COPY CON command is suitable:

```
COPY CON LIST
LAST.TXT
LETTER.BAK
DATA.DBF
TABLE.XLS
START.XLM
GRAPH.CHT

1 File(s) copied
```

Press F6 to place an end-of-file character in the file and then close the file by pressing Enter. Now the **Update** command, along with the list, is passed to the compression program. In PKZIP, this command looks as follows:

```
PKZIP 1 @LIST
```

If you have several list files, these can also be entered more than once in the command line:

```
PKZIP 1 @LIST @DOCS
```

To prevent confusion, PKZIP identifies a list file with the "At" symbol @ (ASCII character 64). Without this character in front of the filename, the compression program would compress the list file itself.

To create the "At" symbol, press the Shift key and the 2 key from the keyboard (not the numeric keypad).

3. Using Compression Programs

Only PKZIP and ARJ support list files.

PKPAK	(Command) ARCHIVE @LIST	Ensure that the end-of-file character (^Z) doesn't appear in the last text line of the list file because this entry won't be recognized.
ARJ	(Command) ARCHIVE !LIST	The exclamation point represents the list file.

Any function that can work with more than one file can be used for "Command" in the above command lines.

LHA doesn't recognize the list files in this way. If you want to use predefined lists with this program, you'll have to use a trick. One of these tricks is called piping, which is used in DOS. With piping, you can redirect input and output channels. (We'll discuss piping in more detail in Chapter 6.)

Excluding files from an archive

Suppose that you've created a lot of files during the day. You want to compress all the files except for a few. You can do this one of two ways:

1. Compress all the files and then delete the unwanted ones from the archive. You'll learn how to do this in Chapter 4.

2. Specify which files should be excluded from the compression process during archiving.

ARJ and PKZIP have this exclusion capability. Both programs use the same switch to do this:

-x "File"

Use "-x" to specify that the subsequent filename shouldn't be bypassed by the program. The exclusion switch can also be used with the other commands, such as **Freshen**, **Update**, and **List**. You can use "-x" with commands which we haven't discussed yet, such as **Unpack** or **Delete Files in Archive**.

The following PKZIP example shows how all the files of a directory are archived, except for program files:

```
PKZIP u ARK -x*.exe -x*.com
```

All files in the current directory are compressed and saved with the ".ARK" extension. The .EXE and .COM files aren't included in the compression process. As you can see from the example, each exclusion must be preceded by its own "-x".

The exception switch can also be combined with file lists:

3. Using Compression Programs

```
ARJ u ARK -x!PROGS
```

If the PROGS file still contains unnecessary entries, such as

```
*.COM
*.EXE
*.BIN
*.SYS
*.OVL
```

you can prevent them from finding their way into your archive program by using a simple exclusion list.

> It's easy to confuse the "-x" switch of ARJ with the "x" command, which is used to decompress files (eXtract).

This confusion doesn't occur with PKZIP because, unlike the other compression programs, PKZIP uses a separate program, called PKUNZIP, for decompressing files. Unlike PKZIP, the PKUNZIP program doesn't let you exclude files.

Compressing Directories

Besides individual files, you can also compress entire directories. This makes it possible to build a complete "package", which can include several directories and subdirectories, into one archive. The directory structure needed to operate a specific program is later rebuilt.

How the subdirectory files are located depends on the compression program. Some programs cannot work with subdirectories. These compression programs are able to represent directories:

- ➢ ARJ
- ➢ LHA
- ➢ PKZIP

Recursive search

ARJ, LHA, and PKZIP use a recursive search to store files in directory trees. The compression process begins at the starting directory entered in the command line. First, all the files in that directory are compressed. Next, the compression program

3. Using Compression Programs

determines whether a subdirectory exists. If there is a subdirectory, the program jumps to this directory and begins processing these files. As with all recursion, only specified files are placed in the archive.

If entire directory trees are archived, the pathnames of the files are very important. The compression program must determine whether the files should be saved with the complete pathname. For example, there is a significant difference between archiving a file as

README.DOC

or

D:\BORLAND\TPASCAL\DOCDEMOS\README.DOC

If files are saved from many different directories, it's possible that two files with the same name would be compressed into the same archive. However, without a pathname, this isn't possible.

Another problem can also occur with archives that don't have complete paths. Because the pathnames are missing, the files may not be able to be restored to the proper directories when they are decompressed.

The following should help you decide if you should create an archive with a complete pathname:

With path data	Select this setting to ensure that the directory structure of the original is accurately backed up, or if some of the files have the same name.
File name only	This setting is sufficient if you only want to back up all files of a certain type within a directory tree.

The default setting used for saving the complete path is different in each compression program. ARJ automatically saves the complete path, while LHA and PKZIP do this only when specifically told to do so.

Using LHA

LHA has two switches that affect how files from different directories are handled:

-r	Recursive collection of files.
-x	Saving files with expanded name data.

These two options work with most command switches. Therefore, it's possible to add files to the archive by using **Update**, **Move**, or **Freshen**. To implement recursive storage, use the -r switch.

3. Using Compression Programs

```
LHA a -r ALLBAK \*.BAK
```

The above command archives all the backup files, of the current drive, that have the .BAK file extension. Press Enter to activate this command. The command may execute without any problems or a message similar to the following may appear:

> Creating archive : ALLTXT.LZH
> Same name in another path "STANDARD.BAK"

This message appears and LHA stops working as soon as two files with the same name are encountered as you try to add them to the same archive. To avoid this problem, you must, in the case of LHA, add an "-x" option. With this switch, you're also adding the pathname to the filename. The result is that even files with the same name can be processed by LHA.

```
C:\TEST>lha a -rx alltxt *.txt>xx.txt

Creating archive : alltxt.LZH

==>   0% XX.TXT
==>  53% README.TXT      o
==>  46% STARS.TXT       ooooo
==>  30% LINES.TXT       oo
==>  41% ASSOC.TXT       o
==>  29% BYTE.TXT        ooooooooooooo
==>  27% BYTE901.TXT     ooooooo
==>  13% BYTECON.TXT     o
==>  12% BYTEDESC.TXT    o
==>  53% JCI.TXT         oo
==>  50% JCI816.TXT      ooo
==>  32% JCI901.TXT      oooooo
==>  41% MAIL819.TXT     oooooooooooooooooooooooo
==>  31% MJCI.TXT        oooooooo
==>  44% PC.TXT          oooo
==>  45% RPT.TXT         o
==>  24% X_JCI.TXT       oooooooooo

C:\TEST>
```

Using recursive collection

As you can see in the above figure, LHA doesn't display the path of a file, even if the path is saved. However, you can display the path information by using the "-l" parameter:

```
LHA u -rxl ALLTXT\*.TXT
```

Now the following will appear on the screen:

3. Using Compression Programs

```
[1/19] XX.TXT
  ==>  45% o
[2/19] STARS.TXT
  ==>  46% ooooo
[3/19] LINES.TXT
  ==>  30% oo
[4/19] BYTE901.TXT
  ==>  27% ooooooo
[5/19] JCI901.TXT
  ==>  32% oooooo
[6/19] MAIL819.TXT
  ==>  41% oooooooooooooooooooooooo
[7/19] MJCI.TXT
  ==>  31% oooooooo
[8/19] PC.TXT
  ==>  44% oooo
[9/19] SUB/BYTECON.TXT
  ==>  13% o
[10/19] SUB/BYTEDESC.TXT
  ==>  12% o
[11/19] SUB/JCI816.TXT
  ==>  50% ooo
[12/19] SUB/MJCI.TXT
  Freezing oooo....
```

Path display during compression

Using PKZIP

Similar to LHA, PKZIP also has a switch that controls recursive storage and another that specifies that pathnames will be saved.

-r	Recursive storage of files. If files with duplicate names are found in a subdirectory, they are passed over without further checking.
-p	Addition of directory names, into which a branch is made during the recursive search.
-P	Addition of the name of the starting directory and recursively branched directories.

The simplest way to use recursive archiving in PKZIP is a command with the "-r" switch:

```
E:\WORD>PKZIP -a -r ALLBAK *.BAK
```

PKZIP searches all subsequent subdirectories for files ending with "BAK" beginning with the current directory (in our example this is the E:\WORD directory). If the program encounters new files with a name that was already assigned, the file isn't archived.

3. Using Compression Programs

```
PKZIP Reg. U.S. Pat. and Tm. Off.    Patent No. 5,051,745

■ 80386 CPU detected.
■ XMS version 2.00 detected.
■ Novell Netware version 3.11 detected.
■ DPMI version 0.90 detected.
■ Using Normal Compression.

Creating ZIP: ALLTXT.ZIP
  Adding: XX.TXT          Deflating (52%), done.
  Adding: STARS.TXT       Deflating (55%), done.
  Adding: LINES.TXT       Deflating (71%), done.
  Adding: BYTE901.TXT     Deflating (76%), done.
  Adding: JCI901.TXT      Deflating (70%), done.
  Adding: MAIL819.TXT     Deflating (63%), done.
  Adding: MJCI.TXT        Deflating (70%), done.
  Adding: PC.TXT          Deflating (58%), done.
  Adding: BYTECON.TXT     Deflating (87%), done.
  Adding: BYTEDESC.TXT    Deflating (88%), done.
  Adding: JCI816.TXT      Deflating (58%), done.
  Adding: BYTE.TXT        Deflating (76%), done.
  Adding: JCI.TXT         Deflating (48%), done.
  Adding: README.TXT      Deflating (47%), done.
  Adding: RPT.TXT         Deflating (54%), done.
  Adding: X_JCI.TXT       Deflating (77%),
```

Simple recursive archiving with PKZIP

During this compression run, PKZIP finds 10 files in the directory tree. If the "p" switch is found on the command line, the path data of directories lying deeper within the directory structure are to be added to the filename.

```
PKZIP -a -rp ALLTXT *.TXT
```

The result of this search already looks slightly different. Both the filenames and the list of names are longer.

```
PKZIP (R)   FAST!   Create/Update Utility   Version 2.04g   02-01-93
Copr. 1989-1993 PKWARE Inc.  All Rights Reserved.  Shareware Version
PKZIP Reg. U.S. Pat. and Tm. Off.    Patent No. 5,051,745

■ 80386 CPU detected.
■ XMS version 2.00 detected.
■ Novell Netware version 3.11 detected.
■ DPMI version 0.90 detected.
■ Using Normal Compression.

Updating ZIP: ALLTXT.ZIP
  Updating: XX.TXT             Deflating (52%), done.
  Updating: STARS.TXT          Deflating (55%), done.
  Updating: LINES.TXT          Deflating (71%), done.
  Updating: BYTE901.TXT        Deflating (76%), done.
  Updating: JCI901.TXT         Deflating (70%), done.
  Updating: MAIL819.TXT        Deflating (63%), done.
  Updating: MJCI.TXT           Deflating (70%), done.
  Updating: PC.TXT             Deflating (58%), done.
    Adding: SUB/BYTECON.TXT    Deflating (87%), done.
    Adding: SUB/BYTEDESC.TXT   Deflating (88%), done.
    Adding: SUB/JCI816.TXT     Deflating (58%), done.
    Adding: SUB/MJCI.TXT       Deflating (70%), done.
    Adding: SUB/MAIL819.TXT    Deflating %00
```

Archiving with pathnames

3. Using Compression Programs

Instead of 10 files, 14 files were archived. Since the pathnames were also saved, the filename "FILE1.TXT" is no longer the same as "TEXTS\FILE1.TXT." No other duplicate files are found.

Remember, the two "P" options are case-sensitive. The lowercase "p" controls files and pathnames in the current directory. However the uppercase "P" specified the directory stated in the command line. Both of these commands

```
E:\WORD>PKZIP -a -rp ALLTXT *.TXT
```

and

```
E:\WORD>PKZIP -a -rP ALLTXT *.TXT
```

produce an identical result because there is no additional subdirectory. However, this isn't the case for these two commands:

```
E:\WORD>PKZIP -a -rp ALLTXT E:\WORD\*.TXT
```

and

```
E:\WORD>PKZIP -a -rP ALLTXT E:\WORD\*.TXT
```

The P command in the first version changes nothing without specific path data, because deviant directories (i.e., those named in the command line) aren't placed in the archive. The files in the first P command can be placed anywhere when they are decompressed. Only the files in subdirectories to E:\WORD get a path prefix. The files in the second P command must be decompressed under the E:\WORD directory. The difference in the P version can now be seen. Because there is a path specification here (E:\WORD*.TXT), it will be attached to all files found.

```
C:\>pkzip -a -rP alltxt c:\text-dir\*.txt

PKZIP (R)   FAST!   Create/Update Utility   Version 2.04g   02-01-93
Copr. 1989-1993 PKWARE Inc. All Rights Reserved.  Shareware Version
PKZIP Reg. U.S. Pat. and Tm. Off.   Patent No. 5,051,745

■ 80486 CPU detected.
■ XMS version 3.00 detected.
■ Novell Netware version 3.11 detected.
■ Using Normal Compression.

Updating ZIP: ALLTXT.ZIP
   Adding: TEXT-DIR/EIGHTH.TXT    Deflating (72%), done.
   Adding: TEXT-DIR/NINETH.TXT    Deflating (72%), done.
   Adding: TEXT-DIR/TENTH.TXT     Deflating (72%), done.

C:\>
```

Complete path information for all files

3. Using Compression Programs

Using ARJ

With ARJ, you don't have to worry about the path when compressing directories. ARJ automatically saves the directory names. If you don't want save the path names, you must specify this. Use the following parameters when working with directories:

-r	Recursively collects files in subdirectories.
-e	Saves filenames without path data.
-a1	Archives empty directories with the others.

By using a brief command, you can immediately save all files, along with their paths, in the archive:

```
ARJ a -r ALLTXT E:\WORD\*.TXT
```

To exclude paths in the archive, use the optional -e switch.

```
Creating archive : ALLTXT.ARJ
Adding     C:\TEST\XX.TXT                   44.9%
Adding     C:\TEST\STARS.TXT                45.5%
Adding     C:\TEST\LINES.TXT                30.5%
Adding     C:\TEST\BYTE901.TXT              25.5%
Adding     C:\TEST\JCI901.TXT               31.3%
Adding     C:\TEST\MAIL819.TXT              38.7%
Adding     C:\TEST\MJCI.TXT                 30.4%
Adding     C:\TEST\PC.TXT                   43.3%
Adding     C:\TEST\SUB\BYTECON.TXT          12.8%
Adding     C:\TEST\SUB\BYTEDESC.TXT         12.2%
Adding     C:\TEST\SUB\JCI816.TXT           42.6%
Adding     C:\TEST\SUB\MJCI.TXT             30.4%
Adding     C:\TEST\SUB\MAIL819.TXT          38.7%
Adding     C:\TEST\SUB\BYTE.TXT             24.7%
Adding     C:\TEST\SUB\JCI.TXT              52.6%
Adding     C:\TEST\SUB\README.TXT           53.4%
Adding     C:\TEST\SUB\RPT.TXT              44.9%
Adding     C:\TEST\SUB\X_JCI.TXT            23.8%
Adding     C:\TEST\SUB\ASSOC.TXT            40.7%
Adding     C:\TEST\SUB\STARS.TXT            45.5%
   20 file(s)

C:\>
```

Compressing with ARJ without path data

What appears on the screen can be misleading. Duplicate filenames appear on the screen, but just the filenames, not the paths, are saved in the archive. However, something is wrong with the previous compression procedure. The ARJ archive now contains several files with the same name. If you display the archive, you'll see the duplicate files.

3. Using Compression Programs

```
XX.TXT           187          84 0.449 93-10-01 12:54:50 78AD06CB A--W B+1
STARS.TXT      36397       16576 0.455 93-09-09 14:13:08 6BE76E31 ---W B+1
LINES.TXT       8774        2672 0.305 93-03-08 14:42:46 0E4DA344 ---W B+1
BYTE901.TXT    49900       12715 0.255 93-09-01 16:44:30 BBB3345B ---W B+1
JCI901.TXT     44541       13950 0.313 93-09-01 16:43:08 5C596E8D ---W B+1
MAIL819.TXT   190519       73646 0.387 93-08-19 08:49:44 B515F05C ---W B+1
MJCI.TXT       59860       18226 0.304 93-08-17 09:14:04 9CE945AA ---W B+1
PC.TXT         26102       11303 0.433 93-06-16 16:14:44 BF6BA4B0 ---W B+1
BYTECON.TXT     2541         324 0.128 93-07-13 13:22:54 A8C43728 ---W B+1
BYTEDESC.TXT    2662         326 0.122 93-06-16 09:22:58 5FC4DF7B ---W B+1
JCI816.TXT     18813        8019 0.426 93-08-17 09:48:20 ABEFAE64 ---W B+1
MJCI.TXT       59860       18226 0.304 93-08-17 09:14:04 9CE945AA ---W B+1
MAIL819.TXT   190519       73646 0.387 93-08-19 08:49:44 B515F05C ---W B+1
BYTE.TXT      113485       28060 0.247 93-08-19 08:43:56 F02A11D0 ---W B+1
JCI.TXT         9080        4773 0.526 93-09-01 16:47:48 96DD78A4 ---W B+1
README.TXT       599         320 0.534 93-09-09 14:49:04 FD704230 ---W B+1
RPT.TXT          323         145 0.449 93-09-01 16:44:30 3AC9C03D ---W B+1
X_JCI.TXT      79403       18863 0.238 93-08-17 09:14:42 7D4F473F ---W B+1
ASSOC.TXT       4322        1758 0.407 93-02-26 11:49:00 63D730BE ---W B+1
STARS.TXT      36397       16576 0.455 93-09-09 14:13:08 6BE76E31 ---W B+1
------------ ----------- ----------- -----
    20 files  934284      320208 0.343

C:\>
```

Duplicate files in the archive

The archive contains duplicate and multiple listings of the same files. For example, "STANDARD.DOC" appears five times. But you also see from the file sizes, dates, and times, that all the files are different. Therefore, files with the same names don't overwrite each other. Actually, with ARJ, it doesn't matter under which names the files are saved under.

> When you decompress the ARJ archive, you must be careful with files that have the same name. If you decompress all files into a directory, several files having the same name cannot be placed in the same directory. So, these files would gradually be overwritten.

Empty directories

You're probably wondering why anyone would compress an empty directory. However, doing this is helpful because it saves you work when compressing a previously-installed program to an archive so you can move the program to a different computer. If you compress the empty directories needed by the program, these directories will be set up, according to the original structure, on the target computer when you decompress the archive. So, you won't have to re-install all the directories or manually create the missing ones.

You can compress empty directories directly only with ARJ. With LHA and PKZIP, you must use a few tricks.

The command for ARJ is as follows:

```
ARJ a -r -a1 ALLDIR *.TXT
```

In the above line, an archive called "ALLDIR" will be created from all the files with the TXT file extension. "-a1" ensures that any empty directories will also be backed up. Whether a file is hidden, is important for the system, or is actually a directory, can be determined from the file attribute, which is controlled by DOS.

Since neither LHA nor PKZIP support this attribute, you must do the following:

1. Determine which directories are empty.
2. Create a "dummy" file in each of these directories.

Although the name of this file isn't important, it must be the same in all empty directories. The easiest and fastest way to create this file is with COPY CON. Therefore, switch to the empty directory and enter:

```
COPY CON LITTLE.ONE
a F6 Enter
```

The file is now complete. Its content is the letter "a" and the end-of-file character ^Z, which is created by pressing F6. You can place any letter in the file. However, remember that you cannot press F6 as the first key, because the file wouldn't contain anything and, therefore, wouldn't be created.

3. Repeat this process for each empty directory or simply copy the file to the appropriate directories.

Now you can compress the data. If you want to retain the directory structure along with the files (as in the ARJ example), the PKZIP command would be:

```
PKZIP -a -rp ALLDIR *.TXT *.ONE
```

or for LHA:

```
LHA a -r -x ALLDIR *.TXT *.ONE
```

With these "dummy" files, both compression programs will now also accept the empty directories (which aren't really empty) into the archive. You don't have to delete these files.

Editing Archives

It's important that you keep your archived well-organized. All the compression programs let you edit the archive once it's created. This involves updating and freshening the files of the archive, as we discussed earlier in this chapter. However, the most important commands for keeping your archives organized are **View**, **Delete**, and **Rename**.

3. Using Compression Programs

Examining the archive

To maintain an archive, you must know what an archive contains. As we discussed in this chapter, the **List** command displays the contents of archives.

With all compression programs, the **List** command is entered with one or two letters and can be modified easily by using a switch. This switch determines how the list is displayed and what information is included.

Various kinds of information can be displayed with the **List** command. You can display a simple listing or very technical information, which provides an in-depth look into the archive.

Except for a few minor differences, using the **List** command provides the following information (in this or a similar format):

Filename	Filename	The number of all archived files is displayed in the last line.
Comment	Comment	If the file in the archive has its own comment, this is displayed. With most compression programs, this occurs automatically, but you'll have to activate it for each option.
Date/Time	Date and time	The original file date and time. On the basis of these dates, archives are updated (Update) or freshened (Freshen).
CRC	CRC code	The CRC (Cyclic Redundancy Check) code of a file is a key calculated from the contents of a file according to a complicated mathematical procedure. The correct compression of the data is checked with these codes.
Length	Original file length	The sum of all file lengths is displayed at the end of the table.
Size	According to file length	The total length of all compressed files is displayed at the end of the table.
	Compression	Compressed files shown.
Ratio	Degree of compression	This value shows by what percent the file size was decreased. Many compression programs also show the size of the compressed file as compared to the original (as a percentage). The average degree of compression is displayed at the end of the table.

PKPAK

PKPAK provides only one command for examining the archive. Activate this command with the "-v" option:

```
PKPAK -v ARC
```

The archive contents are displayed in the following format:

```
C:\TEST>pkpak -v arc

PKPAK    FAST!    Archive Create/Update Utility    Version 3.61    08-02-88
Copyright (c) 1986-1988 PKWARE Inc. All Rights Reserved.  PKPAK/h for help

Searching Archive: ARC.ARC

Filename       Length   Method     Size   Ratio   Date       Time       CRC
--------       ------   ------     ----   -----   ----       ----       ---
BYTE901.TXT    49900    Squashed   20974   58%    09-01-93   16:44:30   E944
JCI901.TXT     44541    Squashed   17305   62%    09-01-93   16:43:08   F2BF
LINES.TXT       8774    Crunched    3510   60%    03-08-93   14:42:46   8C4E
MAIL819.TXT   190519    Squashed   86686   55%    08-19-93   08:49:44   0E5C
MJCI.TXT       59860    Squashed   22130   64%    08-17-93   09:14:04   CC8B
PC.TXT         26102    Squashed   12732   52%    06-16-93   16:14:44   1F91
SAMPLE.GIF      8935    Stored      8935    0%    10-01-93   11:45:24   C16D
STARS.TXT      36397    Squashed   18984   48%    09-09-93   14:13:08   F490
XX.TXT           187    Crunched     114   40%    10-01-93   12:54:50   D483
               ------              ------
0009           425215             191370   55%

C:\TEST>
```

Using the -v option to list archive contents

"V" is an abbreviation for "verbose listing" (i.e., detailed listing). The distinction between a normal and detailed listing originates from other compression programs, which actually have two different List functions.

The PKPAK **List** command provides two options for viewing the file. In its complete form, the command is:

```
PKPAK -v[c][m] (Name)
```

With the "m" option, the screen displays pauses when the output no longer fits on the screen. To continue displaying the output, press a key.

Key	Action
Spacebar	Displays the next screen page.
Enter	Displays only the next line and then stops again.
Esc	Interrupts the listing operation.

If you use "m" with small archives, it doesn't affect the output.

3. Using Compression Programs

Use the "c" parameter to display the individual comments of commented archived files.

```
PKPAK -vc ARC
```

Because there are usually numerous comments, they suppress some of the other information.

```
C:\TEST>pkpak -vc arc

PKPAK    FAST!    Archive Create/Update Utility    Version 3.61    08-02-88
Copyright (c) 1986-1988 PKWARE Inc. All Rights Reserved.  PKPAK/h for help

Searching Archive: ARC.ARC

Filename      Comment                                   Date      Time     CRC
--------      -------                                   ----      ----     ---
BYTE901.TXT                                             09-01-93  16:44:30 E944
JCI901.TXT                                              09-01-93  16:43:08 F2BF
LINES.TXT                                               03-08-93  14:42:46 8C4E
MAIL819.TXT                                             08-19-93  08:49:44 0E5C
MJCI.TXT                                                08-17-93  09:14:04 CC8B
PC.TXT                                                  06-16-93  16:14:44 1F91
SAMPLE.GIF                                              10-01-93  11:45:24 C16D
STARS.TXT                                               09-09-93  14:13:08 F490
XX.TXT                                                  10-01-93  12:54:50 D483
----          ------                                    ------    -----
0009          425215                                    191370    55%

C:\TEST>
```

File list with with area for possible comments

If a file has a general comment, it appears at the top of the listing, even if the "c" parameter isn't used.

LHA and LH-ICE

There isn't much difference in how LHA and the completely compatible ICE display archives.

The difference involves two options. While "l" displays a simple list of archived files, "v" also includes the pathnames. This difference is important because LHA and ICE, unlike PKPAK, can also save files from subdirectories.

```
LHA v ARC
```

This command looks very similar to the PKPAK version. The output is divided into two parts because one screen line is always reserved for the path. Because of this, the listing is difficult to read.

If you don't want to display the pathnames of the files, use the short listing. To do this, use the "l" command instead of "v":

```
LHA l ARC
```

A plus sign appears at the beginning of the line if a file has a subdirectory.

```
C:\TEST>h:lha l reports
Listing of archive : REPORTS.L2H

Name            Original    Packed  Ratio   Date       Time     Attr  Type   CRC
---------------------------------------------------------------------------------
FILE1.DOC             21        21 100.0%  93-10-25  16:37:00  a--w  -lh0-  0561
FILE2.DOC             21        21 100.0%  93-10-25  16:37:00  a--w  -lh0-  0561
FILE3.DOC             21        21 100.0%  93-10-25  16:37:00  a--w  -lh0-  0561
FILE4.DOC             21        21 100.0%  93-10-25  16:37:00  a--w  -lh0-  0561
FILE1.XLS             14        14 100.0%  93-10-25  16:37:32  a--w  -lh0-  2B91
FILE2.XLS             14        14 100.0%  93-10-25  16:37:32  a--w  -lh0-  2B91
FILE3.XLS             14        14 100.0%  93-10-25  16:37:32  a--w  -lh0-  2B91
FILE4.XLS             14        14 100.0%  93-10-25  16:37:32  a--w  -lh0-  2B91
FILE1.DBF             15        15 100.0%  93-10-25  16:38:06  a--w  -lh0-  A96E
FILE2.DBF             15        15 100.0%  93-10-25  16:38:06  a--w  -lh0-  A96E
FILE3.DBF             15        15 100.0%  93-10-25  16:38:06  a--w  -lh0-  A96E
FILE4.DBF             15        15 100.0%  93-10-25  16:38:06  a--w  -lh0-  A96E
---------------------------------------------------------------------------------
   12 files         200       200 100.0%  93-10-25  16:39:06

C:\TEST>
```

Short listing of an LHA archive

LHA and ICE don't provide a Pause function. If the listing is too long, the output scrolls over the screen rapidly. To pause the display, press Ctrl+S.

> A better solution is to use the DOS command MORE, which stops the display. Simply add the MORE command to the command line, separating the two with the pipe "|" character:
>   LHA i ARC | MORE

This character is produced by simultaneously pressing Shift+\.

> The MORE command works with all programs that create line-by-line output. So, it's also possible to pause other DOS commands (for example, DIR or TYPE):
>   DIR | MORE   TYPE README.DAT | MORE   MEM /C | MORE

Temporary directories

Compression programs occasionally run slowly. This is particularly noticeable when files have been archived directly onto diskettes or must be freshened or updated on diskettes.

3. Using Compression Programs

The reason for the slowdown in speed is that diskettes are accessed more slowly than hard drives. However, this isn't directly related to creating and processing archives. For example, in order to use **Freshen** or **Update**, working copies must be created, processed, copied, and again deleted. These are time-consuming processes when using a diskette.

The working copy (compression programs also call it a temporary archive) is usually also created where the archive is located. This can lead to problems with memory space. Therefore, there won't be enough space for a working copy on a 1 Meg archive on a diskette.

To eliminate these waiting periods and avoid memory problems, you should swap the archive copy onto the hard drive. Simply add another parameter to the command line.

```
LHA
ARJ    -w(directory)
PAK,
PKPAK,
PKZIP  -b(directory)
```

The directory for the temporary archive is attached directly to the option letters without a space separating them.

```
LHA/ARJ f -wC:\ B:TEXTS *.TXT
PKPAK/PKZIP -f -bC:\ B:TEXTS *.TXT
```

> The directory must exist; otherwise the compression program will stop working. So, you should use the root directory. Since temporary archives must be deleted again immediately after the end of the operation, there is no danger that your root directory will gradually be filled with garbage data.
>
> Another way to speed up this process is to use a RAM disk, which is a simulated drive. One part of your memory is split off to function like a drive. You can access this drive just like any real drive. However, remember that the data on the RAM disk will be lost as soon as you switch off the computer.

The advantages of a RAM disk are obvious. Because all operations take place directly in main memory, this temporary work place is faster than even the hard drive. You can always use this command, if your RAM disk is large enough.

To install a RAM disk, add the following line to the CONFIG.SYS file:

```
DEVICE=C:\DOS\RAMDRIVE.SYS 512 /E
```

3. Using Compression Programs

This installs a driver called "RAMDRIVE.SYS" and activates it in your DOS directory. The RAM disk will have a size of 512K and use extended memory (/e).

The RAM disk automatically receives the next letter in the alphabet as its drive designation after your last hard drive. For example, if you have drives C:, D:, and E:, the RAM disk will automatically be drive F:. In this case, the commands for the compression program will be:

```
ARJ a -r -wF: TABLES \*.XL?
LHA a -rx1 -wF: TABLES \*.XL?
PKZIP -a -rP -bF: TABLES \*.XL?
```

PKZIP

PKZIP includes many parameters for controlling output. If you access PKZIP's help function, you'll see an entire line of complete listing information:

```
-v[b,c,d,e,n,p,s,r,t]
```

Unfortunately, this line is confusing. You can re-organize the options so that they make sense:

```
-v[b,t,c] [d,e,n,p,s] [r]
```

These letters represent the first letter of each option.

PKZIP provides three different types of lists which you can control via the first parameter group. If you don't use one of these parameters, you'll get the default format, which is similar to the ones used by LHA and PKPAK.

Switch	Effect
b	Display of the list in short form (brief). The CRC value and the file attributes aren't displayed. Now the filenames and the path will fit on the screen.
t	Technical display format. Each file produces almost an entire screen page of information. (technical format).
c	Supplementary display of individual comments.

The options are used for sorting the list. Normally, without additional entries, the list isn't sorted. The files are displayed in the sequence in which they were archived.

3. Using Compression Programs

Parameter	Sort by
d	Date, Time
e	Extension
n	Name of the file
p	Percent of compression
s	Size
r	Reverse sorting

Like LHA, PKZIP doesn't have a switch for stopping the output when the screen is full. Therefore, in this case (as in the case of LHA) use the detour via the DOS command MORE.

```
PKZIP -v ARC | MORE
```

The parameters can be combined in any way. However, PKZIP must be able to understand this arrangement. For example, there is nothing wrong with the following List command:

```
PKZIP -vbcpr ARC
```

This command lists the archive in the short form (brief) with all the comments, sorting in reverse order in terms of the percentage of compression.

In this way, it's possible to arrange the list in any order. However, you'll receive the greatest amount of information if you select the technical format with the "t" option. This format can also be combined with sorting:

```
PKZIP -vt | MORE
```

ARJ

The two commands used for listing in ARJ are "l" and "v". The difference between these two commands is that the listing with "v" also displays the saved pathname for filenames and the current number in the archive.

```
ARJ l ARC
```

The listing looks different from the other listings.

3. Using Compression Programs

```
C:\TEST>arj l arc.arj
ARJ 2.30 Copyright (c) 1990-92 Robert K Jung. Jan 19 1992
NOT REGISTERED for business, commercial, or government use.

Processing archive: ARC.ARJ
Archive date      : 1993-10-01 14:55:30
Filename        Original Compressed Ratio DateTime modified  CRC-32   AttrBTPMGVX
-------------   -------- ---------- ----- -----------------  --------  -----------
XX.TXT               187         84 0.449 93-10-01 12:54:50 78AD06CB A--W B 1
STARS.TXT          36397      16576 0.455 93-09-09 14:13:08 6BE76E31 ---W B 1
LINES.TXT           8774       2672 0.305 93-03-08 14:42:46 0E4DA344 ---W B 1
BYTE901.TXT        49900      12715 0.255 93-09-01 16:44:30 BBB3345B ---W B 1
JCI901.TXT         44541      13950 0.313 93-09-01 16:43:08 5C596E8D ---W B 1
MAIL819.TXT       190519      73646 0.387 93-08-19 08:49:44 B515F05C ---W B 1
MJCI.TXT           59860      18226 0.304 93-08-17 09:14:04 9CE945AA ---W B 1
PC.TXT             26102      11303 0.433 93-06-16 16:14:44 BF6BA4B0 ---W B 1
-------------   -------- ----------
   8 files        416280     149172 0.358

C:\TEST>
```

File list with ARJ

The column with the rather strange heading BTPMGVX contains important information about the archived file. These letters have the following meaning:

Letter	Meaning
B	The file is a backup file.
T	Type of file:
	T Text
	B Binary
	D Directory
P	The file contains path information.
M	Compression method from 1 (basic) to 4 (rapid).
G	File was encoded with a key (garbled).
V	The following parts of the file are on other disks.
X	The file is a part of a larger file.

If a plus sign (+) appears in front of a file date, this indicates that a file is from the 21st century. Any file whose date doesn't begin with "19" is displayed this way. You don't have to scroll through long file lists when using ARJ. The "-jp" option halts the display of the list before it can run off the screen.

```
ARJ l -jp ARC
```

3. Using Compression Programs

ZOO

ZOO contains the "-List"command. It lets you easily display an archive:

`ZOO -L ARC`

It's also possible to display several files at once. Since the ZOO archive normally attaches the .ZOO file extension, the following command line is sufficient:

`ZOO -l *.ZOO`

All archives found in the current directory will be displayed in sequence. Normally the faster commands are used instead of the more complex commands. So, "- List" is used as a fast version of the more complicated "VC" command. The following commands and modifiers can be used for listing files:

Modifier	Effect
L	Displays the standard table, in which the usual information about archived files is displayed.
V	The file information is displayed. Any comments are displayed.
v	File information is displayed. Similar to the "V" parameter but only the archive comments are displayed. Comments about individual files are suppressed. The letter "C" indicates that the file has a comment.
C	Displays the CRC code.

```
C:\TEST>zoo -l *.zoo

Archive arc.zoo:
Length   CF   Size Now   Date        Time
-------  ---  --------   ---------   --------
  49900  56%    22296     1 Sep 93  16:44:30 e944   byte901.txt
  44541  60%    18402     1 Sep 93  16:43:08 f2bf   jci901.txt
   8774  60%     3512     8 Mar 93  14:42:46 8c4e   lines.txt
 190519  51%    94010    19 Aug 93  08:49:44 0e5c   mail819.txt
  59860  60%    23568    17 Aug 93  09:14:04 cc8b   mjci.txt
  26102  50%    13104    16 Jun 93  16:14:44 1f91   pc.txt
  36397  49%    18945     9 Sep 93  14:13:08 f490   stars.txt
    187  39%      115     1 Oct 93  12:54:50 d483   xx.txt
-------  ---  --------              --------
 416280  53%   193952              8 files

C:\TEST>
```

Modifier Effect

3. Using Compression Programs

Using Batch Files to Compress Data

Now that you're more familiar with the various compression programs, you've probably realized that you must remember a lot of parameters in order to use these programs properly.

However, there is a way to simplify the compression procedures that you perform frequently. To do this, use batch files, which you can create quickly and easily. These files execute the commands contained in them again and again. This saves you time because you don't have to type the same commands each time you want to use them.

> Obviously, you can also create batch files for decompressing data, or for entirely different tasks, which aren't related to data compression.

You can begin with a batch file that contains your standard compression command. This procedure is useful only if you always compress your archives in the same way, and don't change names or parameters. Although this may sound inflexible, this is very common. For example, we use our compression program in the same way to archive recently written text files and back them up onto diskettes. In the following example, we'll use ARJ, but any other file compression program can be used for this.

The following is an example batch file that can be used for automatic compressing:

```
COMPI.BAT
@ECHO OFF
REM
REM COMPI.BAT
REM
ECHO Please insert backup diskette in B: and press key
..
PAUSE > NUL
ECHO All text files in E:\WORD are backed up
ARJ u -r -WC:\  B:\BACKUP E:\WORD\*.DOC > NUL

IF ERRORLEVEL 1 GOTO ERROR
ECHO.
ECHO All text files were backed up correctly,
ECHO archiving complete.
GOTO END
:ERROR
ECHO.
```

3. Using Compression Programs

```
ECHO Error during archiving.
EHCO Please repeat process.
ECHO Archiving terminated.
:END
ECHO.
```

The main line in this file is the one that activates ARJ. All text files in the E:\WORD directory are collected recursively. Even subdirectories are included in the search. The BACKUP archive will be updated directly on the diskette. To speed up this process, we used the "W" parameter to set up a temporary C:\ directory. Here the necessary rearrangements of the ARJ archive can be implemented more quickly than on the diskette itself (where it would be done without the switches).

Once the compression procedure is complete, a check is made to determine whether an error has occurred. This can be determined by checking which error code ARJ returns in the DOS variable. Anything other than a 0 is considered an error and is treated as such.

If you want to experiment, you can take a closer look at the error code. Almost all file compression programs return such a code, which provides detailed information about the error. Chapter 8 contains the error table for each compression program.

You can create a separate batch program to determine the code. This batch program can then be incorporated into other batch files like a normal command. You should name this program "ErrText.BAT" (ErrorText).

```
@ECHO OFF
REM
REM ErrText
REM Returns the error code and
REM displays the error text
REM

IF ERRORLEVEL 8 GOTO F8
IF ERRORLEVEL 7 GOTO F7
IF ERRORLEVEL 6 GOTO F6
IF ERRORLEVEL 5 GOTO F5
IF ERRORLEVEL 4 GOTO F4
IF ERRORLEVEL 3 GOTO F3
IF ERRORLEVEL 2 GOTO F2
IF ERRORLEVEL 1 GOTO F1

:No_error
  ECHO
```

```
  ECHO Everything Ok., archiving complete
    GOTO End

:F8
  ECHO.
  ECHO Insufficient main memory available
  ECHO Archiving halted
  ECHO.
  GOTO End

:F7
  ECHO.
  ECHO False parameter in the command line
  ECHO Archiving halted
  GOTO End

:F6
  ECHO.
  ECHO Archive or file cannot be opened
  ECHO Archiving halted
  GOTO End

:F5
  ECHO.
  ECHO Diskette or hard drive is full
  ECHO Archiving halted
  GOTO End

:F4
  ECHO.
  ECHO ARJ backup system damaged
  ECHO Archiving halted
  GOTO End

:F3
  ECHO.
  ECHO CRC file data incorrect
  ECHO Archiving halted
  GOTO End

:F2
  ECHO.
  ECHO Fatal error on diskette or hard drive
  ECHO Archiving halted
```

3. Using Compression Programs

```
    GOTO End

:F1
    ECHO.
    ECHO Error during processing of archive
    ECHO Archiving halted

:End
    ECHO.
```

This routine can be incorporated into COMPI.BAT. Instead of checking for a general error with the following line

`IF ERRORLEVEL 1 GOTO ERROR`

the line is replaced by the call to the ERRTEXT.BAT batch file. The improved version of the batch file appears much smaller after the routine is incorporated into it:

```
@ECHO OFF
REM
REM ERRTEXT.BAT
REM

ECHO Please insert backup diskette in B: and press key ..
PAUSE > NUL
ECHO All text files in E:\WORD are backed up
ARJ u -r -WC:\ B:\BACKUP E:\WORD\*.DOC > NUL

CALL ErrText
```

If you use a different compression program, you must only change the call to the compression program in COMPI.BAT. Finally, the program for returning the error text must still be changed according to the respective compression program.

Decompressing Data

Eventually, an archive must be restored to its original state. Usually this procedure isn't difficult. However, since compression programs are so complex, you may encounter some problems.

In this chapter we'll discuss the different aspects of decompression. Besides the general operations, we'll discuss the characteristics of the individual compression programs in detail.

If you already have complete compressed archives, you can continue immediately. Otherwise, first you should familiarize yourself with compressing files and creating archives. Refer to Chapter 3 for this information.

Integrated or diversified

Not all data compression programs use the same procedure for decompressing files. For some, the dual functions of compressing and decompressing are handled by a single program. The functions are then activated by using command switches. For example, the following command compresses files:

```
LHA a CMPDATA
```

With the following command, the files of the archive are decompressed:

```
LHA e CAMPDATA
```

So, a single letter determines which function is activated.

There are also programs that can perform only one function. For example, the PKZIP/PKUNZIP pair is primarily responsible for packing and unpacking ZIP archives respectively. However, both PKZIP and PKUNZIP include functions for managing files in the archive and providing important information. Therefore, it's possible to delegate all elementary functions to external programs. Actually, several programs deal exclusively with manipulating and processing archives. For example, these programs can do the following (among others):

- List
- Delete
- Repair
- Convert

4. Decompressing Data

Such programs are used on the DOS level along with the specified archives. In the case of PKZIP/PKUNZIP, the command would be:

`PKUNZIP ARCHIVE`

In this case, a command letter isn't needed because PKUNZIP's only purpose is to decompress archives. However, PKUNZIP also contains commands and parameters that make decompressing files more flexible and efficient. You'll learn more about these options later.

Decompressing Archives

The process for opening archives and removing files is usually very simple. Transferring all or only specific files from an archive to a directory requires only a few parameters. Since you can remove files individually or in groups, you don't have to extract all the files from the archive and then delete unneeded files on the DOS level using the DEL command.

With all the compression programs, files with the same name can be overwritten by compressed data. However, if you don't want this to happen, you can use the additional parameters described below. The decompression command is always used the same way:

1. LHA e TRANSFER
2. PKUNZIP TRANSFER *.TXT *.DOC *.WRI
3. ARJ e TRANSFER !TEXTS -x*.BAK

The above examples demonstrate how easy it is to decompress archives. If you've read Chapter 3, you already know what these commands do.

1. LHA decompresses all files contained in the TRANSFER archive.
2. PKUNZIP extracts from the TRANSFER archive only files with the .TXT, .DOC, or .WRI extension.
3. ARJ removes all files from the TRANSFER archive that appear in the TEXTS list file. Only files with the .BAK extension aren't removed.

4. Decompressing Data

Program	Command Line
LHA	LHA e TRANSFER
ICE	ICE e TRANSFER
PKZIP	PKUNZIP TRANSFER
PKPAK	PKUNPAK TRANSFER
ARJ	ARJ e TRANSFER
ZOO	ZOO -extract TRANSFER
	ZOO e/x TRANSFER
PAK	PAK e TRANSFER

Without additional file specifications, the data compression program automatically assumes that all the files contained in the archive should be decompressed into the current directory. However, you can specify an individual file or several files.

If you have the PAK compression program, the command line is as follows:

```
PAK e ARC *.DB? *.XL?
```

The above command decompresses all the files in the ARC archive whose file extensions begin with "DB" or "XL." This example also applies to other compression programs:

```
ARJ e ARC *.DB? *.XL?
PKUNPAK ARC *.DB? *.XL?
LHA e ARC *.DB? *.XL?
```

Besides simply listing filenames, some compression programs also process list files. The filenames, which can then be evaluated by the program, are saved in such files. ARJ and PKUNZIP can process these lists. Simply add the filename to the command line:

```
ARJ e ARC *.DB? *.XL? !TEXTS
PKUNZIP ARC *.DB? *.XL? @TEXTS
```

In the above examples, the direct file entries will return all files in the TEXTS list file. Remember that ARJ and PKUNZIP use different symbols to indicate list files. With ARJ, you must place an exclamation point (!) in front of the list and with PKUNZIP, you must use an "at" symbol (@). These symbols are needed to notify the program that it must evaluate the file contents instead of processing the name of the list file itself.

4. Decompressing Data

ARJ is the only compression program that lets you exclude certain files during decompression. As with compression, it's possible to name a file more than once and combine them with list files by using the "-x" option.

```
ARJ e ARC -x*.BAK -x*.COM -x!NOTT.HAT
```

This command extracts all files from the ARC archive except files with the .COM or .EXE extensions and the files named in the NOTT.HAT list.

> As you know, PKZIP also lets you exclude files from compression. However, for decompressing data, you must use PKUNZIP, which doesn't provide this feature.

Selecting working directories

If you don't want to place the decompressed data in the current directory, you can send the files to any directory on any storage medium. To do this, simply enter the target path of your files after the archive name, such as

```
LHA e ARC C:\REPORT\ *.TXT *.DB? *.XL?
```

or

```
ARJ e ARC C:\REPORT\ *.TXT *.DB? *.XL?
```

As you can see, a trailing backslash (\) is added to the "C:REPORT" path entry. If this backslash was used with the DOS command, an error would occur. However, with compression programs, this backslash is needed for the operation to run.

Enter the path as follows:

```
PKUNZIP ARC C:\REPORT\ *.TXT
PKUNPAK ARC C:\REPORT\ *.TXT
LHA e ARC C:\REPORT\ *.TXT
ICE e ARC C:\REPORT\ *.TXT
ARJ e ARC C:\REPORT(\) *.TXT
PAK e ARC C:\REPORT\*.TXT
```

Remember, the file extension (here *.TXT) must be entered directly after the target path only with PAK. This procedure resembles that of DOS commands (for example, COPY C:\REPORT*.TXT). However, the target directory must already exist.

Creating directories

All the data compression programs listed in the table (except PAK) let you create directories. If a directory doesn't exist, it can be created.

4. Decompressing Data

```
ARJ e ARC C:\WORD\REPORT\
```

In the above command line, ARJ quickly determines that "C:\WORD\REPORT" doesn't exist. In this case, the program prompts for your permission to create this directory.

If you confirm this action, the directory is automatically created. Any additional files will be decompressed into the new directory. If choose not to create the directory, ARJ tries to decompress the files at the designated place, but won't be able to because the target directory doesn't exist. In this case, you must enter a new name for each file or another path.

```
C:\WORD>arj e arc c:\word\report\
ARJ 2.30 Copyright (c) 1990-92 Robert K Jung. Jan 19 1992
NOT REGISTERED for business, commercial, or government use.

Processing archive: ARC.ARJ
Archive date     : 1994-04-18 15:09:02
C:\WORD\REPORT\CD-ROOT.TXT, Create this directory? [YNAQ] y
Extracting CD-ROOT.TXT    to C:\WORD\REPORT\CD-ROOT.TXT  CRC OK
Extracting THIRD.TXT      to C:\WORD\REPORT\THIRD.TXT    CRC OK
Extracting FOURTH.TXT     to C:\WORD\REPORT\FOURTH.TXT   CRC OK
Extracting FIFTH.TXT      to C:\WORD\REPORT\FIFTH.TXT    CRC OK
Extracting SIXTH.TXT      to C:\WORD\REPORT\SIXTH.TXT    CRC OK
Extracting SEVENTH.TXT    to C:\WORD\REPORT\SEVENTH.TXT  CRC OK
    6 file(s)

C:\WORD>
```

A directory is created

> ARJ only creates directories if the target path ends with a backslash. So, if you're sure that the target directory already exists, you don't have to enter the backslash.

LHA and ICE operate basically the same way. Needed directories are created automatically. If you specify that a directory should be created, any additional files will be decompressed immediately. If you choose not to create the new directory, you'll be asked to confirm the compression of each file individually. However, the option of entering the name of the file individually, as in the case of ARJ, doesn't exist.

In the case of PKUNZIP and PKUNPAK, it's important that the directories already exist. Otherwise, an error will occur.

4. Decompressing Data

With PKUNZIP, this behavior can be changed with the "-d" option. If this option is included in the command, the required directories are created automatically. Therefore, the backslash (\) isn't needed.

```
PKUNZIP -d ARC C:\REPORT *.TXT
```

LHA lets you decompress archives directly into several directories simultaneously. This feature is particularly helpful when you've archived many files of different types and then want to work on them separately. Specify this in the command line by entering more than one directory. All the filenames following the name of a directory will be placed in this working directory.

```
LHA e REPORTS C:\WORD\ *.DOC C:\DATA\ *.XL? *.DB?
```

```
C:\TEST>h:lha e reports c:\word\ *.doc c:\data\ *.xl? *.db?

Extracting from archive : REPORTS.LZH

'c:/word/FILE1.DOC' : Make directory? [Y/N] Y
Melted    FILE1.DOC    c
Melted    FILE2.DOC    c
Melted    FILE3.DOC    c
Melted    FILE4.DOC    c
'c:/data/FILE1.XLS' : Make directory? [Y/N] Y
Melted    FILE1.XLS    c
Melted    FILE2.XLS    c
Melted    FILE3.XLS    c
Melted    FILE4.XLS    c
Melted    FILE1.DBF    c
Melted    FILE2.DBF    c
Melted    FILE3.DBF    c
Melted    FILE4.DBF    c

C:\TEST>
```

Separate working directory in LHA and ICE

The italicized options are the working directories. All files with the .DOC extension are compressed into the C:\WORD directory, and all XL- and DB-files are compressed into the C:\DATA directory. If these directories don't exist yet, they are created by LHA after prompting you for confirmation. So, conflicts are no longer possible. If a file was already decompressed into a working directory, it cannot be decompressed again into a different directory. Although it isn't possible with this procedure, duplicating files could be helpful:

```
LHA e REPORTS C:\TO_ME\ *.DOC *.DB? C:\TO_YOU\ *.DOC
```

PAK includes this feature in a similar format. By the entry of several files you can control where certain files will be decompressed. For example, the following command

```
PAK e ARC C:\WORD\*.DOC C:\DATA\*.DB? C:\DATA\*.XL?
```

decompresses the following types of files:

4. Decompressing Data

File	Directory
DOC	Into the C:\WORD directory
XL?	Into the C:\DATA directory
DB?	Into the C:\DATA directory

PAK isn't as flexible as LHA, because if several file types must be decompressed into a directory, you must then enter a separate target path for each in the command line. If the target path is unavailable, PAK will skip decompressing the file ("xxx" skipped).

Preventing prompts

The prompt asking whether a directory, which doesn't exist, should be created during decompression can be suppressed. To do this in LHA, ICE, and ARJ, use the following parameters:

Option	Command
-m	LHA e -m ARC C:\REPORT\
	ICE e -m ARC C:\REPORT\
-y	ARJ e -y ARC C:\REPORT\

Not all data compression programs can easily redirect the output of the extracted file into a different directory (or drive). However, you can use the DOS command CD to jump into the target directory before you begin decompressing. Then you can start the decompression process. In this way, the files will still be placed into the desired directory.

```
C:
CD \WORD\REPORTS
ZOO e ARC
```

Protecting existing files

When you decompress archives, sometimes files with the same name already exist in the current or working directory. Unlike the DOS commands COPY and XCOPY, the compression programs don't immediately overwrite the file in the target directory with the uncompressed version. Instead, the data compression program notice whether files have the same names and then responds as follows:

➤ Skip the file.

4. Decompressing Data

> Indicate that a file of the same name already exists and asks whether the file should be overwritten.

> Compare the ages of the files and overwrite the file in the target directory, if it is older.

> Let you specify another name for the uncompressed file or do this automatically.

The following figure shows how ARJ responds to this situation:

```
C:\UNPACK>arj x arc
ARJ 2.30 Copyright (c) 1990-92 Robert K Jung. Jan 19 1992
NOT REGISTERED for business, commercial, or government use.

Processing archive: ARC.ARJ
Archive date     : 1993-10-01 14:55:30
XX.TXT          is same or newer, Overwrite? [YNAQ] y
Extracting XX.TXT         CRC OK
Extracting STARS.TXT      CRC OK
Extracting LINES.TXT      CRC OK
BYTE901.TXT    is same or newer, Overwrite? [YNAQ] y
Extracting BYTE901.TXT    CRC OK
JCI901.TXT     is same or newer, Overwrite? [YNAQ] y
Extracting JCI901.TXT     CRC OK
MAIL819.TXT    is same or newer, Overwrite? [YNAQ] y
Extracting MAIL819.TXT    CRC OK
MJCI.TXT       is same or newer, Overwrite? [YNAQ] y
Extracting MJCI.TXT       CRC OK
PC.TXT         is same or newer, Overwrite? [YNAQ] y
Extracting PC.TXT         CRC OK
    8 file(s)

C:\UNPACK>
```

ARJ finds files with the same names

ARJ interrupts the procedure and lets you specify what you want to do:

Letter	Effect
Y - Yes!	ARJ decompresses the file in question and overwrites the version already on the disk.
N - No!	The file is decompressed, but you can enter a new name for the archived file. The file will be skipped if you press (Enter).
A - All!	All remaining files are decompressed without additional prompts. Existing files with the same name are overwritten.
Q - Quit!	The decompression procedure stops and the file is not overwritten.

4. Decompressing Data

The other data compression programs provide similar options. However, you usually only have choice between Yes or No.

Switching off safety prompts

Occasionally, you should suppress the compression program's safety prompts and answer all the prompts at once with "Y" ("Yes"). By doing this, the compression procedure won't be interrupted by prompts that you must answer. You should suppress the safety prompts when you want to decompress batch files quickly.

The tables in the following section specify which options should be used to switch off certain safety prompts in the different compression programs.

ARJ

ARJ displays the safety prompt if a file with the same name already exists. The file's age doesn't matter. Therefore, it's dangerous to switch off all prompts. However, by using special options, you can control how the age of files is handled by ARJ.

Option	Function
e	Standard command for decompressing.
-n	New. Decompresses files only if a file with the same name doesn't exist.
-f	Freshen. Decompresses files only if an older version exists in the directory.
-u	Update. Decompresses files only if a file with the same name doesn't exist on the target directory or such a file is older. It combines -n and -f.
-jo	Creates a new name for the archived file when a file with the same name exists.
-y	General 'Yes' to all questions.

Qualified "Yes"

-jy..	Option beginning for qualified YES.
..c	Prompt during creation of a new directory.
..d	Prompt on deleting a file from a directory.
..n	Prompt after a new filename.
..o	Prompt relative to overwriting an existing file.

4. Decompressing Data

The "-y" switch is the simplest YES you can specify in ARJ. It's also the most comprehensive YES, because almost every prompt is suppressed. So, the prompts can be switched off as needed. The introduction of "restricted prompts" is accomplished with the "-jy" switch. You can then attach one or more additional letters to these two, depending on which prompts you want to suppress.

```
ARJ e -jyco ARC C:\WORD\REPORT\
```

The above command prevents prompts from appearing when a new directory is created or when existing files are overwritten. However, instead of deciding whether the current or the archived file contains the more important information, you can have ARJ save both files together.

With "-jo", you tell ARJ to create a new name in the case of a duplicate name for the decompressed files. ARJ simply deletes the file extension and replaces it with a number. For example:

```
LETTER.TXT    ----> LETTER.000
```

Now you must identify the new file and change the name again.

```
C:\UNPACK>arj x -jo arc
ARJ 2.30 Copyright (c) 1990-92 Robert K Jung. Jan 19 1992
NOT REGISTERED for business, commercial, or government use.

Processing archive: ARC.ARJ
Archive date    : 1993-10-01 14:55:30
Extracting XX.TXT        to XX.001         CRC OK
Extracting STARS.TXT     to STARS.001      CRC OK
Extracting LINES.TXT     to LINES.001      CRC OK
Extracting BYTE901.TXT   to BYTE901.001    CRC OK
Extracting JCI901.TXT    to JCI901.000     CRC OK
```

ARJ renames files

LHA and ICE

By default during compression, LHA and ICE do not overwrite files if a newer file with the same name is found in the target directory. Older files are overwritten following the usual prompt.

Use the following options to change this procedure:

4. Decompressing Data

Option	Function
e	Standard command for decompressing archives.
-c	The file date of the archived file is ignored. Therefore, even recent files can be overwritten.
-m	Prevents the safety prompts from being displayed.
-m2	Only for LHA. Decompresses files with the same name, but generates new file extensions in numerical format (for example, LETTER.000).

```
LHA e -c ARC *.TXT
```

With the above command, LHA decompresses all .TXT files in the archive into the current directory. By using the -c option, each file having the same name is overwritten following a prompt, regardless of its date.

```
ICE e -cm *.TXT    (or ICE e -c -m *.TXT )
```

The same result is produced with the above command. However, files with the same name are deleted without the prompt.

```
LHA e -cm2 *.TXT  ( or LHA e -c -m2 *.TXT )
```

If you use the above command, files with the same name aren't overwritten. Instead, the decompressed files receive new names, which are clearly distinguished from the versions in the target directory. "LETTER .TXT" then becomes "LETTER.000" (or another number, depending on which are available).

ICE files can be decompressed by LHA. Also, ICE may be able to decompress LHA files (depending on the age of the programs).

Since LHA is a program descendent of ICE, LHA knows all the compression and decompression algorithms of ICE. However, ICE doesn't know the more recent methods. Therefore, LHA files that were compressed with the current compression method cannot be processed.

```
LHA e ARC.ICE
```

or

```
ICE e *.LZH
```

4. Decompressing Data

PAK

Option		Function
e		Decompression command.
/WP	Write Over- Prompt	Displays a safety prompt, if a file already exists (default setting).
/WN	Write Over Never	Existing files are never overwritten.
/WA	Write Over Always	Existing files are overwritten without prompts.
/WO	Write Over Older	Existing files are overwritten only if they are older than the version in the archive.
/D		Decompresses only those files from the archive which also exist in the target directory. Can be combined with all /Wx parameters.

> If you've defined more than one /W option in a command, the safer option will take priority over the less safe. This means that the option that overwrites the least number of files is the option that will be used. Therefore, /WN has higher priority than /WP, which has higher priority than /WO and /WA.

```
PAK e /WN ARC
```

With the above command, all files from the ARC archive are decompressed into the current directory. If any files in the archive have the same name, they won't be decompressed.

```
PAK e /D /WO ARC C:\TEXTS\*.TXT C:\DAT\*.DB?
```

The above command specifies that files in the ARC archive that have the .TXT file extension will be decompressed into the C:\TEXTS directory and the .DB? files will be decompressed into the C:\DAT directory. Obviously, only the files that appear in the archive and target directory (/D) are included in the selection process. Only relatively old files are replaced by more current ones (/WO).

4. Decompressing Data

ZOO

Option		Function
e,x		Alternative decompression commands.
S	(Supercede)	Existing files are overwritten in the target directory, even if they are more recent than the archived versions.
O	(Overwrite)	The safety prompt doesn't appear.
N	(Neverlands)	The archive is being tested. The files are being decompressed into an empty space.

> ZOO normally (when there are no special parameters) overwrites all older files in the target directory, after the safety prompt appears. If you use the O option with S, archived and obsolete files may overwrite current and important information.

Be sure to use uppercase O.

```
ZOO eO ARC
```

With the above command, ZOO unpacks the ARC archive into the current directory (e) and overwrites older files without safety prompts (O).

```
ZOO eSO ARC
```

With this command, all the files of the current directory will be overwritten by archived files that have the same name, regardless of the age of the file (S). A safety prompt doesn't appear (O).

PKUNZIP

Option		Function
-f	(freshen)	Only files, which are older than the archived files, located in the target directory are decompressed. Safety prompts don't appear.
-n	(newer)	Newer archived files overwrite existing files. A safety prompt doesn't appear.
-o	(overwrite)	Existing files are overwritten without additional safety prompts.
-d	(directory)	Creates necessary directories automatically.

4. Decompressing Data

> Without additional options, PKUNZIP always displays a prompt when there are similar files in the working directory. The difference between -f and -n is that, with -n, files which are not yet present in the target directory are also decompressed. -o overwrites all files, regardless of age.

```
PKUNZIP -o ARC *.TXT
```

The above command decompresses all .TXT files from the ARC archive. Any files in the target directory that have the same name are replaced; safety prompts aren't displayed.

```
PKUNZIP -f ARC
```

With this command, only files present in both the target directory and the archive are decompressed without any safety prompts, if the decompressed files are more current.

PKUNPAK

Option		Function
-n	*(newer)*	Newer archived files overwrite existing files. A safety prompt doesn't appear.
-r	*(replace)*	Existing files are overwritten; safety prompts don't appear.

> PKUNPAK's decompression process is the same as PKUNZIP's process. However, remember that the Freshen option "-f" isn't available in PAK.

```
PKUNPAK -r ARC *.D*
```

The above command decompresses all files which have extensions beginning with "D", from the ARC archive. If files with the same name are located in the target directory, they are deleted, regardless of their age. Safety prompts aren't displayed.

```
PKUNZIP -n ARC C:\TRANSFER\
```

With the above command, all files are decompressed from the archive into C:\TRANSFER. If a file with the same name already exists, this file is overwritten, if it's older. Safety prompts don't appear.

4. *Decompressing Data*

Decompressing Directories

Now that you've learned how to decompress individual files, we'll discuss decompressing entire directories. We've divided these topics into two separate sections because only a few compression programs, such as LHA, ICE, ARJ and PKZIP, can automatically compress entire directory trees.

You can decompress an archive with or without the directory and path information. The second method (without path information) works like the normal decompression of archives. This means that it doesn't disturb directory information. In this case, "e" is used as a command switch, and the files are decompressed together into a directory.

The directory structure is restored in the target directory by decompressing an archive with path information. So, it's possible to archive and move entire directory trees easily. Use "x" as the command letter for this decompression method.

> All the options for the "normal" decompression of files that we've discussed also apply to decompressing directory archives. Therefore, in this section, we'll concentrate on the problems that can occur with archived directories.

Before you can decompress archives with directories, obviously first the archives must be compressed properly. With ARJ, you don't have to worry about correct compression, because path information is incorporated into the archive automatically. LHA and ICE, however, usually store only the filenames. Therefore, these programs need a special command to include the pathnames when the files are compressed. This also applies to PKZIP. (For more information on using the different compression programs, refer to Chapter 3.)

It's easy to decompress archives that have compressed directory structures. Although many parameters were needed for each command during the compression process, the data compression program can (almost) automatically restore the directories in an archive. If the directory tree was originally stored properly, with most compression programs, you can simply enter the correct start command. For example, with LHA, enter the following:

```
LHA x TRANS A:\
```

In this case, an archive, including all files and directories, will be transferred to the diskette. Simply confirm the prompts that appear, if an existing file may be overwritten or a new directory should be created. (As we explained in the previous section, you can switch off these prompts.)

Relative and absolute paths

To understand how directory structures are stored in archives, you must understand the concept of relative and absolute directory positions. We'll explain these concepts by using an example.

Suppose a person rings your doorbell and asks you the quickest way to get to the bus station. You tell this person to go the second traffic light and turn left. The bus station is about 2 miles down, on the right side of the street.

Perhaps this is the quickest way to the bus station from your house. However, these directions are correct only from your current location. If the person had stopped and asked your neighbor on the next street for directions, he/she would have gotten a different answer. So, the directions you've given are valid only from your location at the moment (i.e., they are correct "relative" to your position). This is similar to a relative path.

You could also answer this person's question another way. Instead of using your house as a starting point, you can use a stationary and specific location. Therefore, you could change your directions to "stand with your back to the water tower, go down the street to the fourth traffic signal, turn right, and then left."

Unlike the first description, this way (or path) is based on a fixed location. The starting point of the path (the water tower) is absolute and always the same. In this case, it doesn't matter whether you give these directions while standing on your front porch or from your favorite restaurant.

To apply this example to relative and absolute paths, replace the stationary water tower with the root directory on the hard drive. Regardless of the size of your directory structure, the root directory is unique and can be reached from any location. Therefore, all path descriptions starting from this point reach their goal (if the path is specified correctly).

Restoring directory structures

Restoring directory structures is closely related to compressing data. The following figure of a tree structure should help you understand the examples we'll present in the following sections. In this directory structure (which isn't the only one on drive D:), there are various files which must be archived according to their purpose.

4. Decompressing Data

```
Directory PATH listing
Volume Serial Number is 10F5-0A44
C:.
├──DOS
├──BIN
├──LABELS3
├──WINAPPS
│   ├──CSERVE
│   │   ├──WINCIM
│   │   ├──SUPPORT
│   │   ├──SCRIPTS
│   │   ├──FCABINET
│   │   │   ├──CABINET
│   │   │   │   ├──GENERAL
│   │   │   │   │   └──FOLDER00.000
│   │   │   ├──BASKET.IN
│   │   │   └──BASKET.OUT
│   │   ├──GIF
│   │   └──DOWNLOAD
├──FOXPROW
├──WTM21A
├──BKTOOLS.USR
├──WINWORD
-- More --
```

Typical directory tree

If the archive was compressed properly, it should be easy to decompress the files. Use the following commands to retrieve both files and directories:

```
PKUNZIP -d PASCAL D:\COPIES\
ARJ x -y PASCAL D:\COPIES\
ICE x -x PASCAL D:\COPIES\
LHA x PASCAL D:\COPIES\
```

As you can see, the commands of the individual programs differ only slightly. With all the compression programs, you can decompress the archive wherever you want by specifying a target directory.

In the following sections, you'll learn how to prepare the archive for later compression and which parameters are important for "directory-bound" archives.

PKUNZIP

PKUNZIP needs the -d option to create directories automatically. Without this option, all archived files will be written to the target directory without path information. As a result, the files, which were still separated by a directory in the archive, are now grouped together in the target directory. If there are files with the same names, they won't be decompressed.

Since absolute paths of files aren't saved by PKZIP, they cannot be decompressed by PKUNZIP. Whether the entire directory structure is transferred correctly depends on you.

For example, to archive the BPASCAL directory completely, use the PKZIP command:

4. Decompressing Data

```
PKZIP -a -rP PASCAL \BPASCAL\*.*
```

The P switch saves the complete path in the PASCAL archive. Now you must decompress the archive at the proper location. To do this, use the path entry in PKUNZIP.

```
PKUNZIP -d PASCAL A:\
```

The above command completely restores the archive on diskette. The required directories are created automatically.

```
PKUNZIP -d PASCAL D:\COPIES\ *.BAK
```

With the above command, all files with the .BAK extension are decompressed under the D:\COPIES directory. Any directory containing a .BAK file is created automatically. The new directory structure will appear as follows:

```
C:\TEST>pkunzip -d test c:\unpack\ *.bak

PKUNZIP (R)   FAST!   Extract Utility   Version 2.04g  02-01-93
Copr. 1989-1993 PKWARE Inc. All Rights Reserved. Shareware Version
PKUNZIP Reg. U.S. Pat. and Tm. Off.

■ 80386 CPU detected.
■ XMS version 2.00 detected.
■ DPMI version 0.90 detected.

Searching ZIP: TEST.ZIP
   Inflating: c:/unpack/XX.BAK
   Inflating: c:/unpack/STARS.BAK
   Inflating: c:/unpack/JCI901.BAK

C:\TEST>
```

Decompressed archive with directories

```
PKUNZIP PASCAL C:\BUNCH\
```

In the above command, PKUNZIP decompresses all files in PASCAL into the C:\BUNCH directory, if it exists. Because the "-d" parameter wasn't included, C:\BUNCH and the directories contained in the archive won't be created.

LHA and ICE

Unlike PKZIP, LHA and ICE save the paths as they were defined in the command line during compression. So, the following command line is possible:

```
LHA a -rx PASCAL D:\BPASCAL\*.*
```

4. Decompressing Data

This command always works correctly because it includes the absolute path to the data that must be compressed. To confirm this, use the "v" command:

```
Listing of archive : VB.LZH

    Name        Original    Packed  Ratio   Date      Time      Attr Type  CRC
 -------------  --------    ------  -----   --------  --------  ---- ----- ----
/WINAPPS/VB/SETUPKIT/KITFILES/SETUPWIZ.EXE
                 150670     30388   20.2%  93-04-28  00:00:00  a--w -lh5- B0FF
/WINAPPS/VB/SETUPKIT/KITFILES/SETUPWIZ.HLP
                  22018     14432   65.5%  93-04-28  00:00:00  a--w -lh5- 3555
/WINAPPS/VB/SETUPKIT/KITFILES/COMPRESS.EXE
                  15259      9683   63.5%  93-04-28  00:00:00  a--w -lh5- 864F
/WINAPPS/VB/SETUPKIT/KITFILES/SETUP.EXE
                  15312      8731   57.0%  93-04-28  00:00:00  a--w -lh5- 09D6
/WINAPPS/VB/SETUPKIT/KITFILES/EXPAND.EXE
                  14001      8856   63.3%  93-04-28  00:00:00  a--w -lh5- 7026
/WINAPPS/VB/SETUPKIT/KITFILES/SETUPKIT.DLL
                   7008      2873   41.0%  93-04-28  00:00:00  a--w -lh5- 5B90
/WINAPPS/VB/SETUPKIT/KITFILES/SETUPWIZ.INI
                   3638      1354   37.2%  93-04-28  00:00:00  a--w -lh5- 0D0A
/WINAPPS/VB/SETUPKIT/KITFILES/SETUP.LST
                     40        40  100.0%  93-04-28  00:00:00  a--w -lh0- FD41
/WINAPPS/VB/SETUPKIT/KITFILES/COMPRESS.TXT
                    630       290   46.0%  93-04-28  00:00:00  a--w -lh5- CE11
-- More --
```

Archive with absolute path data

Unfortunately, you may encounter problems when decompressing this LHA archive, because the files cannot be decompressed into any directory other than the main directory. The absolute path entries (the leading backslash makes that clear) will always begin in a \BPASCAL directory when restored.

If you want to be able to decompress the archive into any directory, you should use a different compression procedure. Avoid including absolute paths in the command line. To do this, use two commands instead of one:

```
CD \
LHA a -rx XB BVB\*.*
```

The same files will be compressed. Only the leading backslash in the command line is missing. However, to ensure that the files will be found, the preceding jump to the main directory is important. Now you can decompress the archive into any directory:

```
LHA x VB D:\COPIES\
```

If any directories don't exist on the target drive, they are created automatically by LHA. The "x" command has a built-in confirmation that answers the prompt. If you want to confirm the prompt yourself, add the "-m" option:

```
LHA x -m VB D:\COPIES\
```

4. Decompressing Data

ICE works in almost the same way as LHARC. However, there are a few small differences. The version of ICE we're using (Version 1.14 of 7/15/89) is slightly older than LHARC. Most of these differences involve compression. However, it is important whether the "-r" parameter, for recursive collection, and "-x", for switch on expanded filenames (path information), are switched. In ICE, the correct sequence is:

```
ICE a -xr ...
```

If these options are set up differently, they won't make any sense. In this case, ICE will stop working and display an error message about finding duplicate filenames.

ARJ

ARJ again provides the longest list of options, even if they aren't needed for the decompression. Obviously, the structure of the directory tree is already established in the archive. So, you can immediately begin decompressing the data. Since the directory operations are being used, the command letter "x" is now used instead of "e":

```
ARJ x PASCAL D:\COPIES\
```

If additional options aren't specified, ARJ always saves and compresses the files relatively. Therefore, it's possible to transfer an archived directory tree to any desired location. In the above example, the familiar BPASCAL tree will always fall under the D:\COPIES directory. Remember that with ARJ, even empty directories are again decompressed or created, if you collected them with the "-a1" option during compression.

```
ARJ a -r -a1 PASCAL D:\BPASCAL\*.*
```

The safety prompts, which have appeared several times, can be suppressed. For information on how to do this, refer the first section in this chapter. You can also enter a comprehensive "YES":

```
ARJ x -y PASCAL
```

The "-y" option ensures that the decompression process won't be interrupted by prompts indicating missing directories or duplicate filenames.

You can force ARJ to decompress the archive into the main directory. Simply attach the "-jf" option to the command:

```
ARJ a -r TRANS A:\*.*
```

ARJ archives all files and the entire directory structure on the diskette in drive A. If this structure should be transferred to drive C, use "-jf" to force the data compression program to decompress the archive into the main directory:

4. Decompressing Data

```
ARJ x -jf -y TRANS C:
```

The necessary directories will be created automatically and without any prompts. This is handled by the "-y" switch.

Damaged Archives

Occasionally, you may encounter an archive that cannot be decompressed. In this case, messages, such as "Broken archive", "Bad Data", "Bad Huffman code", "CRC-Error", and "Header damaged" appear. Regardless of the message that's displayed, the result is the same. These messages indicate that the archive is damaged in some way.

This is particularly frustrating when you can no longer access the original files. In this case, there is nothing you can do if the compression program doesn't have a function for repairing the damage.

Errors in the individual files are less serious. Although the file may be lost, the archive itself isn't in danger. The compression program usually indicates an error, if the CRC code of a file is no longer correct. During compression, this code is determined by file contents and saved in the archive. An error occurs when the CRC code, for some reason, no longer matches the original value.

Most of these errors are caused by faulty disk operations. However, even incompatible software cache programs can produce these errors.

As long as the archive is still intact, the damaged file can be removed. To do this, simply use the **Delete** command, which is included in every data compression program. First you must determine which file is damaged. If you didn't notice this during decompression, you should test the archive. Then you'll be able to identify the error.

All the compression programs use the same test command, "t":

```
LHA t COR
PKUNZIP -t COR
ARJ t COR
```

To test the archive, the program decompresses it. However, instead of being written onto the disk, the decompressed data isn't written anywhere. The CRC code can be recalculated and compared with the stored value. Other discrepancies can also be discovered by using this method.

4. Decompressing Data

It can be dangerous to the entire archive if structural information, called the header, is changed. This header contains important information on the location, starting position, length, compression methods, etc. of the files. It's possible that all subsequent data will be lost if the header is unusable.

For example, if the file header of the third archived file is defective and, as a result, the file length cannot be determined, then it will no longer be possible to access the beginning of the next archived file.

A less serious problem involves compressed files that are defective. In this case, there isn't much danger to the archive. However, a defective data region can be disastrous, if an important document happens to be the one that's damaged.

You can easily determine what was damaged by using the integrity test. For example, the KAPUT.LZH archive originally had seven files. However, after a test run, LHA suddenly reports something quite different:

```
LHA t KAPUT
```

```
C:\WORD\PACKER>LHA  t  KAPUT

Testing archive    :    KAPUT.LZH

Testing EXTRAH.BAK   .  .  .  .  .  .
Broken archive.

C:\WORD\PACKER>
```

The archive is damaged

Of the seven files, only one remains and this file is defective. This is indicated by the "Decompressing marker." Not all the points in the circles are filled. This simply means that an error occurred in this archive in the middle of the decompression process.

Because of this error, the file header "EXTRAH.BAK" was apparently overwritten. As a result, the files following it can no longer be located. The program displays the "Broken archive" message. If only the data region of the file is defective, the message "CRC Error" appears and the structure of the archive isn't destroyed. In this case, the only solution in LHA is to try to delete the damaged file. You may be able to do this because you know the name of the defective file, which is probably "EXTRAH.BAK." Use the "d" command to delete this file:

```
LHA d KAPUT EXTRAH.BAK
```

If the response to this command is "EXTRAH.BAK Deleted", the operation was successful. However, if LHA still displays the message "Broken archive", the files are lost forever.

4. Decompressing Data

As you can see in the figure below, our example operation was successful. The EXTRAH.BAK file was deleted. To verify this information, run the integrity test, which provides the remaining files.

```
C:\WORD\PACKER>LHA  t  KAPUT

Testing archive      :    KAPUT.LZH

Testing EXTRAH.BAK   .   .   .   .   .   .   .
Broken archive.

C:\WORD\PACKER> lha d kaput extrah.bak

Deleting from archive:   kaput.lzh
EXTRAH.BAK Deleted
```

The damaged file is deleted

PAK recognizes CRC errors and damaged header files. PAK also looks for and can even find headers, if the archive is not too badly damaged.

Although ARJ and PKZIP/PKUNZIP have special functions for managing damaged archives, these programs cannot miraculously change bad files into good ones.

In ARJ, use the decompression command with the "-jr" option", if header information is damaged and the ARJ archive can no longer be decompressed in the normal way with "e" or "x":

```
ARJ e -jr KAPUT
```

ARJ tries to find the local headers of the individual archives again, if it is no longer possible to locate the files in the archive on the basis of the available information.

"-jr" can be attached to all commands that aren't related to compressing files. So, you can't use this option with a-Add, u-Update, f-Freshen, and m-Move, for example.

If you use "-jr" with damaged files, at the end of the output, you may see a message indicating that ARJ has reached the end of the file unexpectedly. This occurs because ARJ no longer has information about the length of the file in the case of a damaged archive.

4. Decompressing Data

```
C:\TEST>h:arj e -jr test
ARJ 2.30 Copyright (c) 1990-92 Robert K Jung. Jan 19 1992
NOT REGISTERED for business, commercial, or government use.

Processing archive: TEST.ARJ
Archive date     : 1993-10-25 16:34:24
Extracting COMMAND.COM    CRC OK
Extracting WINA20.386     CRC OK
Extracting CONFIG.OLD     CRC OK
Extracting CONFIG.SYS     CRC OK
Extracting AUTOEXEC.BAT   CRC OK
Extracting AUTOEXEC.OLD   CRC OK

Can't read file or unexpected end of file

C:\TEST>
```

Using the -jr option

If PKUNZIP can no longer decompress an archive because the headers are destroyed, then PKZIPFIX is used. This program reconstructs damaged information or finds the next header if the questionable header is completely unusable. PKZIPFIX works relatively successfully, because the ZIP archives contain some structural information that isn't needed.

It's easy to use this program because there aren't any parameters. Simply enter the filename of the archive; the rest is automatic.

The program restores the file information, so the decompression process can be performed. CRC errors and other discrepancies aren't removed. Instead of being located in the original KAPUT.ZIP file, the final result is placed in a separate file called "PKFIXED.ZIP." Now you can decompress the file with the following command:

```
PKUNZIP PKFIXED
```

If an archive was repaired with PKZIPFIX, use the data output by PKUNZIP carefully. Because of defective data, the files can be incorrectly decompressed and completely useless.

To check this data, we produced a test case. We copied a small text file (with legible contents) five times, archived it with PKZIP, and then processed the archive with a disk editor. As expected, PKUNZIP could no longer do anything with the archive and demanded PKZIPFIX.

4. Decompressing Data

PKZIPFIX seems to have taken care of the problem. But after decompressing the repaired archive again with PKUNZIP, it was obvious that the file information was no longer correctly decompressed. Instead of producing readable information, the file contained only garbage characters.

As you can see, after decompressing damaged archives, you must ensure that the decompressed files were correctly restored.

Self-Extracting Archives

Self-extracting archives are extremely helpful because they make it easier to distribute data to others. Not only can you transfer entire directory structures, but, more importantly, the person receiving this data doesn't need a specific compression program or even know anything about data compression.

Unlike a normal archive file, which requires a specific compression program, a self-extracting archive simply needs its own start command, which is actually its own name. So, these archives are easy to use.

The system operators (or sysops) of the many bulletin board systems were the first to use self-extracting archives. These operators placed the data that must be sent to the bulletin board users directly into a self-extracting archive. This helped them avoid many problems caused by users not having the proper version of a compression program in order to extract the necessary data.

Although the file sizes increased because of the automatic compressing, the amount of confusion and frustration among users was drastically reduced. Today, self-extracting archives are widely used.

> Self-extracting archives are also called "SFX archives." We'll use this abbreviation when discussing these archives in this chapter.

Structure of SFX archives

The structure of an SFX archive is actually quite logical. One part is the actual archive, which is built by the data compression program in the usual way, and the other part is the decompressor for the archive.

The decompressor portion is basically the algorithm, which is also used in the actual compression program, in decompression mode. The most important goal of an archive is to save as many bytes as possible.

Obviously, it wouldn't make sense to use compression methods that squeeze out every last bit of room and then cancel this out by using an elaborate SFX portion that requires a great deal of space.

The individual SFX modules (i.e., the portions of the file responsible for automatically decompressing the archive) are significantly different from one another. This is true in performance as well as in length (performance usually has a negative effect on length).

These "mini-modules" are often capable of amazing results. For example, with some SFX files, it's possible to display the contents or update the file without using the compression program.

It's also possible to treat an SFX archive like a normal archive and simply not worry about decompression. So, the following command is acceptable:

```
LHA u ARCHIVE.EXE \PRODUCT\
```

With the above command, the compression program isn't concerned about the archive stuffed into the SFX module. Therefore, it's also possible to execute other operations, for which no provision is made in the self-extracting archive.

Using Self-Extracting Archives

By now you know that an SFX archive is able to decompress itself onto a storage medium. When decompressing archives, you must determine whether a function is already built into the compression program or is implemented as a separate program. LHA and ARJ use the built-in function.

The other data compression programs use self-sufficient programs to make a simple archive into a self-extracting archive. You can identify these programs by their names, such as MAKESFX and ZIP2EXE.

Most data compression programs also include the option of determining whether the SFX module should be large and powerful (with many options) or as small as possible.

When only a limited amount of space is available, it's possible to create the best setup. However, small SFX modules don't have any expanded capabilities, such as decompressing directory structures or updating list functions.

5. Self-Extracting Archives

SFX archives and ARJ

It's easy to create self-extracting archives with ARJ.

As the only program with this capability, ARJ can provide its archive with the SFX module during compression. However, even a complete, normal archive can be equipped with the automatic decompressing function. The other data compression programs also operate according to this principle.

By adding the following parameters to the normal ARJ command lines, you can control the creation of SFX archives:

Parameter	Meaning
-je	An SFX archive is created during compression.
-je1	A small SFX archive is created during compression.
y	The SFX supplement is added to a completed archive.

You can create SFX archives by using all the functions that create normal archives, such as **Add**, **Update**, and **Move**.

```
ARJ u -je DBFS C:\DBASE\*.DB?
```

The above command collects all databases in the dBASE directory on the C: drive and archives them in the SFX archive DBFS. A normal archive is not created with this command (i.e., an archive without the decompressor). Only the .EXE archive is created.

To obtain both a normal ARJ archive, as well as the SFX archive, first you must create a normal archive. This archive is then "SFX-ized" with the "y" option:

```
ARJ u DBFS C:\DBASE\*.DB?   (Creates the archive)
ARJ y -je DBFS              (Creates the supplementary SFX archive)
```

The SFX option "je" can also be used with directory options. Therefore, you can combine entire tree structures, which are then placed on the target drive.

```
ARJ u -r -a1 -je -jf C:\TOTAL A:\*.*
```

With the above command, all files and directories (even if they are empty) on the diskette in drive A: are transferred into the SFX archive "TOTAL" on the hard drive. The "jf" option ensures that the files are saved with their complete path data. To decompress the archive onto another diskette, simply start the SFX archive.

```
TOTAL B:\
```

5. Self-Extracting Archives

All the entries contained in this archive are decompressed onto drive B:. However, before a file is taken from the archive, ARJ first asks you to confirm whether decompression should begin:

```
Processing Archive:    C:\TOTAL.EXE
Archive Date:    1/12/1993        10:40:03
Continue extraction?
```

This prompt appears whenever an SFX archive is started. You can respond with "Yes", "No", or "Quit". During decompression, ARJ always checks whether safety concerns are being impaired, and interrupts the process if files are overwritten or directories must be created.

```
C:\TEST>selfex

ARJSFX 2.30 Copyright (c) 1990,91 Robert K Jung. All rights reserved.
ARJSFX -? for help.

Processing archive: C:\TEST\SELFEX.EXE
Archive date      : 1993-10-26 11:16:56
Continue extraction? y
FILE1.XLS     is same or newer, Overwrite? y
Extracting FILE1.XLS     to FILE1.XLS
Unstoring            14 bytes, OK
FILE2.XLS     is same or newer, Overwrite? y
Extracting FILE2.XLS     to FILE2.XLS
Unstoring            14 bytes, OK
FILE3.XLS     is same or newer, Overwrite? n
Skipped FILE3.XLS
FILE4.XLS     is same or newer, Overwrite? y
Extracting FILE4.XLS     to FILE4.XLS
Unstoring            14 bytes, OK
      3 file(s)

C:\TEST>
```

Safety prompts are included with SFX decompression

You can use the YES option "y" so that all prompts will be automatically confirmed. So, it's possible to have automatic decompression while suppressing all prompts:

```
TOTAL -y B:\
```

ARJSFX features

With approximately 15,000 bytes, the SFX module of ARJ (abbreviated as ARJSFX) is rather large. However, it provides various options and is very powerful. For information about these SFX options, use the ARJSFX Help option "?". For example, to display information about the SFX archive created above, simply enter:

```
TOTAL /?
```

The following Help screen appears:

5. Self-Extracting Archives

```
C:\TEST>total /?

ARJSFX 2.30 Copyright (c) 1990,91 Robert K Jung. All rights reserved.
ARJSFX -? for help.

Usage: ARJSFX [-command] [-switch(s)] [directory\] [file(s)]

Commands:
  e: Extract files              v: Verbosely list contents
  l: List contents              x: eXtract files with pathname (default)
  t: Test contents

Switches:
  a: show ANSI comments         n: only New files (not exist)
  c: skip time stamp Check      p: match with Pathname
  f: Freshen existing files     u: Update files (new + newer)
  g: unGarble with password     y: assume Yes on queries
  i: no progress Indicator

Robert K Jung, 2606 Village Road West, Norwood, MA 02062, USA

C:\TEST>
```

Displaying information about ARJSFX options

> An important difference between the normal ARJ compressor and the SFX archive is that a dash "-" must appear before commands and switches. This ensures that individual files with single-letter names, such as E or X, can be decompressed.

The commands are used as with normal decompression. So it's easy to list or test the archive:

`TOTAL -t`

Only one command switch may appear in the line. However, it's possible to use other switches. For example, the following command displays all the files in the archive named "STANDARD":

`TOTAL -l STANDARD.*`

This is possible because ARJ automatically saves files with their path information or archives files that have the same name. Use the "-P" option to change the display:

`TOTAL -l -p STANDARD.*`

Now files that have only "STANDARD" in their path information will be displayed. This includes the STANDARD.BAK or STANDARD.STY file, but not the \WORD\STANDARD.DOC file.

When updating or freshening, the files in the archive are updated. With the ARJSFX module, use the following switches to determine which files on the target disk should be replaced by archived files:

Switch	Function
-u	Update (new + newer)
-n	Only missing files (new)
-f	Only recent files (freshen)

These options are the same as the ones used during normal decompression. With the following command, you can decompress the TOTAL archive into the current directory. Older files are overwritten without any prompts, and missing files are added.

```
TOTAL -u -y
```

This command is equivalent to the ARJ version:

```
ARJ x -u -y TOTAL.EXE
```

What was created by ARJ can also be canceled. Although it's possible to decompress an SFX archive, delete the .EXE archive, and convert the uncompressed data into a normal archive again, this isn't necessary. Instead, simply use the **Join** "j" command:

```
ARJ j NEW TOTAL.EXE
```

This command links archives. In the above example, the TOTAL archive is "bound" to the NEW archive. The result is a normal NEW.ARJ.

You can combine almost any archives by using the **Join** command. For example, you can create an SFX archive that contains all the smaller SFXs.

Suppose that you archive all your diskettes and create ten individual SFX archives, DISK0 through DISK9, from these diskettes.

```
ARJ u -r -je -jf C:\DISKx A:\*.*
```

In this case, you'll have ten archives in the root directory of the hard drive. With a simple command (join) you can bind these archives together into a single SFX archive:

```
ARJ j -je ALLDISK DISK?.EXE
```

When you delete the individual archives, you'll save 135,000 bytes. This occurs because, for each archive, 15,000 bytes are needed for the SFX module. Now you only have to do that once.

5. Self-Extracting Archives

ARJ's mini mini-module

The short version of the SFX module is called ARJSFXJR. With 5,400 bytes, this SFX module is significantly smaller than the ARJSFX module. As a result, it doesn't include the familiar functions of the larger SFX module.

Although it supports directory structures, ARJSFXJR doesn't display a prompt if a new directory must be created. Instead, it automatically does this. Also, if files of the same name are in the target directory, the files are overwritten.

With these capabilities, the mini-SFXJR module is ideal for passing data to others because the recipient doesn't have to know anything about archiving. However, even if he/she does know how to use the ARJ compression program, it isn't difficult to process an SFXJR module.

SFX archives and LHA

LHA also includes a built-in function for creating self-extracting archives. Unfortunately, LHA cannot directly create .EXE archives. LHA generates an SFX archive with the "s" switch:

```
LHA s EASY *.TXT
```

However, when you activate this command, the following error message appears:

> Archive not found 'EASY.LZH'

This is can be confusing, since the help information indicates that the "s" switch makes a self-extracting archive. However, it's easy to figure out why LHA refuses to run: LHA cannot generate an SFX file while compressing data. Therefore, the sequence of operations must be: First archive, then .EXEcute. In other words, first you must produce a normal LHA archive using the familiar capabilities of LHA. For example, if we use the example in which text files must be packed into an archive called "EASY.LZH", the entry would be as follows:

```
LHA u EASY *.TXT
```

Only then is the "self-decompressor", as these archives are called, created with the "s" option:

```
LHA s EASY
```

Other options aren't necessary. Now the following message appears instead of an error message:

> Making SFX of Archive 'EASY.LZH'

5. Self-Extracting Archives

Then all archived modules are inserted into the SFX module.

LHA's SFX modules

LHA can produce two different versions of the SFX module. The smaller module is automatically used if the "s" switch is used without additional options. However, you can use the following options when creating the SFX archive:

Option	Effect
-x0	Default. Produces the small SFX module.
-x1	Creates the SFX module with expanded capabilities.

The smaller module stores files in an archive and can decompress these files in a target directory. This module doesn't work with directories. Also, the smaller SFX module cannot determine whether a file should be overwritten to update or freshen it. As soon as a file with the same name appears in the target directory, LHA-SFX displays a prompt indicating this.

The SFX module is very small, which is shown by a small file conversion. For example, TOTAL.LZH has a size of 39,384 bytes. After conversion, the result looks like this:

```
LHA s TOTAL
DIR TOTAL
The disk in drive E: is:  It's true!
Directory of E:\WORD\PACKER

TOTAL   EXE      41011   01-13-93   16:08
TOTAL   LZH      39384   01-12-93   18:05
        2 File(s)        80704 Bytes
                       7471104 Bytes Free
```

The SFX archive is only 1,627 bytes larger. Compared with the SFX module of ARJ, this is extremely small. You can also bind the SFX module into the archive. As we mentioned, use the "-x1" switch to do this:

```
LHA s -x1 TOTAL
```

If you compare the larger archive with the normal file, the result is amazing:

```
DIR TOTAL
TOTAL    EXE      41320    01-13-93   16:20
TOTAL    LZH      39384    01-12-93   18:05
         2 File(s)         80704 Bytes
```

5. Self-Extracting Archives

Although the features can't compare with the large SFX module of ARJ, 1,900 bytes are much smaller than 15,000 bytes.

Functions of the LHA SFX module

This small module doesn't provide as many commands as ARJ's module. For example, this module doesn't include a help function. However, the large SFX module does support the restoration of directory structures. With this option, you can send data retrieved from the archive to any location on the hard drive.

TOTAL C:\PRODUCT\DATA

Automatic batch files

LHA also provides a batch file that starts immediately after a large LHASFX archive is decompressed. This file is often called a "telop." In earlier versions of LHA, this file was called "AUTOLARC.BAT." In order for the batch file to start, the following requirements must be met:

1. The SFX module must be created with -x1 (therefore, it's an expanded module).

2. The telop file must be called !.BAT.

3. The SFX archive must be started with the "-!" option.

There are many uses for a telop. For example, you can send the following message to an inexperienced user after an archive is decompressed:

```
@ECHO OFF
CLS
ECHO Bravo, the data are now safe and sound on your hard disk.
ECHO Unfortunately, a tiny error has
ECHO crept in!
ECHO.
ECHO Switch off the screen IMMEDIATELY,
ECHO duck, put your head between your knees and
ECHO protect your neck with your hands.
ECHO RIGHT NOW!!!

ECHO Then count to two hundred and seek
ECHO the help of an expert.

ECHO If none comes, Good Luck!
ECHO.
ECHO Your Data Provider, B. Nice
```

5. Self-Extracting Archives

Regardless of how you use the telop, remember the requirements: You must create the SFX archive with the "-x1" switch, call the telop file "!.BAT", and start the archive with the "-!" supplementary switch. If one of these requirements isn't fulfilled, the batch file won't be executed.

```
TOTAL -!    (Unpacks the SFX archive and then starts !.BAT)
```

> You cannot use tricks to avoid these requirements. For example, if a !.BAT file is located in the target directory, this still won't work. The telop file must be in the archive, because it will be decompressed if the "-!" was entered as the switch.

Either !.BAT is executed (with the "-!" switch) or it is decompressed (without the switch). In the latter case, the batch file isn't started.

SFX archives and PKZIP

As we've mentioned, PKZIP uses many external programs to perform essential functions. Therefore, PKUNZIP is responsible for decompressing the archive. The ZIP2EXE program, in the PK group, creates self-extracting archives. The purpose of this program is indicated by its name, which stands for "from ZIP to EXE." Its only task is to attach an SFX module to a ZIP archive. To distinguish this module from other SFX modules, it's called "PKSFX."

To use the ZIP2EXE program, simply pass the name of the archive to the program:

```
ZIP2EXE Archive[.ZIP] [SFX archive]
```

Use the following command to convert an archive into a PKSFX archive:

```
ZIP2EXE HELLO
```

If a file extension isn't entered, ZIP2EXE assumes you mean a ZIP archive. So, in the above example, a HELLO.EXE archive is created from the HELLO.ZIP archive. It's also possible to create an SFX file, with a different name, from an archive:

```
ZIP2EXE HELLO AUTOMAT.EXE
```

The actual HELLO.ZIP archive isn't transformed. Similar to LHA, a supplementary PKSFX archive is created. This archive can be treated like a normal ZIP file. In this way, a PKSFX is similar to the SFX archives of an ARJ or LHA. Subsequent updating or freshening of a PKSFX is simple:

```
PKZIP -f AUTOMAT.EXE
```

5. Self-Extracting Archives

The above command replaces all files in the AUTOMAT.EXE archive with "new" versions, if any are available. The only difference relative to working with "normal" ZIP archives is that the .EXE file extension must appear in the command line; otherwise PKZIP assumes you want to work on a ZIP archive.

PKSFX archive options

Although a PKSFX module increases the size of the archive by only about 13,000 bytes, it includes many options. To display these options, activate the Help function, which is included with every PKSFX module. To do this, enter the filename, followed by a "/?". These options let you control which files should be decompressed from the self-extracting archive. You can also specify that files with the same name should be overwritten or necessary directories created.

Option	Effect
-n	Overwrites only older files that are present.
-o	Overwrites all files that have the same name.
-d	Creates directories, if they are needed.

These are the same options used with PKZIP and PKUNZIP. Even the command for testing the archive is available. Simply enter the filename, followed by "-t" as you can see in the following figure:

```
C:\TEST>test -t

PKSFX (R)   FAST!   Self Extract Utility   Version 2.04g  02-01-93
Copr. 1989-1993 PKWARE Inc. All Rights Reserved. Shareware version
PKSFX Reg. U.S. Pat. and Tm. Off.

Searching EXE: C:/TEST/TEST.EXE
Testing: TEST.EXE        OK
Testing: SAMPLE.GIF      OK
Testing: LINES.TXT       OK
Testing: MJCI.TXT        OK

C:\TEST>
```

Testing a PKSFX archive

5. Self-Extracting Archives

Since all PKSFX archives can be used with PKZIP or PKUNZIP, other functions from these programs are also available. For example, if saved directory structures should be restored automatically, this is easily done with the PKSFX archive. To do this, enter the "-d" switch in the command line, similar to decompressing normal ZIP archives:

```
"Filename"-d C:\PROJECT\BOSS\
```

With the above command, all files in the AUTOMAT.EXE archive are decompressed into the C:\PROJECT\BOSS directory. The "-d" switch ensures that the necessary directories are created.

SFX archives and PAK

It's as easy to create a self-extracting archive with PAK. The EXEMAKE program converts a PAK archive into an SFX archive.

The information presented above for ZIP2EXE, from the PK family, also applies to EXEMAKE. Simply enter the name of the archive in the command line directly after the conversion command. For example:

```
EXEMAKE ALLDATA
```

Unless additional entries are made, PAK assumes the following:

- ➢ The archive is a PAK file (in our example, ALLDATA.PAK).
- ➢ The SFX file receives the same filename and the .EXE extension (in our example, ALLDATA.PAK becomes ALLDATA.EXE).
- ➢ Decompression occurs in the current directory.

PAK can also work with ARC archives created by PKPAK or the ARC data compression program. If you want to convert such a file into an archive capable of running, the name of the file extension must be specified. This is also true when the SFX file shouldn't have the same name as the archive.

```
EXEMAKE TEXTS.ARC ARCTEXT.EXE
```

In the above command, the -foreign ARC file becomes the self-extracting ARCTEXT.EXE.

An option is then permitted by the executable PAK archive. You can specify the target directory, if you finally decompress the SFX archive.

```
ARCTEXT C:\WORD\DOCUS
```

5. Self-Extracting Archives

> However, the target directory must exist because new directories aren't created. Existing files with the same name aren't overwritten during decompression. Instead, the SFX module prompts you for permission.

PKPAK deviates somewhat from the simple way of constructing SFX archives.

As you learned earlier, a self-extracting file contains two parts, the actual file and a module, which contains the decompression algorithm.

The data compression program (or the appropriate external program, such as EXEMAKE or ZIP2EXE) now generates such an SFX module, copies the archive, and combines the two. This process is as follows:

1. Generate SFX module.
2. Copy archive.
3. Combine the two parts.
4. Then name the result "Filename".EXE.

PKPAK saves itself a lot of work. However, you must use the DOS command COPY /B because you must create an .EXE file. However, don't worry. This doesn't involve programming the SFX module with a program like GW-BASIC. Instead, you must start with the second step listed above.

The SFX module is contained in the PKPAK package. It has the name PKSFX.PGM and must be linked to the archive.

However, the module isn't available. So, you must create it yourself with the MAKESFX program. This program creates the PKSFX module and tailors it to your needs. Simply start MAKESFX and follow the directions:

```
MAKESFX
```

> This procedure must be performed only once. When the PKSFX.PGM module is created, you can immediately start to create the self-extracting archive.

Combining SFX archives

If both the SFX module and the archive are available, simply copy the two parts together into a program. Use the COPY command:

```
COPY /b PKSFX.PGM+ARCHIVE.ARC ARCHIVE.EXE
```

5. Self-Extracting Archives

The COPY command can be used to combine files. To do this, use the plus sign. In the above example, the PKSFX.PGM file is added to the ARCHIVE.ARC and the result is saved in the ARCHIVE.EXE file.

To ensure that the program will run, follow these guidelines:

1. Copy the two parts in the proper sequence. For example, the command "COPY ARCHIVE.ARC+PKSFX.PGM" isn't allowed.

2. Combine only true PKPAK archives with the SFX module.

3. Don't forget the "/B" option when copying.

The "/b" option ensures that the entire file will be copied.

A batch file is useful here. With this file, the self-extracting archive is created easily.

You can simply type this file in your text editor (Norton Commander, EDIT, EDLIN, etc.) and activate it with ARC2EXE.BAT:

```
@ECHO OFF
ECHO.

REM Test of option, and whether files are valid.

IF %1x==x GOTO Error
IF NOT EXIST %1.ARC GOTO Not_there
IF NOT %2x==x IF EXIST %2.EXE GOTO Already_there_2
IF EXIST %1.EXE GOTO Already_there_1

REM Create_the_file

ECHO Create target file ...
IF 2%x==x COPY /b PKSFX.PGM+%1.ARC 1%.EXE>NUL
IF NOT 2%==x COPY /b PKSFX.PGM+1%.ARC 2%.EXE>NUL
ECHO File created.
GOTO end

REM Error messages

:Error
ECHO ARC2EXE - Creates self-extracting archive
ECHO from PKPAK archive.
ECHO.
ECHO Application:
ECHO     ARC2EXE archive [Target archive]
```

5. Self-Extracting Archives

```
ECHO.
ECHO  Tip:
ECHO     The extensions must not be entered,
ECHO     otherwise the program will not run correctly.
ECHO.
ECHO  Examples:
ECHO    ARC2EXE TEST       - Creates the TEXT.EXE FILE from TEXT.ARC
ECHO     ARC2EXE FIRST NEW   - Creates NEW.EXE from FIRST.ARC
GOTO end

:Not_there
ECHO Error!!!
ECHO The file %1.ARC cannot be found, processing terminated.
GOTO end

:Already_there_1

ECHO Error!
ECHO The target file %1.EXE is already present, processing terminated.
GOTO end

:Already_there_2
ECHO Error!
ECHO The target file %2.EXE is already present, processing terminated.

:end
ECHO.
```

This program is self-explanatory, if you read the comments after each REM command. The tests at the beginning of the file are very important. These tests check whether the archive and the target file exist. If ARC2EXE finds an error, the program is interrupted. The COPY command contains two lines because it's also possible to create SFX archives with different names.

Identifying SFX Archives

A confusing aspect of working with SFX archives is distinguishing them from other EXE programs. Obviously, just because a program is an EXE file doesn't automatically mean that it's a self-extracting archive.

5. Self-Extracting Archives

One characteristic that all SFX archives, whether produced by ARJ or LHA, have in common is they all can be processed with the compression program. Normal programs, in other words, .EXE files without archive content, cannot be processed.

Suppose the active directory contains three programs which could be identified as SFX archives. Use the DIR command to display these files:

```
DIR *.EXE
```

```
Disk in drive E: is:  It's true!
Directory of E:\WORD\PACKER\TESTS

SET         EXE     12131   08-02-91   14:53
BA          EXE     13760   04-07-89   12:30
INSTALL     EXE     72927   01-18-93   12:45
    3 File(s)              98818 Bytes
```

Now you can begin testing the files to determine which ones are SFX archives. For our example, we'll use the LHA program. The easiest test is to check the potential archive with the **Test** command:

```
LHA t SET.EXE
```

After you press (Enter), the test results appear:

```
Testing Archive: SET.EXE
No file found
```

The same result occurs with BA.EXE. As you can see in the following figure, only the INSTALL.EXE file is an SFX archive:

```
C:\TEST>lha t install.exe

Testing archive : INSTALL.EXE

Test OK   SET.EXE        cccccccccc
Test OK   BA.EXE         oooooooooooo
Test OK   TEST.ZIP       cccccccccc
Test OK   INSTALL.EXE    oooooooooooooooooooooooooooooo
Test OK   TEST.EXE       oooooooooooo
Test OK   SAMPLE.GIF     cc
Test OK   LINES.TXT      oo
Test OK   MJCI.TXT       oooooooo

C:\TEST>
```

Identifying SFX archives

5. Self-Extracting Archives

Although this method works, using a batch file would be easier. The following batch file, called "IsSFX.BAT", checks whether a specific .EXE file is an SFX file:

```
@ECHO OFF
REM
REM IsSFX.BAT
REM Checks whether a file is an LHA SFX file
REM
If %1x==x GOTO End
IF not exist %1 GOTO Not_there

LHA t %1
IF ERRORLEVEL 1 GOTO Not_an_archive
ECHO The file %1 is an SFX archive
GOTO End

:Not_an_archive
ECHO %1 is not an LHA archive
GOTO End

:Not_there
ECHO File %1 not found.
GOTO End

:End
ECHO.
```

The actual testing takes place in the "LHA t %1" line.

If you're dealing with only one file, you can test this file just as quickly by activating the compression program.

Now suppose that you want to test several .EXE files to determine whether they are associated with various data compression programs. To do this, you must divide the program into two batch files. The first file, IsSFX.BAT, determines the filenames and associates them with the different compression programs. The second file, PTEST.EXE, is the actual test file:

```
@ECHO OFF
ECHO %1
CTTY NUL

:TARJ
  ARJ t %1 > NUL
  IF ERRORLEVEL 1 GOTO TLHA
  CTTY CON
```

```
    ECHO   %1 seems to be an ARJ archive.
    GOTO PEnd

:TLHA
    LHA t %1 > NUL
    IF ERRORLEVEL 1 GOTO TPKZIP
    CTTY CON
    ECHO   %1 seems to be an LHA archive.
    GOTO PEnd

:TPKZIP
    PKUNZIP -t %1 > NUL
    IF ERRORLEVEL 1 GOTO TPAK
    CTTY CON
    ECHO   %1 seems to be a PKZIP archive.
    GOTO PEnd

:TPKPAK
    PKPAK -t %1 > NUL
    IF ERRORLEVEL 1 GOTO PEnd
    CTTY CON
    ECHO   %1 seems to be a PKPAK archive.
    GOTO PEnd

:PEnd
 CTTY CON
```

Although this looks very complicated, it really isn't. The file consists of five parts. Each part tests for a specific compression program. Each of these parts performs the same steps:

1. Calls the **Test** command, along with the file to be checked.

2. Checks whether an error has occurred.

3. In the case of an error, the program concludes that the file isn't an archive. The program then jumps to the next test with GOTO. If an error didn't occur, a message, indicating that the file could be an archive, is displayed.

This structure makes it easy to include a new compression program. Simply insert this command into the file before the ":PEnd" line and change the line with the call to this compression program. For example, to incorporate the (hypothetical) compression program NEWPAK, enter the following:

5. Self-Extracting Archives

```
  ...
  ...
:TPKPAK
  PKPAK -t %1 > NUL
  IF ERRORLEVEL 1 GOTO PEnd
  CTTY CON
  ECHO  %1 seems to be a PKPAK archive.
* GOTO TNewPAK

REM *** here comes the new part ***

:TNewPAK
* NEWPAK test %1 > NUL
* IF ERRORLEVEL 1 GOTO PEnd
  CTTY CON
* ECHO  %1 seems to be a  NEWPAK archive.
  GOTO PEnd

:PEnd
CTTY CON
```

Asterisks precede the lines that have been changed.

However, this program still isn't adequate because it checks only a specific file, whose name must be entered. Now the starting file, IsSFX.BAT, which takes over the rest of the work, is needed to check all the .EXE files of a directory.

```
@ECHO OFF

:Tests
  IF %1x==x GOTO Error
  IF Exist %1 GOTO individually

:Group
  IF %1x==/ex FOR %%V IN (*.EXE) DO CALL PTest %%V
  IF %1x==/Ex FOR %%V IN (*.EXE) DO CALL PTest %%V
  GOTO End

:Individually
  CALL PTest %1
  GOTO End

:Error
  ECHO.
  ECHO IsSFX - Determines whether a program is an SFX archive.
```

```
        ECHO.
        ECHO    Application: ISSFX (file) or /e
        ECHO       ISSFX  P.EXE      - checks P.EXE
        ECHO       ISEXE  /e         - checks all .EXE files in the
        ECHO                           directory
        ECHO       ISSFX             - This Help screen
        ECHO.
        ECHO    Tip:
        ECHO       The program reports only inconsistencies,
        ECHO       not error messages.
:End
        ECHO.
```

Don't let the length of the program intimidate you. The program is easy to use. If you want to check an individual file, activate the batch file as follows:

ISSFX INSTALL.EXE

To check several files, call IsSFX.BAT without filenames, but with the "/E" option:

ISSFX /E

```
C:\WORD>issfx /e
File /e not found.

C:\WORD>issfx1

IsSFX - Determines whether a program is an SFX archive.

   Application: ISSFX (file) or /e
      ISSFX  P.EXE        - checks P.EXE
      ISEXE  /e           - checks all .EXE files in the
                            directory
      ISSFX               - This Help screen

   Tip:
      The program reports only inconsistencies,
      not error messages.

C:\WORD>
```

Checking files with the ISSFX program

5. Self-Extracting Archives

Tips On Self-Extracting Archives

Although SFX archives are easy to use, you should be aware of a few things. In this section, we'll give you some tips on working with self-extracting archives.

Root directories

It's extremely important that the root directory of your hard drive is well-organized. Since the root directory has only a limited amount of space, unnecessary files should be deleted or moved to other directories.

The reason for this space restriction is that the root directory belongs to the system region of the hard drive. This region can contain only 512 entries. So, the root directory cannot contain more than 512 files or directories. Although this may seem like a lot, an archive can include numerous files, which quickly fill up the root directory.

If the root directory is completely filled, no other files can be decompressed. If this occurs, you must delete these files from the root directory. This is easy to do with files that have the same extension but if the archive contains a variety of files, this can be very confusing.

The system files of the root directory may also be overwritten. The following files are especially at risk:

> ➢ COMMAND.COM

and

> ➢ CONFIG.SYS

It's possible that these files will be replaced by files that aren't compatible with your system. If this occurs, your computer may stop working. Because of this possibility, remember that you should always have a backup system diskette available.

Advanced Data Compression Features

Today's file compression programs present the less-experienced computer user with an overwhelming variety of features. You've probably discovered this if you've ever used "ARJ -?" to display the entire ARJ help screen. The few commands needed for normal everyday use are hidden by a jumble of switches, abbreviations, punctuation, and comments.

Because of this, we began this book by explaining the basics of file compression. Now we'll discuss the advanced data compression features, including locked (password-protected) archives, multi-diskette archives, criteria for compressing only selected files, and using file compression in system backups.

As you'll see, some programs provide more options than others. By reading about their various capabilities, you'll be able to choose the compression program that best meets your needs.

We'll start with the functions that are included in most compression programs and then discuss special functions that can be found in only certain programs.

Password Protection

Since the original files cannot be restored without the compression program that was used to compress them, archives are actually encrypted data.

However, to protect an archive completely, you should protect it with a password. The password you type "locks" the compressed data within the archive. Later, the data cannot be uncompressed until the same password is entered to unlock it. Therefore, a password-protected archive is doubly encrypted: Once by compression and again by password locking. The process of uncompressing reverses these steps to decrypt the data into its original form.

6. Advanced Data Compression Features

Scrambling and garbling

Scrambling and garbling are two different methods of locking archived files by using a password. An abbreviation indicates which method the program used.

Working with passwords is always optional. When included, a password follows the associated command.

> Passwords can be used with all commands that involve compressing or uncompressing archives:
>
> Add, Update, Freshen, Move / Extract / Test

You cannot use a password with a command such as List or View because these functions only display filenames. The archive itself isn't affected. Some compression programs, however, display an indicator to show whether an archived file is password-protected.

```
C:\TEST>arj l new
ARJ 2.30 Copyright (c) 1990-92 Robert K Jung. Jan 19 1992
NOT REGISTERED for business, commercial, or government use.

Processing archive: NEW.ARJ
Archive date     : 1993-10-05 14:35:36
Filename        Original Compressed Ratio DateTime modified CRC-32   AttrBTPMGUX<
------------    -------- ---------- ----- ----------------- --------  ------------
SET.EXE            74599      74599 1.000 93-10-04 09:45:46 7B52D732 A--W B 0G
BA.EXE             90369      90331 1.000 93-10-04 09:46:06 6BF3131E A--W B 1G
ISSFX.BAT            326        177 0.543 93-10-05 14:10:52 60C3D4F1 A--W B 1G
TEST.ZIP           74599      74599 1.000 93-10-04 09:45:46 7B52D732 A--W B 0G
TEST.EXE           44898      44567 0.993 93-10-04 09:40:16 41583E67 A--W B 1G
SAMPLE.GIF          8935       8935 1.000 93-10-01 11:45:24 544B2212 A--W B 0G
LINES.TXT           8774       2672 0.305 93-03-08 14:42:46 0E4DA344 A--W B 1G
MJCI.TXT           59860      18226 0.304 93-08-17 09:14:04 9CE945AA A--W B 1G
TOTAL.ARJ         314562     314562 1.000 93-10-05 14:19:34 FD175E96 A--W B 0G
G.ARJ              21050      21050 1.000 93-10-05 14:35:04 D051B126 A--W B 0G
------------    -------- ---------- -----
   10 files      697972     649718 0.931

C:\TEST>
```

ARJ indicates password-protected files

ARJ uses the G-column on the right side of the file list to indicate whether a file is encrypted with password protection. The "G" represents "garble." PKZIP displays password-encrypted files with an asterisk on the normal view screen. The technical view option

```
PKZIP -vt SECRET
```

displays an additional text notation (although it's difficult to see) for such files.

6. Advanced Data Compression Features

Entering the password

A file is password-protected at the time it is compressed. That is why passwords apply to commands that involve the archiving process (Move, Add, Update, Freshen). The password itself can be considered an additional parameter for the command.

ARJ, PAK, and PKPAK use the "g" option (garbling) and PKZIP uses "s" (scrambling). Both parameters have the same syntax:

```
ARJ u -gDIANA SECRET
```

The password parameter immediately follows the other command parameters needed for file archiving. A space isn't inserted between the other parameters and the password parameter. For example:

```
ARJ u -g HELLO SECRET    ( *** wrong!!! )

ARJ u -gHELLO SECRET     ( that's better )
```

This also applies to other programs, as you can see from the following table:

Command	Case-sensitive
ARJ u -gHELLO Archive	yes
PKZIP -a -sHELLO Archive	yes
PKPAK -agHELLO Archive	no
PAK u /gHELLO Archive	no

The above table shows some differences in the way the programs recognize the password option. For PKPAK, the password parameter isn't separated from the other command parameters (in this case, "u" for update). Adding a space causes an error.

With passwords, ARJ and PKZIP/PKUNZIP are case-sensitive. This means that these programs distinguish between uppercase and lowercase characters. So you must remember exactly how you type the password when you lock a file, and use the same capitalization when unlocking it later. To these programs, "HELLO" is a different password than "Hello." PKPAK and PAK, however, aren't case-sensitive. These programs don't distinguish between upper and lowercase characters.

6. Advanced Data Compression Features

ARJ also lets you hide the password while you type it so that no one can see the password on the screen. To hide your entry, type a question mark, instead of a password, directly after the "g" parameter. ARJ requests the password, which will be blanked out on the screen as you type it. For example, if you enter the following command

```
ARJ u -g? NEWARCH *.DBF
```

ARJ will respond with the message:

> Enter garble Password:

If you make a mistake while entering the password, you obviously cannot see it on the screen. So, you'll be prompted to enter the password again to verify that it is correct.

You don't have to use the same password to encrypt every file within an archive. Each file can have its own unique password. However, it would be difficult to remember all these passwords. Also, the archiving process would be very time-consuming because each password must be entered on its own command line, such as:

```
PKZIP -u -sPetER SECRET *.TXT

PKZIP -u -sANnA SECRET *.DBF

PKZIP -u -sX23oSS SECRET RECIPE.GHM
```

The above example uses three different passwords to compress several files into a common archive called "SECRET." Since PKZIP distinguishes between upper and lowercase characters in passwords, you must remember exactly how you entered each password. Of course, you could write down each password, but this defeats the purpose of using passwords.

Accessing protected archives

Passwords actually lock the individual files within an archive, not the archive itself. So, a protected archive is subject to some degree of access, even if all of its data cannot be extracted.

If you forget a password, only files encrypted with that particular password are lost. Any other files stored in the same archive can still be extracted. The password itself isn't stored in the archive. Instead, it is used by a mathematical algorithm in the CRC (Cyclic Redundancy Check) calculation. Encrypted files are followed by unencrypted ones.

6. Advanced Data Compression Features

Note that only the first files are locked. When you try to extract archived data, the program doesn't tell you if you enter an incorrect password. It simply reports a CRC error.

```
ARJ e -ghello SECRET
```

```
C:\TEST>arj x -ghello secret
ARJ 2.30 Copyright (c) 1990-92 Robert K Jung. Jan 19 1992
NOT REGISTERED for business, commercial, or government use.

Processing archive: SECRET.ARJ
Archive date     : 1993-10-05 14:49:14
Extracting SET.EXE       CRC error!
BA.EXE        is same or newer, Overwrite? [YNAQ] y
Extracting BA.EXE        Bad file data, CRC error!
ISSFX.BAT     is same or newer, Overwrite? [YNAQ] y
Extracting ISSFX.BAT     Bad file data, CRC error!
TEST.ZIP      is same or newer, Overwrite? [YNAQ] y
Extracting TEST.ZIP      CRC error!
TEST.EXE      is same or newer, Overwrite? [YNAQ] ^C


C:\TEST>
```

CRC error resulting from incorrect password

The only thing wrong in the above example is that the password isn't capitalized. Since the password used in archiving was "Hello", the extract command fails. As with archiving commands, ARJ lets you hide password entry during extraction. Again, simply type a question mark in place of the password on the command line. For example:

```
ARJ x -g? SECRET
```

> If your files are so private that you must use password protection, you may want to delete the originals once they are safely archived. The Move command does this automatically.

```
PKZIP -m -sIMPORTANT! SECRET *.DBF *.TXT *.XLS
```

Protecting SFX archives

PKZIP and ARJ support password protection for self-extracting archives. The other programs do not.

It's easy to use passwords with SFX archives. For PKZIP, simply convert the protected archive, as shown below:

6. Advanced Data Compression Features

```
PKZIP -a -sVERY SECRET     (first pack with scrambling)

ZIP2EXE SECRET     (then convert)
```

It's also easy to do this in ARJ. The command line simply includes an additional option to make the archive into a protected SFX file:

```
ARJ -a -je -gVERY SECRET
```

In both examples, a self-extracting archive called "SECRET" is built from the files in the current directory and protected with the password "VERY". For extracting, just use the same option ("s" or "g") again.

```
SECRET -sVERY     (for PKZIP archive)
```

or

```
SECRET -gVERY     (for ARJ archive)
```

The files are then unpacked as usual.

> The password options are supported only by the large models of the ARJSFX and PKSFX modules. Remember that these programs also are case-sensitive.

Password protection limitations

Obviously, passwords cannot make your data completely safe from intrusion or carelessness. As we mentioned, passwords lock only the individual files within an archive instead of the archive itself. This means that the archive can still be deleted, copied, or edited with special programs.

Actually, even the files themselves are protected only against unauthorized extraction. They can still be deleted, renamed, or overwritten from the hard drive by unprotected versions.

We'll use an example to demonstrate this problem. Suppose that a disk contains the archive CRITICAL.ARJ, as shown below. You discover that all the files are garbled (a "G" appears on the right side of the listing). However, despite this protection, these files can still be accessed. For example, the following command, which deletes all archived batch files, works normally without a password:

```
ARJ d CRITICAL *.BAT
```

6. Advanced Data Compression Features

```
C:\TEST>h:arj d critical *.bat
ARJ 2.30 Copyright (c) 1990-92 Robert K Jung. Jan 19 1992
NOT REGISTERED for business, commercial, or government use.

Updating archive  : CRITICAL.ARJ
Archive date      : 1993-10-26 11:24:18
Deleting AUTOEXEC.BAT
    1 file(s)

C:\TEST>
```

Deleting files in CRITICAL.ARJ

The next command, which updates all the protected backup files with the extension .BAK, is also executed without any interruption from the program:

`ARJ u CRITICAL *.BAK`

Only the P file and the program remain protected, since neither operation affected them directly.

> As this example demonstrates, password protection has its limitations. Still, passwords are a good way to help keep private information safe. LHA and ZOO don't support password protection of archived files.

Comments

If you do a lot of archiving, you probably know how difficult it is to keep track of your compressed files. At the very least, you should use meaningful filenames that provide clues to the file's contents. Also, almost all compression programs are able to attach comments to entire archives or to individual compressed files. These comments provide information about the file.

When using comments, remember that they occupy disk space. However, since comments aren't compressed, you can easily determine how much they increase the storage requirement for an archive: Each character uses one additional byte.

6. Advanced Data Compression Features

Using comments in PKZIP

In PKZIP, it's easy to add comments to archives. Two commands let you attach comments to an entire archive or to individual files. The following table shows the control parameters:

Option	Description
-z	Comment refers to archive (ZIP comment).
-c	Comment refers to an individual archived file (file comment).
-C	Used with Update or Add to attach comments only to new files being archived.

Comments can have a maximum length of 60 characters. The text of the comment isn't entered on the command line. Instead, PKZIP prompts you for the text on a separate line after you enter the command.

`PKZIP -c SECRET`

With the above command, you can create or edit comments for each file in an archive. If a file already has a comment, first it's displayed.

Simply type the desired comment for each file at the program prompt. If there is an old comment, your entry overwrites it. Press [Enter] to keep an existing comment and move to the next file. To delete an existing comment, type a space and then press [Enter].

`PKZIP -c -u SECRET *.TXT`

The above command updates all .TXT files in the archive called "SECRET." You are prompted for a comment for each new file that's written to the archive.

Use the **View** command to display file comments. PKZIP displays comments either in the long technical format (vt) or as an extra line on the usual columnar format (vc). Both of these formats are special options of the **View** command.

`PKZIP -vt SECRET *.BAT`

The above command shows, for example, all the .BAT files in the SECRET archive in long technical format. Among the information displayed for a given file is any comment currently attached to it. The columnar view, which shows several files on the same screen, is easier to read. The following command activates this format:

`PKZIP -vc SECRET`

6. Advanced Data Compression Features

Creating specific comments for each file in an archive is time-consuming. An alternative is to attach a general comment to the archive itself. An archive comment is displayed whenever the archive (ZIP file) is processed. The switch for an archive comment is "-z" (ZIP comment).

```
PKZIP -z SECRET
```

After you enter the above command, PKZIP prompts you for the archive comment. If one already exists, it's displayed before the prompt. You can revise this comment or replace it with new text. Like at the DOS level, you can copy the comment to the edit line using [F3] or the [→] key. By doing this, you don't have to re-type the text that doesn't have to be changed. The 60-character limit that applies to file comments isn't effective in this case. So, you can type up to one and a half lines before PKZIP sounds a warning beep and stops further entry. Press [Enter] when you're finished typing.

The program now displays the archive comment each time you work with the archive, whether you're extracting, freshening, or even simply viewing the archive contents.

Comments in ZOO

ZOO provides the same types of comment options as PKZIP but the comments can be up to 64K in length. The following commands process file or archive comments:

Option	Meaning
-c	Create or edit the file comment.
c	Same as -comment .
cA	Create or edit archive comment. You must use the same capitalization when typing this command.

```
ZOO -c ARCHE *.TXT
```

The above command lets you add or revise comments for all .TXT files in the archive called "ARCHE." Any existing comments are first displayed. ZOO uses an unusual entry format here. After each comment, on a line by itself, you must type "/END" (or "/end"). So, an entry such as

```
this is my favorite archive /END
```

is interpreted as an unfinished comment that includes the /END sequence as part of its text. The correct format is the following two-line entry:

```
this is my favorite archive [Enter]
/END [Enter]
```

6. Advanced Data Compression Features

Now that the termination sequence is correctly placed on its own line, pressing [Enter] updates the file comment and lets you continue with the next file. Pressing [F6] and [Enter] exits the file-commentating process.

To delete an existing comment, enter the following on the first line:

```
/END
```

> If you frequently delete comments, you should activate the ZOO **Pack** command occasionally. This actually removes old comments, which have been deleted, from the hard drive.
>
> ```
> ZOO P ARCHE    (Pack archive)
> ```

A simple addition to the comment command lets you adds comments to the archive itself:

```
ZOO cA ARCHE
```

In the above command, the added letter "A" (uppercase required) indicates an archive comment. As with file comments, an existing archive comment is displayed before you're prompted for your entry.

To display all the comments, use the **-list** command.

```
ZOO -l ARCHE
```

With the above command, each file in the archive is listed, along with any comments. Because of the large size allowed for comments, you may want to use the DOS command MORE to pause the display when the screen is full.

```
ZOO -l ARCHE | MORE
```

Add the MORE command to page through the information and read it at your own pace.

Comments in ARJ

Of all the programs, ARJ provides the largest selection of options for handling comments. Not only can you create and edit comments for both archives and their individual files, but you can also automatically apply comments that you've already created and saved in a text file. This is very helpful if, for example, you must add a general comment to several BBS archives.

```
ARJ c COPIES
```

6. Advanced Data Compression Features

In ARJ, the **c** command applies comments. You can move through the archive in dialog mode, editing mode, or add the comments for one file at a time. Existing comments are displayed as they are encountered.

ARJ accepts up to 25 lines of comments per file.

At the prompt, enter the desired comment and press `Enter`. To keep an existing comment, press `Enter` without typing any text. To delete a comment, type a space and then press `Enter`.

Instead of entering a comment from the screen, you can have ARJ read it from a text file. To do this in dialog mode, type an exclamation point followed by the filename. This is a useful way to apply long comments.

To display all the comments in an archive, use the (expanded) format. Simply add the "v" command:

```
ARJ v COPIES
```

The display is in tabular form, with each file comment immediately below its associated file entry. If you have long comments, add the "-jp" option to keep the information from scrolling off the screen before you can read it:

```
ARJ v -jp COPIES
```

When used alone, the **c** command applies to both archive and file comments. However, you can add an optional parameter on the command line to distinguish between the two types of comments.

Option	Type
-z	Archive comments
-jz	File comments

The ARJ program's ability to read comments from text files helps create identical comments for archives.

```
ARJ c -zLABEL.TXT COPIES
```

The above command applies a comment to the COPIES.ARJ archive. The text for the comment is taken from a file called "LABEL.TXT". The filename immediately follows the parameter. If a space is added before the filename, an error occurs. The "-z" parameter specifies that the comment should apply only to the archive itself. The individual files aren't affected. If you want to assign your own comments to the files, the command line might look as follows:

```
ARJ c COPIES -zARCHIVE.TXT -jzFILE.TXT
```

6. Advanced Data Compression Features

Now the comment for the COPIES archive is taken from the file called "ARCHIVE.TXT." The text from a different file, called "FILE.TXT", is applied as a comment to each of the compressed files. In this example, the parameters follow the archive name. You can also place them in front of it, as in the previous example.

It's also possible to apply a general comment to all the archives on a disk drive. This is easy to do with ARJ. First prepare the text of the comment and save it in a file. Then search the root directory and all the subdirectories and apply the prepared comment to each archive that's found.

For example, suppose that you're responsible for supplying ARJ archives to several people within your department on a regular basis. You could include the following comment:

```
Please refer problems or questions to
Don Michler - Ext. 5456
```

After saving the comment in a file called "REFER.TXT", you can attach it to every ARJ archive on your hard drive with a single command:

```
ARJ c -r \*.ARJ -zREFER.TXT
```

The "-r" parameter specifies that all subdirectories under the specified directory should also be processed.

By using the DOS term "NUL" instead of a filename, you can delete comments this way. The rest of the command remains the same.

```
ARJ c COPIES -zNUL
```

The above command deletes the archive comment from the COPIES archive. With the following command, all archive and file comments are deleted from all the archives on the current drive:

```
ARJ c -r \*.ARJ -zNUL -jzNUL
```

The following table summarizes the command options for handling comments in ARJ:

6. Advanced Data Compression Features

Option	Meaning
c	Create or edit comments in an archive.
-z	Do archive comments only.
-jz	Do file comments only.
-jzFILE	
-zFILE	Automatically attach comments found in FILE to an archive.
-jzNUL,	
-zNUL	Automatically delete comments from an archive.

Time Stamps

Your computer keeps a record for each file and directory to show the date and time when it was last updated. This is called a time stamp. To display time stamps, use the DOS command DIR.

```
 Volume in drive C is DRIVE_C
 Volume Serial Number is 1AA3-4492
 Directory of C:\

DOS          <DIR>        08-13-91   1:35p
NWLITE       <DIR>        10-12-92  11:31a
BPL_TEST     <DIR>        10-18-93   9:11a
TD_TEMP      <DIR>        10-20-93   9:07a
TD_ORIG      <DIR>        10-20-93  11:33a
COMMAND  COM        52925 03-10-93   6:00a
WINA20   386         9349 03-10-93   6:00a
CONFIG   OLD          210 05-27-93   8:33a
CONFIG   SYS          274 10-26-93   9:51a
AUTOEXEC BAT          499 10-26-93   9:51a
AUTOEXEC OLD          659 05-27-93   8:32a
DBAPPS       <DIR>        10-21-93   5:01p
ST           <DIR>        10-25-93   3:50p
TEST         <DIR>        10-25-93   4:04p
ALLTXT   ARJ         1180 10-25-93   4:46p
WORD         <DIR>        10-26-93  11:00a
DATA         <DIR>        10-26-93  11:00a
       17 file(s)       65096 bytes
                      6567936 bytes free

C:\>
```

Displaying time stamps

6. Advanced Data Compression Features

Time stamps are important in both compressing and uncompressing files. Except for the **Add** command, every operation that moves a file to or from an archive works with the time stamp. The **Update** and **Freshen** commands rely on this information to determine which archived files should be overwritten. For this reason, the time stamp for every file in an archive is carefully preserved, despite the extra storage space that's needed. You can observe this when you use the **View** command, for example, to display a ZIP archive.

In some compression programs, time stamps aren't limited to these functions. In addition to the **Update** and **Freshen** commands, various file selection options can be controlled by time stamps. ARJ can select files, for example, that were created either:

- On a certain date,
- At a precise time on a certain date, or
- Within a certain time span.

In PKZIP, you can check for files that were created or modified on or after a certain date. The option for this is "t." If a date isn't specified, the current date (today) is assumed.

```
PKZIP -urpt TODAY *.XL? *.DB? *.DOC
```

Regardless of how much work you do on your PC in a given day, you can easily update your archive with all the new or changed files by using a command like the one above. The parameters have the following meanings:

Parameter	Meaning
u	Update files.
r	Recursing all subdirectories.
p	Storing paths recursed along with filenames.
t	But only include those files that were created or modified today.

The file extensions further limit the types of files (text, Excel, and database) that will be processed.

PKZIP also lets you specify a date with the -t parameter. If you've been too busy to compress your files, just specify the date when you last did so. For example, the above command adapted for archiving files from the 20th of January, 1993, is:

```
PKZIP -arpt012093 TODAY *.DOC *.XL? *.DB?
```

6. Advanced Data Compression Features

> The time stamp parameter can be used only in compression operations with PKZIP. It doesn't work with commands such as **View**, or for extracting files from an archive. The extraction program PKUNZIP uses the "-t" option to test for data corruption.

ARJ and time stamps

With ARJ, you can examine time stamps more precisely. You can specify not only a date, but also time to the nearest second. Also, there are two separate options for selecting time stamps either before or after a specified cutoff. Finally, time stamps can be used with additional commands for archive file management and extraction operations. For example, you can delete all archived files older than a certain date.

ARJ requires the date/time in descending order (from years to seconds), without separation characters. The format is as follows:

YYMMDDHHMMSS

The letters represent numeric digits in the positions shown.

YY	For the year	MM	For the month	DD	For the day

For example, January 23, 1993 at 7:07:28 pm, would appear as:

930123190728

Although this is difficult to read, you usually don't have to enter the actual time of day.

Option	Meaning
-o[YYMMDDHHM	Selects only files that were created or modified on or after this date/time.
-ob[YYMMDDHHM	Selects only files that were created or modified before this date/time.

With both options, if the date/time is omitted, the current (today's) date is automatically used.

By using these options, you can easily find and archive your old, inactive files. Based on their time stamps, simply move the outdated ones to an archive with the **Move** command, and make room on your hard drive for more current data.

6. Advanced Data Compression Features

Remember that some important files are almost never updated. So, be careful when clearing old files from your hard drive because you may accidentally delete an important file. For example, using the following command to delete files, that are over a year old, from your hard drive could be disastrous:

```
ARJ m -rob920101 DEEPSIX \*.*
```

> Remember, the "*.*" wildcard refers not only to data files, but also to program files. These files usually aren't changed once you install them on your hard drive. So, with one command, you can destroy your operating system files. Then your computer will stop working because you no longer even have the command interpreter COMMAND.COM.

However, with a little care, you can limit the operation only to files that can safely be deleted. For example, most files created by application programs would fall into this category. You can identify many text files (DOC, TXT, WRI), worksheets (XL?, WK?), databases, and graphics by their extensions.

```
ARJ m -rob920101 DEEPSIX \*.DOC \*.TXT \*.WRI ...
```

The above command is much safer than the previous one. We can even improve this command further. Instead of entering all the extensions on the command line, create a list file and pass it to ARJ for processing. For example, with any text editor, you can quickly create a file called "DEEPSIX.DAT", which looks like this:

```
\*.TXT
\*.DOC
\*.WRI
\*.XL?
...
```

Then you can execute the following command:

```
ARJ m -rob920101 DEEPSIX !DEEPSIX.DAT
```

The **Move** command compresses all the appropriate files to your archive and then deletes the uncompressed originals.

> Once you've deleted all the desired files, you should check the contents of the archive. This is important because you may have accidentally deleted an important file. In this case, extract it separately from the archive.

6. Advanced Data Compression Features

Using Attributes to Select Files

Besides a file's size and time stamp, DOS also keeps track of certain information about each file. Programs often check these file attributes and use them as the basis for decisions about file processing. The archive attribute is one of the most common attributes. Whenever a file is created or changed, DOS sets the bit for its archive attribute. This tells backup programs that the file should be archived, because it contains new or changed information. Every file has a bit for each of the attributes listed below:

Attribute	Meaning
Archive	Set by DOS when a file is updated. Backup programs check this bit, then reset it after backing up the file.
Hidden	If this bit is set, the DIR command doesn't display the file, but it can be edited.
Read-only	Files with this attribute cannot be modified or deleted. If you try to do this, the DOS message, "Access denied", appears.
Directory	Indicates an entry is a subdirectory.
System	Indicates a system file, such as IO.SYS or MSDOS.SYS. System files are also hidden.

Compression programs cannot access some of these attributes. Also, compression programs don't use all the attributes that are available. The ability to take advantage of file attribute information can be an important factor in choosing a compression program. With a special attribute switch in ARJ, for example, you can identify empty directories and compress them.

Another consideration is how hidden or read-only files are processed. You'll want to know whether they can be overwritten, archived, excluded from particular types of processing, etc. All compression programs support file privacy. If the hidden or system attribute of a file is set, the file won't be compressed. You can test this yourself by changing to the root directory of your boot drive (the drive your PC starts from) and trying to compress the system files:

```
LHA a TEST *.SYS
ARJ a TEST *.SYS
PKZIP TEST *.SYS
...
```

With the possible exception of HIMEM.SYS, most likely only your CONFIG.SYS file will be compressed. The system files IO.SYS and MSDOS.SYS, which both have the system attribute set, aren't included.

6. Advanced Data Compression Features

PKZIP and ARJ have special parameters for overriding this protection. It is important to understand the implications of file attributes, especially in archiving files. PKZIP recognizes the following attribute parameters:

PKZIP File attribute options	
-w[h,s]	Include
	h hidden
	s system
	files in archive. The two parameters h and s can be combined.
-W[h,s]	Exclude hidden (h) or system (s) files from archive. This is the default.

In ARJ, attribute parameters are handled differently:

ARJ-File attribute parameters	
-a	Compresses every file, regardless of attributes.
-a1	Compresses every file (like -a) and empty directories.
-b	Compresses only updated files, which carry the archive attribute (also called backup bit).
-b1	Compresses updated files (like -b) and clears the archive attribute.
-b2	Clears the archive attribute only. Is not a selection parameter.

The "s" and "h" options in PKZIP let you specify whether system and/or hidden files should be included in the archive.

```
PKZIP -whs ROOT C:\*.*
```

This command saves your root directory in an archive called ROOT. Even the hidden system files IO.SYS and MSDOS.SYS (IBMBIOS.COM and IBMDOS.COM in PC-DOS systems) are included. To do this in ARJ, use the "-a" parameter.

```
ARJ a -a ROOT C:\*.*
```

6. Advanced Data Compression Features

```
D:\WORD\PACKER>pkzip -whs root -x*.000

PKZIP (R)   FAST!   Create/Update Utility    Version 2.04c   12-28-92
Copr. 1989-1992 PKWARE Inc. All Rights Reserved.   Shareware Version
PKZIP Reg. U.S. Pat. and Tm. Off.   Patent No. 5,051,745

 ▪ 80486 CPU detected.
 ▪ XMS version 3.00 detected.
 ▪ Novell Netware version 3.11 detected.
 ▪ Using Normal Compression.

Creating ZIP: ROOT.ZIP
   Adding: ANSI.SYS       Deflating ( 1%), done.
   Adding: KEYBOARD.SYS   Deflating ( 2%), done.
   Adding: COUNTRY.SYS    Deflating ( 2%), done.
   Adding: RAMDRIVE.SYS   Deflating ( 1%), done.
   Adding: KEYBRD2.SYS    Deflating ( 2%), done.
   Adding: HIMEM.SYS      Deflating ( 1%), done.
   Adding: CHKSTATE.SYS   Deflating ( 2%), done.
   Adding: AUTOEXEC.BAT   Deflating (28%), done.
   Adding: TEST.BAT       Deflating (58%), done.
   Adding: TEST1.BAT      Deflating (58%), done.
   Adding: CONFIG.SYS     Deflating (29%), done.

D:\WORD\PACKER>
```

Including the system and hidden files

The above figure shows that the files in question are compressed. With ARJ, you cannot distinguish between system and hidden files. However, by adding the "-a1" switch, you can save empty directories, which isn't possible in PKZIP. This makes sense only if you specify the recursion switch as well, so all subdirectories are thoroughly searched.

```
ARJ a -ra1 ALL C:\*.*
```

The above command compresses every file on the hard drive. The "-r" switch invokes subdirectory recursion, and the "-a1" ensures that protected files and empty directories will also be included.

A look at the ARJ archive after compressing with the following command reveals an unexpected result.

```
ARJ l  -a1 ROOT
```

The five "files" with a size of 0 bytes are obviously subdirectories. However, they are definitely not empty. The "-a1" switch cannot determine by itself whether a subdirectory is empty. Since the recursion switch was omitted, the subdirectories cannot be searched. ARJ simply archives everything for which there is an entry in the directory (and a subdirectory is simply another entry), regardless of attributes.

6. Advanced Data Compression Features

```
Copr. 1989-1992 PKWARE Inc. All Rights Reserved. Shareware version
PKUNZIP Reg. U.S. Pat. and Tm. Off.

■ 80486 CPU detected.
■ XMS version 3.00 detected.

Searching ZIP: ROOT.ZIP

 Length  Method   Size  Ratio   Date     Time   CRC-32    Attr  Name
 ------  ------   ----  -----   ----     ----   ------    ----  ----
   6427  DeflatN  6365    1%   09-02-93  06:20  08ec1093  --w-  ANSI.SYS
  10290  DeflatN 10115    2%   03-10-93  06:00  6030a026  --w-  KEYBOARD.SYS
   3860  DeflatN  3808    2%   09-02-93  06:20  ae2d5090  --w-  COUNTRY.SYS
   3241  DeflatN  3227    1%   03-10-93  06:00  9b5bf024  --w-  RAMDRIVE.SYS
  11703  DeflatN 11470    2%   09-02-93  06:20  dba363fc  --w-  KEYBRD2.SYS
   8465  DeflatN  8385    1%   09-02-93  06:20  78ec80d6  --w-  HIMEM.SYS
  15733  DeflatN 15531    2%   03-10-93  06:00  d8ab415f  --w-  CHKSTATE.SYS
    341  DeflatN   248   28%   10-02-93  11:03  cd0857c6  --w-  AUTOEXEC.BAT
    557  DeflatN   238   58%   09-10-93  09:08  09d70847  --w-  TEST.BAT
    547  DeflatN   235   58%   09-14-93  09:02  01ca15da  --w-  TEST1.BAT
    333  DeflatN   239   29%   10-05-93  09:22  d60a07f0  --w-  CONFIG.SYS
 ------          -----   ---                                    --
  61497          59861    3%                                    11

D:\WORD\PACKER>
```

What has happened to the directories in the archive?

When you view archives in PKZIP and ARJ, you'll see that the attributes of the compressed files are indicated by certain symbols. The ARJ display shows these in five columns on the right. Each attribute has a letter abbreviation, as follows:

A	Archive (backup)
S	System
H	Hidden
R	Read-only
D	Directory

PKZIP has only three columns, since the archive and directory attributes are not recognized. The attribute status of a normal file looks like this:

```
--w   DOCUMENT.DOC
```

The "w" stands for "writeable", indicating that the file can be changed. This means that its read-only bit is switched off (as are the hidden and system bits). Other files have some of their attribute bits switched on. They might appear as:

```
shr IO.SYS
-hw BYE.DAT
```

IO.SYS carries the system, hidden, and read-only attributes. The BYE.DAT file is hidden, but it can be written.

6. Advanced Data Compression Features

Attribute masking

The term "masking" refers to setting, resetting, or checking particular bits. In the context of archiving, these bits are the file attribute bits. By clearing one or more of the hidden, system, and read-only bits, PKZIP can alter the attributes of a file as it's compressed into an archive. In normal use, PKZIP leaves the file attributes unchanged. The "-j" parameter can clear individual attribute bits. Therefore, a hidden, read-only system file can be turned into a normal writeable file.

-j[s,h,r]	Deletes the specified attribute(s) by resetting the appropriate bit(s) when used with one or more of the three letters: s System h Hidden r Read-only
If a file has none of the attributes specified, its status is unchanged.	

```
PKZIP -whs -jhrs ROOT C:\*.*
```

The above command compresses all files below the root directory into the archive called "ROOT." The "-w" parameter ensures that hidden (h) and system (s) files are also included. The "-j" option clears the packed files of all hidden (h), read-only (r), and system (s) attributes.

Data Compression Methods

The various compression programs use several data compression methods, including "squashing", "squeezing", "crunching", and "imploding." Certain methods are specifically designed for particular file or data types. Some compression programs analyze a file's content and choose a method that will produce the maximum compression.

PKZIP and ARJ are the only compression programs that actually give you a choice of methods. Although other programs may offer options for different compression algorithms, they do this only to maintain compatibility with older versions.

ARJ: Six methods

ARJ provides the largest selection of options for data compression methods. Instead of specifying a particular algorithm, you indicate the relative importance of speed versus packing density. According to the ARJ documentation, every improvement in speed is obtained only by sacrificing density. The switch for faster compression is "-m" and a number from 1 to 4.

6. Advanced Data Compression Features

Option	Meaning
-m1	Maximum (highest density) compression.
-m2	Somewhat less compression, slightly faster.
-m3	Faster still, but with less compression.
-m4	Maximum speed.

In addition to the "-m" switch, there is another option for optimizing compression density with m1 and m2.

Option	Meaning
-jm1	Maximum (highest density) compression (improvement of m1).
-jm2	Improvement of m2.

> The "-j" optimizing switch should be used with m1 and m2 only. If it's used with m3 or m4, the results are uncertain.

You're probably wondering whether having such precise control over packing density and speed is really useful. Usually differences in the results of the various options are small. For testing purposes, we built a directory consisting of Word documents, ASCII files, and binary files in equal proportions. Then we archived the directory using each of the ARJ compression modes. The following table shows some surprising results:

```
ARJ a -jm MAX *.*
```

Method	Time	(Cache)	Size	Compression rate
-jm1	1:14	(0:17)	436,051	43.2%
-jm2	1:12	(0:16)	436,568	43.2%
-m1	1:13	(0:11)	436,573	43.2%
-m2	1:11	(0:08)	440,346	43.6%
-m3	1:07	(0:18)	450,985	44.6%
-m4	1:10	(0:17)	496,031	49.1%

6. Advanced Data Compression Features

Methods m1 to m4 are not radically different in terms of time or compression. All compression rates remain under 50%, which is fairly good for mixed data with a high proportion of binary files. m4, the fastest algorithm, is only four seconds faster than the slowest. An extra 60K of memory was required for this gain in speed.

> - The m0 method archives files without any compression.
> - The ARJ-SFX module does not support the m4 method.
> - The jm3 and jm4 methods are undefined and lead to unpredictable results.

> Use a memory cache to speed up hard drive access during data compression. Doing this can save a significant amount of time, as shown by method m2. The entire compression process was shortened from 1 minute 11 seconds to just 8 seconds.

However, this is only possible because ARJ accesses the hard drive so intensively. Since PKZIP does less disk accessing, it can perform much faster. However, using a cache doesn't improve PKZIP's performance. This is shown in a table later in this section.

An archive listing shows the compression method that was used for each file:

```
D:\WORD\PACKER>arj l test
ARJ 2.30 Copyright (c) 1990-92 Robert K Jung. Jan 19 1992
NOT REGISTERED for business, commercial, or government use.

Processing archive: TEST.ARJ
Archive date     : 1993-10-05 15:31:22
Filename      Original Compressed Ratio DateTime modified  CRC-32   AttrBTPMGVXx
------------  -------- ---------- ----- -----------------  --------  ------------
ANSI.SYS          6427       6358 0.989 93-09-02 06:20:00 08EC1093 A--W B 1
KEYBOARD.SYS     10290      10099 0.981 93-03-10 06:00:00 6030A026 A--W B 1
COUNTRY.SYS       3860       3796 0.983 93-09-02 06:20:00 AE2D5090 A--W B 1
RAMDRIVE.SYS      3241       3221 0.994 93-03-10 06:00:00 9B5BF024 A--W B 1
KEYBRD2.SYS      11703      11457 0.979 93-09-02 06:20:00 DBA363FC A--W B 1
HIMEM.SYS         8465       8376 0.989 93-09-02 06:20:00 78EC80D6 A--W B 1
CHKSTATE.SYS     15733      15565 0.989 93-03-10 06:00:00 D8AB415F A--W B 1
AUTOEXEC.BAT       341        243 0.713 93-10-02 11:03:16 CD0857C6 A--W B 1
TEST.BAT           557        239 0.429 93-09-10 09:08:04 09D70847 A--W B 1
TEST1.BAT          547        235 0.430 93-09-14 09:02:00 01CA15DA A--W B 1
CONFIG.SYS         333        233 0.700 93-10-05 09:22:48 D60A07F0 A--W B 1
------------  -------- ---------- -----
    11 files     61497      59822 0.973

D:\WORD\PACKER>
```

Compression method shown on right

6. Advanced Data Compression Features

The M-column on the right side of the display indicates the compression method the program used to compress the file. If this seems complicated, don't worry. ARJ automatically recognizes the compression method used and chooses the appropriate extraction method accordingly.

While using ARJ, we didn't place any restrictions on archiving time or memory requirements. The standard m1 setting was sufficient.

> If such considerations are a matter of concern, you should be aware of the following memory requirements associated with the different compression methods.

ARJ Memory Requirement	
Method	Requirement
-m1	at least 300K
-m2	at least 282K
-m3	at least 250K
-m4	at least 235K

PKZIP is flexible

PKZIP offers two compression methods and options for applying them according to file type.

Imploding	Very thorough compression. This is the default setting.
	Requires less memory (90K). Regardless of the option specified, this is always the method used when memory is a limiting factor.
Shrinking	Very fast
	Requires somewhat more memory (128K). Regardless of the option specified, this is always the method used for files under 320 bytes.

Imploding is the default method. The "-e" option lets you override the default setting with your own choice of methods.

```
-e[x,s,a,b]  Compression method options
```

6. Advanced Data Compression Features

Option	Meaning
-ex	All files are compressed by imploding (default).
-es	All files are compressed by shrinking.
-ea	ASCII files are compressed by imploding, binary files by shrinking.
-eb	ASCII files are compressed by shrinking, binary files by imploding.

Processing time and compressed file size vary considerably depending on the option used. The following table shows the performance figures for archiving a directory with PKZIP. These are the same files tested earlier with ARJ.

```
PKZIP -a -es SPEED *.*
```

Method	Time	(Cache)	Size	Compression rate
none	:21	(:16)	464,621	46.0%
-ex	:21	(:16)	464,621	46.0%
-es	:10	(:04)	574,170	56.8%
-ea	:18	(:14)	531,955	52.7%
-eb	:11	(:06)	506,836	50.2%

As you can see, there's a significant difference from ARJ. Even with exclusive use of imploding, PKZIP took only 21 seconds. The fastest method took half that time. Although the compression achieved isn't quite so good, this speed is remarkable for processing 1,010,032 bytes of data.

Although the times were further reduced by caching, the differences are much less dramatic than with ARJ. This indicates that PKZIP accesses the hard drive less than ARJ.

Compatibility of compression methods

Other programs use different methods of compression for compatibility reasons. Most newer compression programs are downwardly compatible. However, you may still encounter problems with some archives.

LHA uses the "-o" option to produce archives that are compatible with the older compression method. Then these archives can also be processed by LHARC Version 1.13c.

```
LHA a -o OLD *.*
```

6. Advanced Data Compression Features

Despite maintaining compatibility, LHA achieves tighter compression than LHARC 1.13. Because of the various possibilities it provides, PAK is more confusing. The standard compression method of PAK is crushing. However, PAK archives can be converted to the archive formats of ARC and PKARC.

Option	Meaning
/C	Use crunching method (ARC, PKARC).
/S	Use squashing method (PKARC).

Existing archives can be converted with the "C" command. The format for new archives is specified in conjunction with the **Add**, **Update**, or **Move** commands.

```
PAK c /c CONVERT
```

```
C:\TEST>pak c /c convert
Pak 2.51 Copyright 1988-90 NoGate Consulting
---------------------------------------------
Unregistered evaluation copy

C:CONVERT.PAK
Converting CRITICAL.ARJ  Analyzing CRITICAL.ARJ  Crunched (10%), finished.
Converting LINES.TXT     Analyzing LINES.TXT     Crunched (60%), finished.
Converting MJCI.TXT      Analyzing MJCI.TXT      Crunched (57%), finished.
Converting SAMPLE.GIF    Analyzing SAMPLE.GIF    Stored, finished.
Converting SECRET.ARJ    Analyzing SECRET.ARJ    Stored, finished.
Converting TEST.EXE      Analyzing TEST.EXE      Stored, finished.
Archived files increased in size 7212 bytes.

C:\TEST>
```

Converting a PAK archive

The above command converts the archive called "CONVERT" to crunched format. Use the following command to create a new archive in squashed format:

```
PAK a /s NEW
```

6. Advanced Data Compression Features

Using ARJ As a Multi-packer

There used to be only one way to transfer large quantities of data from one computer to another. First, you had to store the desired files from the source computer on several diskettes by using the DOS BACKUP command. Next, the contents of the diskettes had to be placed on the target computer's hard drive by using the RESTORE command. Problems could occur if both computers had different versions of DOS. For example, a system running DOS 2.1 couldn't RESTORE an archive created by the BACKUP command of DOS 3.3.

Today's data compression programs have solved this problem. However, ARJ is the only program capable of high-volume archiving. When an archive must span multiple diskettes, ARJ effortlessly performs the necessary management for you. You don't have to worry about file sizes, disk space, or what goes where.

The "-v" switch lets an archive span more than one volume. Several other options provide added flexibility and power to the multi-volume archiving process. Used with every possible option, the "-v" switch looks like this:

```
-vvwa360sCOMMAND
```

The following table should clarify this command line:

Option	Meaning
-v	Creates a multi-volume archive.
v	Sounds a beep between volumes.
w	Prevents archived files from being split across volumes.
360	Specifies maximum volume size in bytes. Units of 1000 (not 1024) can be abbreviated as K.
a	Checks space available on target medium before starting a new volume.
s	Executes a command or batch file before starting a new target volume. Spaces between the 's' and the command or filename aren't permitted.

Creating a simple multi-volume archive

Despite the confusing array of parameter options, creating a multi-volume archive is easy. For example, if you want to archive all files in the current directory to diskettes, simply type:

```
ARJ a -va A:TRANSFER
```

6. Advanced Data Compression Features

The "-v" switch ensures that the archiving process isn't aborted if the diskette in drive A: becomes full. The "-v" alone, however, isn't sufficient. ARJ must know how large the individual archive volumes can be. Maximum volume size is controlled by the "a" option, as used above, or by specifying a size directly.

When a divided archive requires another diskette, ARJ prompts you to insert one in the target drive.

After inserting the new diskette, simply enter "Yes" to continue compressing. ARJ checks to see that there is free space on the diskette. If there isn't, you can switch diskettes and enter "Yes" again. The "v" option tells ARJ to prompt you with a beep when it's time to change diskettes.

```
ARJ a -vva A:TRANSFER
```

ARJ beeps before starting a new archive volume.

> Unlike most of the other switches, the "-v" switch requires that options be entered in a specific order. To activate the warning beep, you must place the "v" option directly after the "-v" switch:

```
ARJ a -vav HELLO    ( **** wrong )
ARJ a -vv HELLO     ( **** right )
```

The "a" switch specifies that ARJ should automatically determine the maximum volume size. Before starting to write a new volume, the program checks to see how much free space is on the target storage medium (ARJ doesn't overwrite existing data). The available free space becomes the maximum size for that volume.

> If you use the "a" switch with other options, remember to place it on the command line correctly (after "v" and "w"). For example:
> ```
> ARJ a -vvwa b:HELLO
> ```

You can divide an archive into multiple volumes even on your hard drive. In this case, the "a" switch isn't appropriate, since you want to restrict the volume size to less than the available free space. To do this, you can specify the size limit directly, as in the following examples:

```
ARJ a -v360000 B:\TRANS -wC:\
```

or

```
ARJ a -v360K B:\TRANS -wC:\
```

6. Advanced Data Compression Features

The above command creates a multi-volume archive called "TRANS" on drive B:. Regardless of the type of diskette you insert in the drive, the size of a single volume is limited to 360,000 bytes. (To save time, a temporary archive is also created on the C: drive.)

The only difference between the second command and the first is that thousands are expressed as K. Remember that, in this instance, K means 1,000 instead of 1,024.

If the specified amount of storage isn't available, ARJ warns you before starting the new volume.

> WARNING! Only 38,122 bytes of free disk space. Continue?

You can respond to the warning with the usual "Yes", "No", "All", or "Quit" ARJ commands.

ARJ recognizes size abbreviations for the four popular diskette formats. For example, instead of "362000", you can simply use "360".

Abbreviation	Meaning
360	362,000 bytes
720	730,000 bytes
1200	1,213,000 bytes
1440	1,457,000 bytes

```
ARJ a -v360 A:HELLO

ARJ a -v1440 D:TRANS
```

The first example creates a multi-volume archive named "HELLO" on the A: drive. Volume size is limited to 360K. The second command creates an archive named "TRANS" on the D: drive, whose volumes are each limited to 1440K.

Each volume of a divided archive needs a unique name. ARJ uses the normal extension ARJ for the first volume, then assigns ascending numbers after the letter "A" to subsequent volumes. For example, the command:

```
ARJ a -v10000 PARTS \*.TXT *.BAT
```

might create the following volumes:

6. Advanced Data Compression Features

```
Volume in drive C has no label
Volume Serial Number is 10F5-0A44
Directory of C:\NEW

.            <DIR>         10-05-93   3:43p
..           <DIR>         10-05-93   3:43p
PARTS   ARJ          9,156 10-05-93   3:44p
PARTS   A01          9,193 10-05-93   3:44p
PARTS   A02          9,191 10-05-93   3:44p
PARTS   A03          9,172 10-05-93   3:44p
PARTS   A04          9,129 10-05-93   3:44p
PARTS   A05          9,182 10-05-93   3:44p
PARTS   A06          9,161 10-05-93   3:44p
PARTS   A07          9,144 10-05-93   3:44p
PARTS   A08          9,194 10-05-93   3:44p
PARTS   A09          9,171 10-05-93   3:44p
PARTS   A10          9,214 10-05-93   3:44p
PARTS   A11          9,296 10-05-93   3:44p
PARTS   A12          9,181 10-05-93   3:44p
PARTS   A13          9,205 10-05-93   3:44p
PARTS   A14          3,964 10-05-93   3:45p
       17 file(s)      132,553 bytes
                    19,161,088 bytes free

C:\NEW>
```

Naming archive volumes

File extensions for all but the first volume start with A01 and go through A00. This limits the normal number of volumes in a single archive to 101. It sounds like a generous limit, but even this can be overridden.

To allow for as many as 1,000 volumes (this should be sufficient), specify the file extension .000 (or you could start with some other number, such as 00, allowing for a lesser total). The command would look like this:

```
ARJ a -v20K PLENTY.000
```

ARJ will name the first volume with the extension you specify and number subsequent ones sequentially. The last possible volume would have the extension .999. However, if necessary, the volume size can still be increased.

Optimizing memory space

In filling archive volumes, ARJ tries to use the available space as completely as possible. This may involve splitting a file that cannot fit at the end of a volume and continuing it at the beginning of the next. With this technique of space optimization, the program can come within 200 bytes of the maximum volume size.

You can prevent ARJ from splitting files by adding the "w" switch to the command line. Remember, this option must be placed after the "v" (prompt with beep) and before the "a" (automatic volume size) or specified volume size.

```
ARJ a -vwav ...   ( wrong )
ARJ a -vvwa ...   ( right )
ARJ a -vw360 ...  ( right )
```

6. Advanced Data Compression Features

When files cannot be split, more space is wasted. To demonstrate this, we'll compare two commands. The only difference between these commands is the "w" option. Both operations compress the text files *.TXT to a 50,000-byte-per-volume multi-volume archive on the hard drive.

The optimized archive is called "OPT_Y" and is created with the following command:

```
ARJ a -r -v50K OPT_Y \*.TXT
```

The non-optimized archive is called "OPT_N" and is created with the following command:

```
ARJ a -r -vw50K OPT_N \*.TXT
```

The effect of optimization is apparent in a DIR listing:

```
DIR OPT_Y

Volume in drive D: is all my lovin'
Volume Serial Number is 1702-76A9
Directory of D:\WORD\PACKER

OPT_Y    A01      49204 01-27-93  18:24
OPT_Y    A02      49188 01-27-93  18:24
OPT_Y    A03      49236 01-27-93  18:24
OPT_Y    A04      38137 01-27-93  18:24
OPT_Y    ARJ      49162 01-27-93  18:24
```

The listing of the OPT_N archive shows the difference:

```
DIR OPT_N

Volume in drive D: is all my lovin'
Volume Serial Number is 1702-76A9
Directory of D:\WORD\PACKER

OPT_N    A01      47633 01-27-93  18:21
OPT_N    A02      49837 01-27-93  18:21
OPT_N    A03      49824 01-27-93  18:21
OPT_N    A04      29885 01-27-93  18:21
OPT_N    ARJ      46535 01-27-93  18:21
```

It's obvious that the non-optimized archive has more volumes. Now let's compare the average volume size. Not counting the last (partial) volume in each archive, we arrive at the following figures:

Archive	Average size
OPT_Y	49200 bytes
OPT_N	40562 bytes

6. Advanced Data Compression Features

As you can see, not using space on diskettes efficiently is a serious problem. Therefore, allowing files to be split by omitting the "w" switch can save both time and diskettes.

> Sending multi-volume archives to the hard drive can save a lot of time, even if the individual volumes are later copied to diskettes. In this case, you can suppress the message
>
> OK to process to next Volume
>
> by using the "-y" switch:
> ```
> ARJ a -r -v360 -y TEXTS C:\*.TXT
> ```

Combining commands

Now let's return to the task we discussed at the beginning of this section. All the files in a directory must be archived to diskettes (assuming more than one is needed) on the A: drive.

```
ARJ a -va A:TRANSFER
```

Each time a diskette on the target drive is full, ARJ prompts you to insert another diskette and indicate that you're ready to continue. If the new diskette doesn't have enough free space, the following warning message appears:

> Insufficient disk space!

At this point, you cannot delete files or format the diskette. So, you must have a sufficient supply of formatted blank diskettes ready before executing the above command.

It's also possible to alter the ARJ command by attaching a DOS command to it. Before ARJ starts a new volume, the DOS command will be executed. This gives you a chance to interrupt ARJ and format the diskette or delete files. The "s" switch is used for attaching the command. This option immediately follows the command, without being separated by a space. ARJ accepts the following:

- ➤ Internal DOS commands (e.g., DIR)
- ➤ Programs (e.g., FORMAT, COMMAND)
- ➤ Batch files

6. Advanced Data Compression Features

Batch files can be used to automate all the necessary steps for dealing with diskettes and the hard drive. The "s" switch must be placed after all others.

```
ARJ a -vvwasCOMMAND.COM A:SAVE
```

The above command is an excellent example for creating a multi-volume archive, using all the available options in the correct sequence. The "s" switch ensures that the command interpreter COMMAND.COM runs before ARJ begins each volume of the SAVE archive, including the first. So, when you execute the command, you'll see the following DOS message first instead of the usual filename and percent display (assuming that you're using DOS 5.0):

> Microsoft(R) MS-DOS(R) Version 5.00
> (C)Copyright Microsoft Corp 1981-1991

This takes you a level higher in the operating environment and places ARJ in the background. The diskette can be processed as required, using DIR, FORMAT, DELETE, etc. The only thing that could cause problems is calling ARJ again.

You'll return to ARJ automatically, once you've finished the necessary disk management tasks, by simply leaving COMMAND.COM with the EXIT command.

```
EXIT
```

ARJ now proceeds as normal. When a new volume must be started, COMMAND.COM is called again, and the process is repeated.

Be careful when using a command that contains a space. For example, the following command

```
ARJ a -vsDIR A:\ A:HMMM
```

will cause problems, because ARJ will interpret the archive name as "A:\" (an invalid construction), instead of the intended "HMMM on drive A:." The solution is simple. Enclose the entire multi-volume parameter string, beginning with "-v", in quotes:

```
ARJ a "-vsDIR A:\ " A:HMMM
```

> Notice that we've deliberately left a space between the backslash and the closing quote. If we didn't do this, ARJ would interpret the quote as part of the path because the program expects the path to be terminated by a space. So, remember when specifying a path, put a space before the closing quote.

6. Advanced Data Compression Features

Using batch files to check files

Batch files can make the archiving process even easier. The following tasks in the multi-volume archiving process could be automated by using a batch file:

> Determine whether a diskette has data on it.

> If it does, delete the data from the diskette.

Only a simple DIR command is needed to check a diskette for existing files. Deleting files is slightly more complicated. The batch file can indicate whether the diskette contains data but you must decide whether the data should be deleted. Also, a batch file cannot accept and interpret your instructions without some help.

First, a routine, which accepts input from the keyboard, is needed. To do this, you'll need the DOS program DEBUG and a small text file you can create yourself. Let's call this file "KEYS.DEB." Copy the coding for the text file exactly from the following lines:

```
a 100
MOV AH,07
INT 21
MOV AH,4C
INT 21

r cx

8

n KEYS.COM

w

q
```

The KEYS.DEB text file now contains the commands that should be passed to the DOS debugger to create a program called KEYS.COM. To do this, type the following:

`DEBUG<KEYS.DEB`

If an error doesn't occur, KEYS.COM is now ready. However, when you call the program with

`KEYS`

6. Advanced Data Compression Features

there is no apparent response. However, when you type any character, you return to normal processing. This occurs because KEYS simply waits for a character from the keyboard. When it receives one, it checks it and saves it in the DOS variable called ERRORLEVEL. Now a batch file can see which key was pressed and take an appropriate action.

Let's look at a batch file, called DTEST.BAT, that can perform these tasks. First it provides a directory listing for the selected drive, then reacts to a YES/NO user response to delete any files.

```
@ECHO OFF
  REM
  REM  DiskTest.Bat
  REM    Makes sure a diskette is ready
  REM    for multi-volume archiving.

  ECHO.
  If %1x==A:x Goto Continue
  If %1x==B:x Goto Continue
  If %1x==a:x Goto Continue
  If %1x==b:x Goto Continue

  ECHO No diskette drive was given (A: or B:).
  ECHO.
  Goto End

:Continue
  DIR %1 /p
  ECHO.
  PAUSE
  ECHO.
  ECHO Should diskette in %1 be erased ???
  ECHO Please enter (y)es or (n)o.
  ECHO.

  KEYS
  IF ERRORLEVEL 121 Goto Delete
  IF ERRORLEVEL 110 GOTO End
  IF ERRORLEVEL 89  GOTO Delete
  IF ERRORLEVEL 78  GOTO End
  GOTO End

:Delete
  ECHO y | DEL %1\*.*
  ECHO.
```

6. Advanced Data Compression Features

```
:End

 ECHO Press any key
 ECHO to return to ARJ.
 ECHO
 Pause>NUL
```

To use DTEST.BAT with ARJ, simply type:

`ARJ a "-vvasDTEST A: " A:OK`

Before starting a new volume of the OK archive on drive A:, ARJ runs the DTEST program. This in turn ensures that the diskette on the indicated drive is ready for writing. If the DTEST drive parameter is omitted, the diskette isn't checked.

Extracting multi-volume archives

Extracting multi-volume archives is even easier than creating them. Simply type the "-v" switch to tell ARJ that the archive is divided. Any of the special options used in creating the archive can be omitted from the extraction command.

`ARJ x -v B:LONG`

This command extracts a multi-volume archive beginning with the volume called LONG.ARJ. The numbering of the file extensions for subsequent volumes makes it possible for ARJ to restore all files and directories in an orderly sequence. If you assigned your own extensions instead of using the default naming scheme when you archived your text file, you must provide the full name of the first volume when extracting:

`ARJ x -vv B:LONG.A01`

or

`ARJ x -vv LONGER.000`

If you extract or otherwise process a divided archive without the "-v" switch, the volume specified will be handled as normal, but processing will not continue to subsequent volumes. For example, the following command extracts the first volume, but ignores the remaining 999:

`ARJ x B:LONG.000`

It's easy to access a particular file or group of files in a divided archive. For example, to extract all text files (TXT or DOC) from the multi-volume TEXTS archive, use the command:

`ARJ x -v TEXTS *.DOC *.TXT`

6. Advanced Data Compression Features

The only difference between this and the usual extracting command is the "-v" switch, which ensures that all volumes will be searched for the specified files.

If the "-v" is omitted in this example, only the first volume will be searched.

Listing multi-volume archives

The **List** and **View** commands can also be applied to multi-volume archives. Again, it's important to include the "-v" switch if you want to display all the volumes.

```
ARJ l -v TEXTS
```

Beginning with TEXTS.ARJ, the program lists all volumes of the TEXTS archive. The screen pauses so you can change diskettes.

EXE Compressors

By now you've realized that the biggest advantage of file compression is the ability to save disk space. However, before you can use compressed data, it must be restored to its original format. This fact causes problems for many of today's comprehensive software packages. Although programs cannot run until they are decompressed, the decompression process itself takes up both space and time.

The French programmer Fabric Bellard developed an alternative to the conventional concepts of data compression. In the Bellard system, a program resides in compressed form on the disk and is decompressed directly into memory when it's executed.

His program, called LZEXE, quickly became popular. Commercial developers like Microsoft have offered similar products, but LZEXE is more successful.

Now other shareware programmers have developed their own programs using the Bellard system. In this chapter, we'll discuss LZEXE, PKLite, and DIET.

How EXE Compressors Work

Data compression is a complex subject. Many techniques have been developed for compressing programs into executable archives. Authors of advanced program-compression products must thoroughly understand compression schemes, the inner workings of the operating system, and program file structures.

Certain file types are indicated by their filename extensions. For example, COM and EXE are program extensions. Each indicates certain criteria according to the way the program is structured. A process that decompresses a program into memory must consider the program's structure carefully; otherwise problems will occur. The main differences between COM and EXE files are program size and the way the program code is constructed.

As we mentioned, the program resides in compressed form on the disk and must be decompressed into memory for execution. Similar to a self-extracting (SFX) archive, the EXE archive containing the compressed program also contains a small module that performs the extraction process. Its final action, once the executable code has been loaded into memory, is to start it running.

7. EXE Compressors

Since the compressed version still remains on the disk, there is no need to recompress the program after using it. The executable version in RAM can simply be deleted.

COM and EXE file structures

COM files are a simpler and more compact type of program than EXE files. The COM format is based on the old CP/M (the standard operating system before MS-DOS). It's characterized by its maximum program size of 64K. The 64K barrier is a characteristic of the 80x86 processor.

A computer's total memory area is divided into of 64K segments. You can imagine this as a street with a million people living along it. Instead of each person having a separate house with a separate address (such as, 5 RAM St.), the people are crowded into high-rise apartment buildings. So, a person's address could be 1,267 RAM St., Apt. 45,600.

The COM program, however, is confined to a single segment. All its data and instructions are referenced relative to the beginning of the segment, in which the program is loaded. This makes it easy to determine addresses. "House numbers" (segment addresses) aren't needed. In a COM program, you need only the "apartment number" to locate the desired "resident." Because of this, it's also easy to work with compressed COM files.

EXE programs are more difficult for compressors to manipulate, because the 64K limit does not apply to them. Therefore, EXE programs can be as large as the available memory. They can even be larger than the available memory if overlays are used. Overlays are sections of a program that can be moved in and out of memory as needed.

Segment boundaries aren't an obstacle for EXE programs. To return to our high-rise apartment building example, a complete address would now consist of both a house number and an apartment number. In other words, besides the relative location within a segment, we must specify the segment itself. However, since we can never be sure just where in RAM a program is loaded, the segment addresses used in an EXE program must be calculated at run time.

This makes it very difficult to extract an EXE file directly into memory.

Limitations of program compressors

Although they are powerful, program compressors still have their limitations. These compressors especially have problems with certain EXE models.

7. EXE Compressors

Programs written for MS-Windows belong to this problem category. Their EXE format differs from that of "normal" EXE files written for DOS. Windows programs contain a lot of information that isn't part of the classical model assumed by the EXE compressors.

To use memory effectively, by swapping program sections in and out, an EXE file uses overlays. EXE compressors can handle normal overlays. However, if overlays must be linked at specified memory locations, EXE compression probably won't work.

Some programs (e.g., Turbo Pascal) modify themselves. Instead of being written to an external file, which usually occurs, configuration data can be placed at a specified location directly within the EXE file. This isn't compatible with the concept of compression, where the executable code resides only temporarily in memory.

The last group of problem programs are ones that perform a self-test before starting, such as Microsoft's debugger, CODEVIEW.EXE. Each time it executes, CODEVIEW checks to see whether the program has been changed. The manipulations performed by an EXE compressor will be detected, and the program won't continue.

Using EXE compressors

The program compressors are much easier to use than normal archiving programs, because almost no optional parameters are needed. Except in DIET, which is actually more than a program compressor, the **Run** command is reduced to a simple program conversion request, similar to the following:

```
LZEXE program
```

```
PKLITE program
```

In the following sections, we'll discuss the various EXE compressors in more detail.

LZEXE

LZEXE is the classic program compressor. The French author Fabrice Ballard made this special-purpose compression program available to PC users by releasing it as shareware. We'll discuss Version 0.91. LZEXE was originally written in French but some English-language versions exsist. The English help screen is as follows:

7. EXE Compressors

```
H:\DOSAPPS\UTIL\PACK>lzexe
LZEXE.EXE Ver 0.91 (ENG) (c) 1989 Fabrice BELLARD
High Performance Executable File Compactor

Syntax: LZEXE <filename> (.EXE)
<filename> is the name of the .EXE file you wish to compact
The (.EXE) file extention may be omitted.
The output file will be written to the current directory

For more information, please read L2EXE.DOC  (.ENG)

    This program was concieved and designed by Fabrice BELLARD who
    graciously decided to submit this version into FREEWARE.
    If you have any problems or any suggestions about this program,
    please write to:           Fabrice BELLARD
                           451 chemin du mas de matour
                               34790 GRABELS   (FRANCE)
    or send a message in BAL on RTEL or QBSS under the name: FAB

H:\DOSAPPS\UTIL\PACK\LZEXE>
```

LZEXE help screen

The syntax of LZEXE is:

`LZEXE <<filename>>.[.EXE]`

The only parameter that's needed is the program name of the EXE file to be compressed.

`LZEXE PKUNZIP`

The above command tells LZEXE to compress the program PKUNZIP.EXE.

```
H:\DOSAPPS\UTIL\PACK>lzexe
LZEXE.EXE Ver 0.91 (ENG) (c) 1989 Fabrice BELLARD
High Performance Executable File Compactor

Compacting - - PKZIP.EXE
Reading the Header
Reading the Relocation Table
Compacting the .EXE File - This may take time
Writing the De-Compactor
Writing the Compacted Relocation Table
Updating the Header

Compactor Finished

Compressed 41462 > 46268 bytes

Sorry, the compactor was ineffective
Erasing the file    LZEXE.TMP

H:\DOSAPPS\UTIL\PACK\LZEXE>
```

LZEXE work report

The following happened:

> ➢ The (original) PKUNZIP.EXE file was renamed "PKUNZIP.OLD".
>
> ➢ The new PKUNZIP.EXE file was successfully compressed.

7. EXE Compressors

You can try it out right away. Start the compressed EXE version as you normally would:

```
PKUNZIP
```

Without any noticeable delay, PKUNZIP should start.

Windows programs and LZEXE

Although the LZEXE documentation warned against it, we tried to compress a Windows program called PIFEDIT.EXE.

```
LZEXE Pifedit
```

The attempt failed although the compression rate looked amazing at first:

```
PIFEDIT.EXE     651
PIFEDIT.OLD   55168
```

If you think this looks too good to be true, you're right. We got an error when we tried to start the program under Windows, which "proves" what we already know: Windows programs should not be compressed with LZEXE.

An error occurs with Windows programs

Compressing COM files

LZEXE cannot handle COM files. So, these files must be converted to EXE files before they are compressed with LZEXE. The accessory program COMTOEXE is used for this purpose. COMTOEXE is easy to use. For example, suppose that you want to compress the DOS program MODE.COM. Use the following commands:

```
COMTOEXE MODE.COM
LZEXE MODE
```

These commands had the following effect on memory space:

```
MODE.COM      23521
MODE.OLD      23553
MODE.EXE      15931
```

Once you've determined that the procedure was successful, you should delete MODE.COM and MODE.OLD to reap the benefits of the compression.

PKLite

PKLite is from the company that produces PKZIP/UNZIP. Like PKZIP, PKLite displays a help screen, which can be called without any parameters.

```
PKLITE (tm)   Executable File Compressor   Version 1.00   12-01-90
Copyright 1990 PKWARE Inc. All Rights Reserved.

Usage: PKLITE [options] [d:][/path]Infile [[d:][/path]Outfile]
Options are:
  -a = always compress files with overlays
  -b = make backup .BAK file of original
  -e = make compressed file unextractable (* commercial version only *)
  -l = display software license screen
  -n = never compress files with overlays
  -o = overwrite output file if it exists
  -r = remove overlay data
  -u = update file time/date to current time/date
  -x = expand a compressed file

(*) See documentation and license screen for more information

If you find PKLITE easy, and convenient to use, a registration of $46.00
would be appreciated.  Registration includes one free upgrade to the
software and a printed manual.  Please state the version of the software
that you currently have.  Send check or money order to:
                        PKWARE, Inc.
                        7545 N. Port Washington Rd.
                        Glendale, WI 53217
C:\>
```

PKLite help screen

As you can see, you can control PKLite's options by using special parameters.

Compressing programs

In its simplest application, without any options, PKLite is as easy to use as LZEXE. In fact, it's actually easier because COM programs can be compressed directly, without converting them first.

Although PKLite doesn't provide a lot of information, it does indicate which files were reduced, from what size, to what size. It doesn't distinguish between COM and EXE files. The compressed version overwrites the original file.

If you want to save the original, add a different name for the compressed version to your command.

7. EXE Compressors

```
PKLITE MODE.COM CMODE.COM
```

In the above example, the new file is named "CMODE.COM." If the new file already exists, PKLITE asks if you want to overwrite it.

```
C:\WORD>pklite mode.com cmode.com
PKLITE (tm)   Executable File Compressor   Version 1.00   12-01-90
Copyright 1990 PKWARE Inc.  All Rights Reserved.

Compressing: MODE.COM into file CMODE.COM
Original Size: 23569  Compressed Size: 15598  Ratio: 33.9

C:\WORD>
```

Compressing with PKLite

The "-o" option lets you skip this prompt. If the new file already exists, the program overwrites it automatically.

```
PKLITE -o MODE.COM CMODE:COM
```

The "-b" option is the opposite of the "-o" option because it provides added security against the possibility of accidental file destruction. Remember, PKLite usually overwrites the original file with the compressed version.

```
PKLITE MODE.COM
```

The above command creates a compressed version of MODE.COM and saves it under the same name. Therefore, the original version is lost. To prevent this from happening, use the "-b" option.

```
PKLITE -b MODE.COM
```

With this command, the compressed file is saved as MODE.COM, like before. However, now the original is saved as a backup version called "MODE.BAK." If you still want to run this version, you must rename it. However, don't call it MODE.COM because this name already exits.

```
REN MODE.BAK OLDMODE.COM
```

7. EXE Compressors

You can control whether PKLite updates the compressed program's time stamp. It will be updated to the current date and time if the "-u" option is specified. Otherwise, it remains as is. You might want to use this option to differentiate multiple copies of the same compressed program.

```
PKLITE -u MODE.COM
```

The above command compresses the MODE program and updates its time stamp. Extract protection involves an intensive compression process that results in a smaller than usual file. More importantly, the "-x" (extract) option cannot subsequently be used to decompress the program. The "-e" option provides extract protection. However, this option isn't supported by the shareware version of PKLite.

EXE files usually contain certain information that isn't needed by the program. This data takes up valuable memory space. With PKLite, you can use the "-r" option to remove this information.

```
PKLITE -r NEWPROG.EXE
```

> Use this option carefully, since the data will be permanently deleted. It cannot be reconstructed, even by using the "-x" option to decompress the file.

Also, other programs sometimes use this information. For example, a debugger needs it to interpret internal data structures and addresses.

Overlays

As we mentioned, overlays and program compression don't always mix. When you try to compress a program that has overlays, PKLite usually reports this and asks whether it should continue.

You can prevent this from happening by using the "-a" option, which tells PKLite to always proceed with compression, even if overlays are present.

> When you use this option, save the compressed version under a separate name. For example:
>
> ```
> PKLITE -a BIGPROG.EXE SMALL.EXE
> ```

With the "-n" option, you can tell PKLite never to proceed with compression if overlays are present:

```
PKLITE -n BIGPROG.EXE
```

7. EXE Compressors

Decompressing programs

Programs that were compressed by PKLite can also be decompressed to their original form. The "-x" option decompresses the data and removes the decompression module from the file:

```
PKLITE -x MODE.COM
```

If the specified file wasn't compressed, PKLite realizes this and displays a warning message.

Many software developers use compression as a way to protect their programs. Since it is a type of encryption, it protects copyright information, copy-protection schemes, and other important data from tampering. However, such protection is canceled if anyone can simply restore the original code by using the "-x" option. The "-e" option prevents this by providing extract protection. As we mentioned, this option isn't available in the shareware version. It's well worth the cost of registration to obtain the full version.

Options

The following table provides an overview of all the options available in PKLite. The syntax is as follows:

```
PKLITE [Options] [Path]PROG [[Path]NEWPROG]
```

Option	Meaning
-a	Always compress, even if program has overlays.
-b	Save a backup of the original file renamed as .BAK.
-e	Compress in such a way that decompression isn't permitted.
-l	Display license screen.
-n	Do not compress a program that has overlays.
-o	Overwrite the target file if it already exists, without prompting for confirmation.
-r	Remove extraneous data from an EXE file. The data cannot later be restored, even with the "-x" parameter.
-u	Update time stamp to current date and time.
-x	Extract (decompress) program to original form.

7. EXE Compressors

DIET

The DIET program, written by Teddy Matsumoto of Japan, is the most comprehensive EXE compressor. This program can process data files as well as programs.

If you think of DIET as a cross between PKLite and PKZip, you're partially right. However, this program offers much more. Data files compressed by traditional compression programs must be restored to their original form before they can be used. However, this isn't necessary in DIET. If you install DIET as a sort of monitor in memory, it starts the data transfer process and decompresses compressed files as they are read from the disk, right into memory.

Now you can leave even your large data files permanently compressed. Whenever a program accesses one of these files, DIET automatically performs the required manipulations.

To be able to do this, DIET must constantly monitor the flow of data to and from the disk. This means it must remain memory-resident in order to compress and decompress data automatically.

Besides this permanent monitoring function, DIET can be used in non-resident mode to handle the various batch operations of a conventional file archiver. This includes compressing programs into executable archives.

In the following sections, we'll explain how to use DIET, both as a free-standing file compressor and as a memory-resident module.

Compressing files

DIET works with all types of files. COM, EXE, and ordinary data files are all supported. Let's start by reviewing DIET's functions. To do this, call the program without any parameters:

```
DIET
```

One of the easiest archiving tasks is compressing the entire current directory. To do this, enter the following:

```
DIET *.*
```

You can also specify which files you want to compress:

```
DIET *.EXE

DIET PROF.TXT

DIET TEXTS.TXT EXTRA.XLS
```

7. EXE Compressors

The first command compresses all EXE program files in the current directory. The second compresses a single file called PROF.TXT, and the last one compresses two named files together.

```
D:\WORD\PACKER>diet
<<<< exciting file slimming exerciser 'DIET' version 1.44 >>>>
      .... copyright(c) 1992,1/22  by Teddy Matsumoto ....

Usage:  DIET [option] filename [filename]...

 -X      compress as executable file        -L     list out DIET files
 -D      compress as data file              -H     check DIET files
 -R      retrieve data files                -L     check original DIET.EXE
 -RA     retrieve all files                 -B     compare by byte size
 -G      choose great SFX routine           -I     ignore warnings
 -K      kill tmporary file at program end  -J     JAPANESE message
 -$      compress recorded files manually   -A     set R/O attribute

 -Z[n]   stay on memory    (n=0,1,2:EMS mode)  -P  recompress melted files
         / change status (if already stayed)   -W  compress newly created files
 -ZR     remove from memory                    -N  not compress automatically
 -ZA     activate TSR function    (DIET ON )   -M  no message output
 -ZD     deactivate TSR function (DIET OFF)    -S  set original file size

 -Cxxxx    copy files with compressing/retrieving (check timestamp)
 -Oxxxx    output file / directory designation
 -Txxxx    temporary file directory designation

D:\WORD\PACKER>
```

DIET help screen

DIET doesn't preserve the original files. However, you can add the "-O" option to compress them under new names or in a different location:

```
DIET -O*.BAK *.TXT
```

The above command compresses all .TXT files found in the current directory. Instead of storing these files under the original names, it creates new copies, which have the .BAK extension. This method isn't very useful for COM and EXE files because they need their extensions in order to run. In this case, you can place the new files in a different directory:

```
DIET -OC:\NEWVER\ *.EXE *.COM
```

All programs in the current directory are compressed and placed in the directory called "C:\NEWVER." Remember that the path must end with a backslash. If this is missing, DIET displays the following message:

> -DISK I/O error!

The target directory must also exist because it won't be created automatically.

The following figure illustrates a feature of DIET that isn't included with other compression programs:

7. EXE Compressors

```
D:\WORD\PACKER>diet *.com
<<<< exciting file slimming exerciser 'DIET' version 1.44 >>>>
     .... copyright(c) 1992,1/22  by Teddy Matsumoto ....

Compress 'FORMAT.COM' ......
Compressing failed! (22731 to 24497 bytes : same cluster size)

Compress 'GRAPHICS.COM' .....
Success! (19742 to 11742 bytes)

Compress 'MODE.COM' ......
Success! (23569 to 15567 bytes)

Compress 'COMMAND.COM' .............
Success! (54933 to 34968 bytes)

Compress 'VSAFE.COM' ...............
Success! (62576 to 32606 bytes)

Compress 'CAPTURE.COM' ...............
Success! (59247 to 14345 bytes)

D:\WORD\PACKER>
```

Programs are compressed

DIET *.COM

As you see from the command, all COM programs in the current directory are compressed and saved under the original names. The above figure shows that most of the files were compressed. For the programs DOSKEY.COM and MORE.COM, DIET reports that the compression wasn't successful.

This "failure" indicates how DIET evaluates the outcome of compression. In this case, the memory space needed on the storage medium is considered instead of the size of a file itself. This is due to a basic disk management unit called the cluster.

While a diskette cluster is 512 bytes, units of 2048 or even 4096 may be used on hard drives. The data for a file is stored in a series of clusters. It's not possible for a file to take up less than one cluster on a disk. For example, on our hard drive, with a cluster size of 2K, a 12-byte file would require a full 2K.

Now let's return to DIET. The program doesn't consider compression a success unless the compressed version uses fewer clusters than the original. This is the only value that represents a usable gain in disk space. The two files that weren't compressed successfully have the following values:

File	Before	After	Space used
DOSKEY.COM	5883	4579	3 clusters
MORE.COM	2545	2964	2 clusters

7. EXE Compressors

With the 2K cluster size, both files used the same number of clusters after compression as before.

```
D:\WORD\PACKER>diet -b diskcomp.com copy.com
<<<< exciting file slimming exerciser 'DIET' version 1.44 >>>>
     .... copyright(c) 1992,1/22  by Teddy Matsumoto ....

Compress 'DISKCOMP.COM' ...
Success! (10668 to 6996 bytes)


D:\WORD\PACKER>
```

Now the compression is successful

Compressing with the "-b" option tells DIET to evaluate its success by comparing "before" and "after" sizes in bytes instead of clusters. DOSKEY.COM is considered successfully compressed with this command:

```
DIET -b DOSKEY.COM
```

Managing files

Since there isn't a special filename extension identifing files compressed by DIET, these files look at first like normal files. Use the "-L" option to determine which files are compressed:

```
DIET -L
```

```
C:\WORD>diet -l
<<<< exciting file slimming exerciser 'DIET' version 1.44 >>>>
   .... copyright(c) 1992,1/22  by Teddy Matsumoto ....

←[0m  TEST-2.EXE   #←[7mMODE.COM    ←[0m   CMODE.COM    #←[7mCD-ROOT.TXT ←[0mn
#←[7mTHIRD.TXT    ←[0m
         #←[7mFOURTH.TXT  ←[0m  #←[7mFIFTH.TXT    ←[0m  #←[7mSIXTH.TXT    ←[0m  #←[7mSEVEE]
TH.TXT ←[0m  #←[7mSTEVE.DOC    ←[0m
    #←[7mARC.ARJ     ←[0m


C:\WORD>
```

Locating compressed files

Now you can easily see which files were produced by DIET. A number sign (#) precedes each file; if your PC is equipped with the ANSI.SYS driver, the compressed files are highlighted.

DIET can also check compressed files for errors. This function is similar to the CRC testing performed by other compression programs. The letter used for this option is "-h":

```
DIET -h *.*
```

This command checks all files in the current directory. A file mask is required. If one isn't specified, the help screen appears instead.

DIET can even check itself to make sure it is intact. Although DIET wouldn't let us compress it, suppose that another program were to change it somehow. DIET performs a self-test with the "-!" option, so you can make sure the program is still working:

```
DIET -!
```

Compressing problem files

Overlays can present problems for DIET, just as they do for other program compressors. Normally files with overlays are reported to the user and excluded from processing. You can change this by using the "-I" or "-V" option.

```
DIET -V BIG.EXE
```

7. EXE Compressors

The above command compresses the program BIG.EXE. If it has overlays, DIET notes this but compresses it anyway.

```
DIET -I BIG.EXE
```

The "-I" option directly affect overlays, but it ignores warnings and exception processing. If you use this parameter, a program with overlays would simply be compressed.

DIET can also compress a special type of program called a device driver. These programs work in the background of your system to control input and output from peripheral devices.

Device drivers have the .SYS filename extension and contain instructions like regular programs. However, instead of being called separately, device drivers are loaded into memory and started when you boot your computer. While the computer is running, they remain in memory to monitor and control certain events. The drivers installed on startup are specified in the CONFIG.SYS file, which, despite its name, is not a device driver. Each device driver is specified in a command that begins as follows:

```
DEVICE=....
```

A popular device driver is HIMEM.SYS, which lets you access to memory beyond 1 Meg:

```
DEVICE=HIMEM.SYS
```

Device drivers are structured differently than COM and EXE programs. For this reason, you must use a special option when compressing them. This is the letter "-D":

```
DIET -d -b *.SYS
```

Don't be confused by the "-b" in this command line. Remember, this option simply indicates that you want DIET to compare exact file sizes in bytes when reporting whether the compression was successful.

Something else is also confusing. HIMEM.SYS is compressed as a device driver, but CONFIG.SYS, even though it has the .SYS extension, isn't. To make this more confusing, CONFIG.SYS can be compressed with the normal command

```
DIET CONFIG.SYS
```

while this returns an error for HIMEM.SYS. The reason why this occurs is actually quite simple. DIET examines a file before compressing it. If the "-D" option is used, the file must be a device driver, which is indicated by the value 255 255 (or FF FF) in the first two data bytes. CONFIG.SYS doesn't have these bytes. This is easily seen by displaying its contents:

7. EXE Compressors

```
TYPE CONFIG.SYS
```

CONFIG.SYS is just a simple text file.

```
D:\PACK\PACKER>type c:\config.sys
device=c:\adeptec\aspi4dos.sys /d
DEVICE=C:\DOS\HIMEM.SYS /machine:1
DEVICE=C:\DOS\EMM386.EXE NOEMS X=C600-C6FF
BUFFERS=10,0
FILES=40
DOS=UMB
Lastdrive=P
FCBS=16,0
REM BUFFERS=30,0
DEVICEHIGH /L:2,12048 =C:\DOS\SETVER.EXE
DEVICE=C:\DOS\SMARTDRV.EXE /DOUBLE_BUFFER
SHELL=C:\DOS\COMMAND.COM C:\DOS\ /e:600 /p
STACKS=9,256

D:\PACK\PACKER>
```

Displaying CONFIG.SYS

Using a driver after compression is very easy. If the compressed version remains in the original directory, you don't have to do anything at all. The CONFIG.SYS entry references the same filename, which hasn't changed. Special parameters aren't required.

If you put the compressed version in a different directory, however, you must change the path in your CONFIG.SYS file. For example, use the drivers ANSI.SYS and COUNTRY.SYS. Your CONFIG.SYS file has the corresponding commands:

```
...
DEVICE=C:\DOS\ANSI.SYS
DEVICE=C:\DOS\COUNTRY.SYS
...
```

So, the original drivers are in the DOS directory on your C: drive. Now suppose that you create compressed versions of both drivers in the root directory and want to use them:

```
DIET -D -OC:\ C:\DOS\ANSI.SYS C:\DOS\COUNTRY.SYS
```

The CONFIG.SYS entries must be changed as follows:

```
...
DEVICE=C:\ANSI.SYS
DEVICE=C:\COUNTRY.SYS
...
```

7. EXE Compressors

> Remember, the new versions won't be implemented until you reboot your computer. Also, you shouldn't try this without having a boot diskette available, in case something goes wrong.
>
> Compressing device drivers can only save disk space, not memory. The file itself may be smaller, but when you call the driver, the code is decompressed as it loads into memory. If you want to compress your device drivers, make sure you actually reduce the number of clusters and don't retain any original versions. Otherwise you won't save any disk space.

Decompressing files

The compression process can also be reversed. The "-R" option is used for this, combined with the "A" option, if desired.

Option	Meaning
-R	Reverses compression for specified data files (not programs or drivers).
-RA	Reverses compression for all files specified (including programs and drivers).

A file filter must be included in the command:

```
DIET -R *.*
```

Although the above command specifies all files, only data files are actually decompressed. COM, EXE, and SYS files ("true" SYS files, not CONFIG.SYS) are skipped. If there are no compressed data files in the current directory, DIET displays the following message:

> No files to be processed!

If the -L command indicates that the directory contains compressed files, try this command again but use the "A" option:

```
DIET -RA *.*
```

This reverses all compressed files, regardless of type, to their original format.

> If you want to decompress only selected files or file types, you shouldn't use "-RA". To decompress only EXE and COM files, for example, use the following command:
>
>   DIET -RA *.EXE *.COM

> You can use the "-O" option with decompression to place the restored files in a different directory. Don't forget to end the target path with a backslash.
>
>   DIET -RA -OC:\BIG\ *.EXE *.COM

Memory-resident DIET

At the beginning of this chapter, we mentioned DIET's memory-resident capabilities for handling compressed files. Now we'll take a closer look at how this works. DIET can function as an extension of MS-DOS, so that it interacts in any exchange of data between memory and the disk. In order to do this, it must be installed as resident in RAM. All options for using DIET in resident mode begin with "Z." To install the program permanently in memory, use the following command:

```
DIET -Z
```

DIET will load into memory and stay there permanently. A program capable of doing this is referred to as a "terminate and stay resident" program, which is abbreviated as TSR. From now on, it monitors all read operations. A message like the following indicates that the installation was successful:

> Stayed in Memory!
> auto recompress: off
> Temp. directory: current

Any message other than "Stayed in Memory!" indicates that a problem has occurred. The items "auto recompress" and "temporary directory" can be changed with parameters. We'll discuss this in more detail later.

When you install any code as memory-resident, you should determine how much space it takes away from other programs. To do this, use the DOS command MEM:

```
MEM /C | MORE
```

The /C parameter displays a table of all the programs currently in memory. DIET will be one of the entries:

7. EXE Compressors

```
Conventional memory:

Name      Size      (decimal)     Size (Hex)

MSDOS     12432     (12.1KB)      3090
HIMEM      1072     ( 1.0KB)       430
EMM386     3216     ( 3.1KB)       C90
COMMAND    3776     ( 3.7KB)       EC0
DIET      24688     (24.1KB)      6070
FREE         64     ( 0.1KB)        40
FREE        240     ( 0.2KB)        F0
FREE     609648     (595.4KB)    94D70

Total FREE:        609952        (595.7KB)
```

Your listing may look a little different, but DIET should occupy 24K.

Temporary directory

Like other compressors, DIET needs extra temporary storage space to do its work. This normally goes in the current directory. With diskette operations you may want to change this, since diskette access is slow and space is limited.

You can specify a temporary directory by using the "-T" option with the installation command:

```
DIET -Z -TC:\DOS\TEMP\
```

The above command tells DIET to use the directory C:\DOS\TEMP for any work that requires data swapping.

> The ending backslash is required. Now the installation response from DIET will show the specified work directory:
>
> ```
> temp. directory: C:\DOS\TEMP\
> ```

You must ensure that the directory exists. Although DIET shows the path you specified, it doesn't actually check for it. It simply assumes that it exists.

Deactivating DIET

There are two ways to deactivate DIET after installing it as memory-resident:

- Remove it from memory.
- Deactivate it temporarily, but keep it in memory so that it can be re-activated at any time.

Obviously, the most extreme method is to remove DIET from memory. The "R" option is used for this:

7. EXE Compressors

```
DIET -ZR
```

The response should be:

> Removed from Memory!

If you activate this command when the program isn't memory-resident, the response is:

> Not stayed in memory!

It's also possible to switch off DIET's monitoring function temporarily and then re-activate it later. The "D" option is used for this:

```
DIET -ZD
```

DIET responds with the following message:

> TSR-Function is deactivated

Once placed on standby, the program can be called back to work at any time by using the "A" option:

```
DIET -ZA
```

DIET indicates that it's ready to work by displaying an appropriate message. The auto recompress and temp directory settings are also shown.

> Normally after you install DIET with the "-Z" option, the background monitoring mode is immediately activated. If it doesn't seem to be working, try activating it manually:

```
DIET -ZA
```

Sometimes DIET deactivates itself. This can happen when the user interrupts a compression or decompression process by pressing [Ctrl]+[Break] or [Ctrl]+[C]. You can reactivate it using "-ZA".

As we explained, DIET automatically intervenes in the DOS process of reading a file. When a program writes to the file, however, the data isn't necessarily compressed as it goes to the disk. If you want this to happen, you must specify the "-P" option.

```
DIET -Z -P
```

7. EXE Compressors

The above command activates the auto recompress mode. You can use this command to install the program or after it's already resident. In the latter case, DIET is not actually reloaded.

> Unfortunately, the Recompress function isn't completely reliable. Some programs won't work with it properly, so they still write data in uncompressed form. You should check your files after one of these programs has used them. If they aren't compressed, simply compress them with the usual command:
>
> `DIET *.DOC`

When a problem occurs with write compression, DIET reports an error. You can suppress error messages with the "-M" option:

`DIET -Z -P -M`

Example

We'll use an example to demonstrate this process. First, we'll compress a file. We've chosen ABACAT.DOC, a simple text file. The figure below shows the contents of the file before it's compressed.

`MORE<ABACAT.DOC`

```
C:\WORD>more<abacat.doc

To: All Persons:

This is just a note to remind you to register all the shareware
products that are on the companion disk with the book

PKZip, LHArc and Co.

Thank you, Abacus


C:\WORD>
```

Contents of a text file

Now we can perform the compression:

`DIET -b ABACAT.DOC`

7. EXE Compressors

Since the file is already less than one cluster, DIET won't consider it successfully compressed unless we also use the "-b" option. Now the program will compare the before and after sizes in bytes instead of clusters.

```
C:\WORD>diet -b abacat.doc
<<<< exciting file slimming exerciser 'DIET' version 1.44 >>>>
      .... copyright(c) 1992,1/22  by Teddy Matsumoto ....

Compress 'ABACAT.DOC' .
Success! (187 to 179 bytes)


C:\WORD>more<abacat.doc

{L=↑¥ëdïz ó K ╖   To: All Persons╫√:
■This ²   just a note to r ñemind you⌐ü≡g│ ⁊r■⌐╖∩≈th │sha∞⌡"±⌐product╛zäδa╛∅ Ñ≤∩■cooı
pani²╫pd├k wiδ⌡!=bookâPK ╔Zip, LHArc╙ôCo.n≤x<┬ä∑Abac\ hô
C:\WORD>
```

Garbage characters

The compressed file is now unreadable to an ordinary program. We can see this by trying to read its contents again by using MORE.

As expected, all we see are "garbage" characters.

Now we'll install DIET in memory-resident mode.

```
DIET -Z
DIET -ZA
```

The first command performs the installation, and the second one ensures that the program is activated. Now things have changed. A third attempt to read ABACAT.DOC, without explicitly decompressing it first, works without any problems:

```
MORE<ABACAT.DOC
DIET parameters
```

We'll end this chapter with an overview of the DIET parameters:

7. EXE Compressors

Compression Options

Option	Meaning
-B	Use the number of bytes in the original and compressed versions to determine whether compression was successful. Without this option, the number of clusters is used.
-D	Compress device drivers.
-I	Ignore warnings during compression.
-V	Compress programs with overlays.
-O<target>	Do not overwrite original files; produce backup copies.

Decompression Options

Option	Meaning
-R	Decompress (reverse compress) all specified data files.
-RA	Decompress all specified data files, programs, and device drivers.
-O<target>	Do not overwrite original files; produce backup copies.

Resident-mode Options

Option	Meaning
-Z	Install DIET as memory-resident. If EMS memory is present, a page of it is reserved.
-ZR	Remove DIET from memory-resident mode.
-ZA	Activate DIET in memory if it was deactivated. Cannot be used until DIET has been installed with the "-Z" option.
-ZD	Deactivate DIET in memory, but keep it resident. This status can be reversed with "-ZA".
-P	Activates the auto recompress mode.
-M	Suppresses any messages.

Command Summary And Switches

In this chapter, we'll summarize the features of each of the compression programs we discussed in this book. As you'll see, these programs provide a variety of options, especially ARJ.

Each section is divided into syntax, commands, and switches (or options). When needed, we used examples to clarify the information.

Errorlevel basics

Errorlevel is a variable that can be tested following program execution to determine whether certain problems occurred. This approach is used in batch mode, where a program cannot interact with the user by sending error messages directly to the screen.

If you use compression programs in batch files, you should check for errors immediately after each command. Be careful about testing values with the DOS IF command. This command works differently than the same command in a normal programming language.

You're probably familiar with programming statements like the following:

```
IF Errorlevel = 20 Then ...

IF Errorlevel = 25 Then ...
```

Each of the above examples tests the variable for an exact value. Coding the same task for DOS is less straightforward. DOS performs a greater-or-equal test on the value of Errorlevel. We'll use an example to demonstrate the implications of this test.

Suppose that a program can return any code from 0 through 10. If you're interested in a value of 3, you must eliminate the other possibilities. Here's how it works:

```
ARJ a PAN Peter.*
IF Errorlevel 4 ECHO Unimportant error
IF Errorlevel 3 GOTO Important
IF Errorlevel 1 ECHO Unimportant error
IF Errorlevel 0 ECHO No error
```

The first line checks for codes greater than or equal to 4. The next line checks for codes greater than or equal to 3, but everything greater than 3 has already been eliminated. Consequently, if this condition is true, we know that the code equals 3.

Not all programs return a specific code for each possible outcome. However, the value 0 is almost always used to indicate error-free execution, while other values mean that something went wrong. A batch file that checks for successful completion of an operation might contain the following lines:

```
...
LHA e GAMES *.* C:\GAMES
IF Errorlevel 1 GOTO Error
ECHO Extract successful
```

ARJ 2.30

Syntax

```
ARJ <Command> [-<Switch>[-/+]<Switch>]...] <Archivename>[.ARJ]
[<filenames>...]
```

Please note the following concerning the syntax:

- ➢ No distinction is made between upper and lowercase characters.
- ➢ Switches may be placed anywhere after the command letter.
- ➢ Entries enclosed in square brackets ([]) aren't required.

Restrictions

Although you probably won't encounter them in everyday use, the following restrictions apply to ARJ:

- ➢ 64 filenames or wildcards per command line.
- ➢ 16,000 filenames resulting from the use of wildcards.
- ➢ 8,000 filenames or wildcards to be excluded.
- ➢ 8,000 ARJ filenames resulting from the use of wildcards.
- ➢ 2,048 characters per comment (25 lines or a comment file of up to 2,048 characters).

8. Command Summary And Switches

Memory requirements

ARJ takes up a lot of memory, especially when operating in its most intensive compression mode. This takes about 290,000 bytes, while extracting files from an archive takes about 166,000 bytes.

Memory limitation is the reason for the 16,000 file restriction noted above.

Commands

The following is the complete command reference for ARJ. As you can see by the number of commands that are provided, ARJ is a versatile and powerful program.

We've divided this section into two parts:

1. Commands

    All the command letters of ARJ are listed alphabetically. The explanation of the command may include cross-references to related commands or switches.

2. Switches

    Switches modify commands. Since there are so many switches, it's not practical to list the applicable ones with each individual command. Therefore, they are arranged alphabetically in a separate section.

---

a   add

Add places the specified files into an archive. Files with the same names are overwritten.

Examples:

```
ARJ a archive
```

Compresses all files from the current drive and directory into the archive file called ARCHIVE.ARJ.

```
ARJ a e:\pics\graphics c:\windows\*.bmp
```

Compresses all files ending in ".BMP", from the WINDOWS directory on the C: drive, into an archive file called GRAPHICS.ARJ in the PICS directory on the E: drive.

```
ARJ a -r -vv1440K b:\archive c:\*.*
```

Compresses all files from drive C: into the archive file(s) ARCHIVE.ARJ (A01, A02, ...) on 3.5-inch, 1.44 Meg diskettes in drive B:.

8. Command Summary And Switches

The **Add** command allows for a multi-volume archive with up to 99 extension volumes. A beep sounds with each prompt for a new formatted diskette in drive B:.

b   batch command

The "b" command lets you temporarily extract archived files for processing with DOS commands or programs. For example, you can use this command to check the contents of an archived file with the DOS TYPE command.

The extracted files receive the default names ARJTEMP.XXX (XXX represents a series of numbers beginning with 001). The temporary files are deleted when the operation is complete.

Examples:

```
ARJ b archive *.TXT
```

Enter system command: type *.TXT

The above command temporarily extracts all .TXT files from the ARCHIVE.ARJ archive and displays their contents on the screen. The TYPE command is entered after the following prompt:

Enter system command:

The following switches can be used with this command:

Switch	Description
-jw	Rename extracted files
-jq	Execute command

```
ARJ b archive chess.pas -jwCheckmat.pas "-jqTURBO Checkmat.pas"
```

This command temporarily extracts the file called "CHESS.PAS" from the archive called "ARCHIVE." The temporary file is then renamed from "ARJTEMP.001" to "CHECKMAT.PAS." Finally, a program called "TURBO" is called to process CHECKMAT.PAS.

c   comment

This command lets you attach comments to archives themselves or to individual files within archives. There are two modes for attaching comments:

> ➢ You can type up to 25 lines directly in dialog mode. Terminate the entry by pressing [Enter] to create a blank line.

8. Command Summary And Switches

> ➤ You can pass a previously created text, of up to 2,048 bytes, to the specified archive file using the "-z" switch.

Examples:

```
ARJ c archive
```

The above command activates the dialog mode for entering comments, first for the archive itself and then for each packed file.

```
ARJ c archive -z
```

Only a comment for the archive file is requested.

```
ARJ c archive -zNOTES.TXT
```

The contents of NOTES.TXT (maximum 2,048 bytes) is automatically attached as commentary to the archive.

```
ARJ c archive -zNUL
```

Attaches the contents of the NUL file as commentary to the archive. Since NUL is empty, this deletes any current comments.

```
ARJ c archive -jzNUL
```

Deletes all comments for individual archived files.

```
ARJ c archive -zNUL -jzNUL
```

Deletes all comments, both for the archive itself and for all individual archived files.

> Comments aren't compressed. Therefore, the more comments you include, the lower the overall compression rate will be for the archive.

d   delete

The "d" command deletes one or more compressed files from an archive.

When wildcards are used with the "-q" switch, a confirmation prompt appears before the deletion of each file.

Examples:

```
ARJ d archive *.TXT
```

All files ending in ".TXT" are deleted from the archive.

```
ARJ d -q archive *.TXT
```

You're asked to confirm each .TXT deletion individually.

e   extract

This command extracts one or more compressed files from the specified archive to the current or specified directory.

You must confirm a safety prompt before an existing file is overwritten. To suppress the prompt and assume a "yes" response, include the -y switch with this command.

Directory information stored in the archive is ignored. This means that every extracted file is placed in the specified directory.

Examples:

```
ARJ e archive
```

All files in the ARCHIVE.ARJ archive are extracted to the current directory.

```
ARJ e -y archive b:\Letters *.TXT
```

All files ending in ".TXT" are extracted to the target directory "Letters" on drive B:. Existing files are overwritten without a prompt.

f   freshen

Freshen replaces archived files with more current versions.

A file, from the source disk, that isn't already in the archive won't be added to it. (To do this, use the Update "u" command).

Example:

```
ARJ f -r document *.TXT *.DOC
```

This command freshens the archive called "DOCUMENT" by updating archived files ending in ".TXT" and ".DOC" with newer versions from the current directory and subdirectories.

g   garble files

Garble provides password protection for archived files. Garbled files cannot be decompressed without the correct password.

8. Command Summary And Switches

"g" is used as a command to add password protection to files in an existing archive. To garble the files as they are placed in the archive, use it as a switch ("-g") in combination with the appropriate command (Update, Add, etc.).

Remember the following:

> ➢ Password protection in ARJ is case-sensitive.

> ➢ Each file in an archive can have its own password. Usually the number of different passwords is kept to a minimum.

The "g" command can also be combined with the "-g" switch, which lets you type the password directly on the command line.

Example:

```
ARJ g archive -gjoshua
```

With this command, all files in the ARCHIVE.ARJ archive are garbled with the password "joshua."

---

i   **integrity of ARJ.EXE**

This command checks the ARJ.EXE program itself and reports a CRC error if a problem occurs.

Example:

```
ARJ i ARJ.exe
```

This command checks the integrity of ARJ.EXE (to detect changes introduced by viruses or other file compressors, for example).

---

j   **join**

Join combines two or more archives to make a single archive. It also turns executable SFX archives back into normal archives.

Examples:

```
ARJ j letters texts.arj doc.arj
```

This command combines the archives TEXTS.ARJ and DOC.ARJ into a single archive called "LETTERS.ARJ."

```
ARJ j -r archive *.arj
```

8. Command Summary And Switches

The above command is a simple way to combine all archives from the current directory and subdirectories into a single archive called "ARCHIVE.ARJ."

```
ARJ j games games.exe
```

The executable SFX archive GAMES.EXE is converted to a normal archive called "GAMES.ARJ."

---

k   delete backups

Archived files designated as backups are deleted with this command. Backup files are extra copies of compressed files within an archive.

Examples:

```
ARJ k backup *.*
```

All files marked as backups in the BACKUP.ARJ archive are deleted.

```
ARJ k -q document *.TXT
```

All .TXT files marked as backups in the DOCUMENT.ARJ archive are deleted after you confirm the safety prompt for each file.

---

l   list

List shows the contents of an archive on the default output device (normally the screen). The compressed files are listed in the order in which they were stored.

-jp	This switch lists the output a page at a time.

Example:

```
ARJ l -jp passcr *.pas
```

All .PAS (Pascal source code) files in the PASSCR.ARJ archive are listed on the screen a page at a time.

An extended variation of the List command is Verbose list (v).

---

m   move

Move archives the specified files and then deletes the original versions.

8. Command Summary And Switches

A safety prompt doesn't appear before each deletion. For added security, use the "-jt" switch with this command. It ensures that the compressed versions are good before deleting the originals.

-jt	Tests archived files before deleting original versions.

Example:

```
ARJ m dbase *.dbf -r -jt
```

The above command archives all dBase data files from the current directory and subdirectories into an archive called "DBASE.ARJ." After a successful integrity test on the compressed files, it also deletes the originals.

n   rename

Rename assigns new names to archived files.

The new names are assigned in dialog mode. ARJ asks for a new name for each file that's specified. To keep the same name, press Enter.

Example:

```
ARJ n texts *.TXT
```

When this command is activated, you'll be asked to enter a new name for each .TXT file in the TEXTS archive.

o   order archive

This command rearranges the files in an archive. Files specified on the command line are placed at the beginning of the archive. The desired sequence can also be specified in a text file. You cannot use wildcards (*, ?).

Examples:

```
ARJ o archive offers.TXT orders.TXT invoices.TXT
```

The three files specified in this command are moved to the front of the ARCHIVE.ARJ archive. The order of any other files in the archive doesn't change.

```
ARJ o texts !textsort.lst
```

This command rearranges the TEXTS.ARJ archive. The new file sequence is specified in a text file called "TEXTSORT.LST."

8. Command Summary And Switches

p   print to standard output

This command prints the contents of compressed files to the standard output device. Unlike List, which simply indicates which files are present, this command prints the actual contents of the files.

Example:

```
ARJ p document
```

Displays the contents of all files in the DOCUMENT archive on the screen.

```
ARJ p document >NUL
```

The output is nulled. Since the files must first be extracted, this is another way of testing the integrity of the archive.

```
ARJ p document >PRN
```

The output is directed to the printer.

---

r   remove pathnames

This command removes all pathnames for the archived files, leaving only the filenames. If a file isn't specified, paths are removed from all files in the archive.

The Remove command has the same effect on an existing archive as the switch -e has when an archive is created. Paths removed in this way cannot be restored.

Example:

```
ARJ r archive *.TXT
```

Path information is removed from all .TXT files in the ARCHIVE.ARJ archive.

---

s   sample

Sample displays the contents of an archived file on the screen. This command is similar to the Print (p) command, but the display automatically pauses for a user response after each full screen. Also, lines are truncated after the 79th character and control characters are replaced by question marks.

Example:

```
ARJ s document contract.DOC
```

This command displays the file CONTRACT.DOC from the DOCUMENT archive one screen at a time.

8. Command Summary And Switches

t   test

Test checks the integrity of compressed files within an archive. If a file isn't specified, every file in the archive is tested. If the test fails, a CRC error is reported.

Example:

`ARJ t imprtant`

This command tests all files in the IMPRTANT.ARJ archive for error-free compression and storage.

---

u   update

Update replaces files in an archive with newer versions and adds those not yet present. The time stamp is used to control updating.

Example:

`ARJ u passcr`

Compresses all files, in the current directory, that don't exist yet in the PASSCR.ARJ archive or that exist there as older versions.

---

v   verbose List

Similar to the "l" command, Verbose list provides a listing of an archive's contents. However, complete paths are displayed and the compressed files are numbered sequentially.

The numbers can be used instead of filenames to reference the files.

-#	Switch used to access files by position number.

Examples:

`ARJ v texts -jp`

All files in the TEXTS archive are listed along with their sequential position numbers. The display pauses between pages.

`ARJ e texts -# 3 12`

The third and twelfth files are extracted from the TEXTS archive.

8. Command Summary And Switches

w   where is text?

This command searches archived files for a particular text string. Case-sensitivity is optional, along with the ability to show the desired string in context by listing additional lines.

The following switches can be used:

-jp	Pause when screen is full.
-jv	Display ASCII characters with codes 128 to 255 (IBM graphic characters).
-jq	Input search information on command line.

Normal input for this command is interactive, through a question-and-answer dialog box.

Examples:

```
ARJ w texts
```

This command asks you to enter the search string and specify case-sensitivity and the number of lines to print. All files in the TEXTS archive are then searched for the string, which is displayed when found.

The search can also be initiated directly from the command line without entering dialog mode. This is done by using the "-jq" switch with the following syntax:

```
-jq<ignore-case><line-count><delimiter><search-text>
```

The required entries are:

Ignore-case	"-" to observe case, "+" to ignore case.
Line-count	Number of lines to print with the specified string.
Delimiter	A separation character between line-count and search-text. Usually a plus or minus sign.
Search-text	The exact string to be located. If this consists of more than one word (if spaces are included), the entire -jq group is enclosed in quotes.

```
ARJ w texts -jq+5+offer
```

This command tells ARJ to search all files in the TEXTS.ARJ archive for the word "offer." Case is ignored. If the search is successful, five lines of text will be displayed along with the located string.

```
ARJ j w texts "-jq+5-invoice nr. 007"
```

8. Command Summary And Switches

Although it's similar to the previous example, this command uses "-" as the text delimiter and includes spaces in the text string.

---

x   extract extended

This command extracts archived files using complete path information. If a specified directory does not exist, it's created after you confirm the prompt that appears.

Example:

```
ARJ x invoices c:\firms
```

All files from the INVOICES.ARJ archive are extracted, along with their complete path structures, to the FIRMS directory on the C: drive. Archived files may be specified as belonging to subdirectories, such as REPORTS or QUARTER. If this directory structure doesn't exist on the target storage medium, you're asked to confirm that it should be added. The files are then extracted accordingly.

---

y   copy with new options

This command copies an existing archive and applies new features. It can be used to make a self-extracting (SFX) archive from a normal archive. The original archive is also retained.

Example:

```
ARJ y archive -je
```

With this command, a second copy of ARCHIVE.ARJ is created as a self-extracting archive called "ARCHIVE.EXE."

Switches

A switch modifies an ARJ command in a certain way. There are two types of switches: Normal and extended. An extended switch consists of two letters, the first one being "j." The following applies to all switches:

- ➢ Case is ignored.
- ➢ A switch is meaningless without a command (except for the help switch).
- ➢ A switch can appear anywhere on the command line after the command itself.

8. Command Summary And Switches

-? Help screen

The question mark displays the entire ARJ help text a screen at a time.

```
ARJ -?
```

-- No more switches

This switch indicates that additional switches won't be found on the command line. You'll need this switch if you use filenames beginning with "-."

Example:

```
ARJ a texts -- -info.TXT
```

The file called "-INFO.TXT" will now be recognized as such and processed by ARJ. Without the "--" switch, ARJ would interpret the filename as a wrongly-coded switch.

-+ environment

This switch disables the standard environment variable ARJ_SW and/or replaces it with another variable.

Example:

```
ARJ a archive -+ARJ_ENV
```

The environment variable ARJ_SW is replaced by ARJ_ENV.

-& critical error handler

This switch traps critical error messages from the operating system (Abort, Fail, Retry) and invokes custom error handling.

You should use this switch when ARJ is working in "unsupervised" mode.

Example:

```
ARJ a b:\archive -&
```

In case of trouble (e.g., an unreadable sector), a custom routine handles the error, so the archiving process doesn't have to be aborted.

8. Command Summary And Switches

-!   alternative list symbol

This switch specifies an alternative character for list file processing (the standard symbol is "!").

Example:

```
ARJ a archive -!@ @sort.lst
```

The standard symbol used by LHA and PKZIP ("@") is defined as the list symbol.

-$ volume name

Adds the name of the current volume (volume label) on the indicated drive to an archive. A single archive can have more than one volume label.

The volume label is displayed with the DOS VOL command.

Example:

```
ARJ u texts -$C:
```

The volume name of the C: drive is added as a file to the TEXTS.ARJ archive.

-#   file number

Selects files in an archive by position number. The verbose list (v) command shows the position number for each file.

Example:

```
ARJ e texts -# 1 5 10 12
```

The first, fifth, tenth, and twelfth files are extracted from the TEXTS.ARJ archive.

-a   file attributes

The file attributes switch provides access to all files regardless of attributes. With the default setting in ARJ, Hidden and System, files are ignored.

-a	Allow all file attributes.
-a1	Include empty directories.

8. Command Summary And Switches

-b   Backup

When the backup switch is specified, the archiving process checks the backup (archive) attribute of each file to determine the desired processing.

DOS sets this attribute when a file is added or changed. A backup program can then determine which files should be saved and which have remained untouched since the last backup.

-b	Saves only those files whose archive bit is set.
-b1	Saves only those files whose archive bit is set. Clears the bit after archiving is complete.
-b2	Resets the archive bits for the specified files. Unlike -b and -b1, this switch does not in itself serve as a file selector.

Examples:

```
ARJ a a:backup c:\*.TXT -r -b1
```

In the above example, all .TXT files on drive C: that carry the archive attribute are compressed to the BACKUP.ARJ archive on drive A:. The archive bits are cleared as the files are saved. For this reason, files wouldn't be saved on a subsequent execution if the same command was immediately repeated.

```
ARJ a c:backup *.dbf *.xls -b
```

All files in the current directory that carry the archive attribute and end in ".DBF" or ".XLS" are packed to the BACKUP.ARJ archive.

```
ARJ a c:Backup \*.DOC -b2
```

Every .DOC file on the current drive is saved to the BACKUP.ARJ archive regardless of the setting of its archive bit. If the bit was set, it's cleared after the file is saved.

-c   skip time check

This switch eliminates checking of file time stamps. Normally the time stamp controls which files the "f" and "u" commands will save. With the "-c" switch, all files are saved regardless of when they were last updated.

-d   delete

This switch indicates subsequent deletion of selected files. All files processed will be deleted after the associated command is executed.

8. Command Summary And Switches

Example:

```
ARJ a texts *.DOC -d -y
```

All .DOC files will be compressed to the TEXTS.ARJ archive. The originals will be deleted without a safety prompt.

-e   no pathname

This switch eliminates path information from archived files. Only the filename is stored. The "x" command cannot restore the original directory structure.

-e	Do not save paths.
-e1	Do not save output directory.

Example:

```
ARJ a archive c:\dos\*.* -e1
```

All files in the DOS subdirectory are archived without path information (therefore, also without the DOS output directory).

-f   freshen

When used with the "e" or "x" command, this switch ensures that only newer versions of files already present on the target storage medium will be decompressed. When used with the "m" command, this switch ensures that only newer versions of files already present in the archive will be moved to it.

Example:

```
ARJ e texts *.TXT -f
```

A .TXT file will be extracted to the disk, only if it already exists there, but with an older date and time.

-g   garble with password

When used with an archiving command, this switch applies a password to the archived files.

-gXX	Password is entered directly after the switch.
-g?	Password is entered in dialog mode.

8. Command Summary And Switches

This switch is also used to unlock password-protected files from an archive. If the wrong password is used, ARJ reports a CRC error or bad file data.

ARJ is case-sensitive with regard to passwords.

Examples:

```
ARJ a secret c:\private\*.* -gjoshua
```

All files from the PRIVATE subdirectory are packed to the SECRET.ARJ archive and locked with the password "joshua."

```
ARJ a secret c:\private\imprtant.TXT -g?
```

A password is requested in dialog mode (to be entered twice) and applied to the IMPRTANT.TXT file saved in the SECRET.ARJ archive.

```
ARJ e secret -gjoshua
```

All files with the password "joshua" are extracted.

-i   **no indicator**

With this switch, a progress indicator bar isn't displayed (default setting). By including the "-i1" switch with an archiving command, you can display a bar indicating the progress of the compression process.

-i	Progress indicator is not displayed.
-i1	Progress indicator is displayed.

-j   **shifted switch**

This switch changes the meaning of the switch that follows to its alternative value. For example, "-a" is different from "-ja" but the same as "-jja." The combination "-jae" means the same as "-ja je." Extended switches are listed at the end of this section.

-k   **backup of archive**

This switch creates a backup (.BAK) copy of an archive when it's changed. An existing .BAK file with the same name will be overwritten.

8. Command Summary And Switches

-l   list file

Creates a list file, which is a text file containing the names or wildcards for the files affected by the command.

Examples:

```
ARJ a texts c:\winword\*.DOC *.TXT -llist.TXT
```

After packing all .DOC and .TXT files from the WINWORD directory to the TEXTS.ARJ archive, the program creates a text file containing the filenames selected.

```
ARJ l texts -llist.lst
```

Since this command doesn't specify selected files to be listed, the LIST.LST text file will contain the wildcard string "*.*".

-m   method

Specifies the compression method:

-m0	No compression.
-m1	Highest compression (standard).
-m2	Somewhat less compression, slightly improved speed.
-m3	Still less compression, more-improved speed.
-m4	Lowest compression, highest speed.

Example:

```
ARJ a archive *.* -m4
```

All files are compressed using the fastest processing method and the lowest-density compression.

-n   new files

This switch selects only new files. When used with a decompression command, only files not already in the target directory are decompressed. When used with an archiving command, only files not already present in the archive are added to it.

8. Command Summary And Switches

-o   on or after

The "o" switch selects files according to time stamps. You can use it to screen for files of a certain age.

-o	On or after the date-time specified in YYMMDDHHMMSS format.
-ob	Before the date-time specified in YYMMDDHHMMSS format.

By combining both switches, you can define an interval during which a file must have been created or modified. A year less than 80 will be considered in the twenty-first century.

Examples:

```
ARJ a archive -o930312
```

Archives all files created or modified on March 12, 1993, or later.

```
ARJ a archive -o930301 -ob930312
```

Archives all files created or modified from March 1, 1993 up to March 12, 1993.

-p   match pathname

If files with the same name exist under different pathnames, you can use this switch to specify the path of the desired file.

-q   query on file

This switch tells ARJ to display a prompt for each file processed. It's especially useful as a safety feature with commands that involve file deleting. You must confirm a query before each file is deleted.

Example:

```
ARJ d document *.DOC -q
```

All .DOC files should be deleted from the DOCUMENT archive. ARJ will ask you to verify each deletion.

-r   recurse subdirs

This switch tells ARJ to recurse all subdirectories encountered during processing of the specified files. This allows you to preserve the original directory structure in the archive.

8. Command Summary And Switches

Appropriate switches:

-a	Hidden and system files will also be archived.
-a1	Empty directories will also be archived.

Examples:

```
ARJ a secure c:\*.bak -r
```

All backup (.BAK) files in the C: root and its underlying subdirectories will be compressed to the SECURE.ARJ archive.

```
ARJ a secure c:\*.bak -r -a -a1
```

Same as above, but hidden and system files as well as empty directories will also be archived.

-s   **archive time-stamp**

This switch applies the time stamp from the most recently archived file to the archive itself.

-t   **file type**

The "-t" or "-t0" switch indicates that the specified files should be handled as binary files (the standard setting). With the "-t1" switch, the files are handled as text files.

> This version of the program does not support any setting besides the default, -t0.

-u   **update**

This switch updates and adds new files. When it's used with a decompression command, ARJ extracts only those files not already present in the target directory or whose date-time precedes the archived version.

> When the switch is used with the "m" command, only those files not already present in the archive are moved to it.

8. Command Summary And Switches

-v   multiple volume

This switch allows an archive to extend across multiple volumes.

The volumes are identified by sequential numbers assigned when the archive is created. The following variants are possible:

-vv	A beep signals the end-of-volume condition, file size message, and prompt for new diskette.
-vw	Files cannot be split between volumes.
-va	ARJ automatically determines the maximum available file space on the specified drive.
-vs	A DOS command is executed before a new diskette is started.
-v36	Creates archives at 360K.
-v72	Creates archives at 720K.
-v12	Creates archives at 1.2 Meg
-v14	Creates archives at 1.44 Meg
-vNN	Creates archives at NN bytes

Examples:

```
ARJ a b:\backup c:\*.* -vv1440 -r
```

All files on the C: drive are archived to multiple 3.5-inch HD (1.44 Meg) diskettes on drive B:. A beep sounds when a new diskette is needed. The first volume of the archive is given the suffix ".ARJ", the second ".A01", the third ".A02", etc.

```
ARJ m -v360 -y -jt -r d:\backup c:\*.*
```

The above command initiates the archiving of all files on the C: drive to multiple volumes of 360K on drive D:. The original files are deleted without a prompt, since automatic confirmation is indicated by the "-y" switch.

```
ARJ a b:\backup -vvwasCOMMAND c:\*.TXT -r
```

This command saves all .TXT files from the C: drive to the BACKUP archive on drive B:. Multiple volumes are allowed. Each new volume is signaled by a beep (v), files will not be split (w), disk space is analyzed automatically (a), and COMMAND.COM is executed before each volume (s).

8. Command Summary And Switches

-w   work directory

This switch specifies a work directory that ARJ can use during compression or extraction.

The program can store and manipulate an archive there temporarily, then copy it to the target drive and release the file space when the operation is complete. This usually speeds up processing.

> This technique is especially effective if you place the working directory on a RAMDISK.

Example:

```
ARJ a -we:\ a:\archive *.TXT
```

The .TXT files in this example are compressed temporarily to the E: drive in RAM and subsequently copied to a diskette on drive A:. If copying is interrupted, both the temporary and the target archive are deleted.

-x   exclude files

This switch excludes certain files from processing.

When used with an archiving command, files specified by name or with wildcards after the switch won't be compressed. Multiple names or wildcards are allowed, as is the use of a list file with the "-!" switch.

Examples:

```
ARJ a source *.* -x*.pas -x*.bas
```

All files except Pascal and Basic source files are compressed to the SOURCE.ARJ archive.

```
ARJ a source *.* -x!excl.lst
```

The contents of EXCL.LST specifies the files to be excluded.

```
ARJ a passrc c:\tp6\*.pas -r -x\tp6\*.pas
```

It's also possible to completely exclude directories. In fact, you can exclude a directory, and still have its subdirectories compressed. This is what happens in the example shown above. All Pascal files in subdirectories of the C:\TP6 directory are compressed into an archive named "PASSRC.ARJ."

8. Command Summary And Switches

-y   assume yes

All prompts during processing of the associated command are answered "yes" when this switch is used. You should use this switch when ARJ is executing a task automatically.

Example:

```
AUTOARC.EXE -y
```

The self-extracting archive AUTOARC begins extracting files without further prompts.

-z   zipfile comment

Assigns a comment to an archive. When used with the "c" command, this switch assigns commentary to an archive itself, instead of to an individual archived file.

Example:

```
ARJ c hello -zPETER.TXT
```

Assigns the contents of PETER.TXT as a comment to the HELLO archive.

Extended switches

Extended switches are used exactly like normal switches. They are used only because some letters must be duplicated in order to accommodate all the necessary options. An extended switch always begins with "j."

-jb   backup

The -jb group relates to backups of files within archives.

The following variants are possible:

-jb	Indicates an archive as a backup archive.
-jb1	Erases the backup indicator for an archive.
-jb2	Erases the backup indicator for an archived file.
-jb3	Indicates an archived file as a backup file.

8. Command Summary And Switches

-jc   exit after count

This switch terminates a command after a certain number of files have been processed.

Examples:

```
ARJ l texts -jc5
```

The first five files from the TEXTS.ARJ archive are listed on the screen.

```
ARJ a texts -jc5
```

The first five files under the current directory are archived to TEXTS.ARJ.

-jd   disk space

This switch ensures that a specified amount of disk space remains free on the target drive when files are extracted. If the limit is reached, ARJ will stop processing and report errors for the files that haven't been extracted yet.

```
ARJ e -jd 100000 archive
```

ARJ extracts as many files as possible from ARCHIVE.ARJ until the available disk space on the target drive falls below 100K.

-je   SFX-archive

This switch creates a self-extracting (SFX) archive. Unlike LHA and PKZIP, ARJ creates the SFX archive during the archiving process. In conjunction with the "y" command, this switch can be used to make a self-extracting archive (.EXE) from a normal archive (.ARJ). The following variants exist:

-je	Creates the normal SFX module.
-je1	Creates a SFXJR (SFX-Junior) module, with limited capabilities and lower memory requirement.

-jf   full path

This switch saves the full path of each file that is archived.

-jf	Saves full path.
-jf1	Saves path without drive.

8. Command Summary And Switches

-jg   select backup files

This switch selects archived files marked as backups. This makes it possible to use backup files in operations when they aren't usually accessible. The "k" and "y" commands are the only ones that normally work with backups. With the "-jg" switch, other commands like "e" or "d" can process them as well.

Example:

```
ARJ d -jg backup *.bak
```

All backup files with the suffix .BAK are deleted from the BACKUP.ARJ archive.

-jh   huffman buffer

This switch lets you specify a size for the Huffman buffer.

Buffer size can affect processing speed. So many factors play a role here that experimenting is the best way to determine a reasonable size.

Examples:

```
ARJ a DOC *.TXT -jh2048
```

Here the minimum buffer size of 2,048 bytes is used.

```
ARJ a DOC *.TXT -jh65535
```

Here the buffer is increased to the maximum size of 64K.

-ji   index file

Creates an index file with the specified name.

An index file lists all the files that were selected by a given command. This is especially useful when backing up a lot of data on several diskettes. The index helps you locate a desired file more easily.

Example:

```
ARJ a -jiindex.lst -r pics *.pcx
```

All PCX files archived in PICS.ARJ are listed in an index file called "INDEX.LST". You can display the index later using the TYPE command to locate specific files.

8. Command Summary And Switches

-jk   keep temp archive

This switch retains the temporary archive after an abort or error that would normally delete it. The name of the temporary archive is "ARJTEMP.$00."

-jl   display only filespec

Only file-specific information is displayed with this switch. Path and drive designations are suppressed to make the screen easier to read.

-jm   maximum compression

ARJ assumes an enhanced compression (tighter packing) mode with this switch.

-jm works in conjunction with "-m1" or "-m2." Compression is noticeably slower, however. About 1% to 8% higher compression is usually possible.

> Use of the -jm switch with -m3 and -m4 is undefined.

-jn   restart at

This switch is used to specify a file at which a previously interrupted multi-volume archiving can be resumed. It's used in conjunction with "-jx."

Example:

```
ARJ a archive -v360 -r -jn\pascal\turbo.exe -jx1000
```

The above command skips all files up to TURBO.EXE and resumes archiving from there, starting with file position 1000.

-jo   query/unique

ARJ interprets this switch differently for compressing versus unpacking procedures.

In connection with the "m" or "a" command, it queries the user before overwriting archived files.

8. Command Summary And Switches

With extracting commands, it generates a unique extension where needed to avoid duplicate filenames in the target directory.

Numeric extensions from 000 to 999 are used.

-jp   **pause after screen**

A command that fills the screen will pause before continuing when this switch is used.

Example:
```
ARJ v whole -jp
```

-jr   **set string parameter**

This switch is used to input search information on the command line.

-jr	recover archive

This switch is used for recovering data from defective archives.

In the event of a CRC failure or "Bad file data" error, part of the archive may still be salvaged using "-jr."

Example:
```
ARJ e -jr archiv
```

The above command tries to extract data from the archive in spite of errors.

-js   **store by suffix**

This switch specifies, by suffix, certain types of files that should be archived without compression.

Normally this switch is used to avoid trying to compress files that are already in compressed form.

> ARJ, ZIP, LZH, PAK, and ARC are the default suffixes for this option. Other types of files can be stored without compression by specifying the appropriate endings.

8. Command Summary And Switches

Example:

```
ARJ a uncomp -js.arj.lzh.gif.tif
```

All files with the specified suffixes are stored in the UNCOMP.ARJ archive in their current form.

-jt   test temp archive

ARJ tests a new archive before deleting existing files when this switch is specified. If an error occurs, the original data won't be overwritten or deleted. You can also use this switch to do an integrity check on an archive before extracting files from it. If an error occurs, the files won't be extracted.

Example:

```
ARJ m archive -jt
```

Before deleting the originals, ARJ checks the compressed files for errors.

```
ARJ e archive -jt
```

Before extracting the compressed files, ARJ checks them for errors.

-jv   verbose display

This switch calls for detailed screen output when used with the "t" or "x" command. When used with the "v" command, compressed files are shown without paths.

-jw   extract output name

You can use this switch in an extract command to specify an output device.

Example:

```
ARJ e texts appl.TXT -jwPRN
```

The APPL.TXT file is sent to the printer.

-jx   extended position

This switch lets you resume processing at a particular file position.

8. Command Summary And Switches

A multi-volume archiving procedure that aborted with an error can be continued from the file where the interruption occurred. You restart the process by manually entering the correct file position with this switch. An interrupted restore (extraction) can be similarly resumed.

Example:

```
ARJ a archive1.a01 readme.TXT -jx100000
```

The above command contains a manual restart command for the archiving of the README.TXT file at position 100000 on the ARCHIVE1.A01 volume.

-jy   **assume yes**

This switch indicates an automatic "yes" response for certain questions. The "-jy" switch is much more limited than the "-y" switch. The specific question that is to be confirmed is coded along with the switch.

The following can be specified:

a	APPEND when extracting split files.
c	Create directory.
d	Delete file.
k	Available memory.
n	New filename.
o	Overwrite existing file.
r	Delete keyboard buffer.
s	Text search.
v	Multi-volume archiving.
y	Accept letter responses (Y/N/A/Q).

Example:

```
ARJ x archive -v -jyaco
```

This command suppresses the questions for appending files, creating directories, and overwriting files and assumes that all these actions are permitted.

8. Command Summary And Switches

-jz   zipfile comment

This switch indicates that a comment refers to an individual file in an archive. It's closely related to the "-z" (archive comment) switch and the "c" command.

Examples:

```
ARJ c archive TOC.TXT -jzcomment.TXT
```

The above command assigns a comment, which is taken from a file called COMMENT.TXT, to the TOC.TXT file in ARCHIVE.ARJ.

```
ARJ c archive *.TXT -jzNUL
```

The comments for all .TXT files in ARCHIVE.ARJ are deleted.

ERRORLEVELS

The following table shows which error codes ARJ may return in the ERRORLEVEL variable. A batch file can check the value of this variable.

Code	Meaning
0	No error
1x	Warning
	Specified file not found, NO to continue query
2	Fatal error
3	CRC failure
	Archive or archived file
4	ARJ integrity error
	Registered version only
5	Disk full or write error
6	Cannot open archive or file
7	User error, wrong parameter
8	Insufficient memory

8. Command Summary And Switches

LHA 2.13

Syntax

```
LHA <Command> [/<option> ARC [[DIR\] [File]...]... [-+012ºWDIR]...]
```

Commands

a   **add**

Adds files to the specified archive. Existing files are overwritten regardless of age. If the archive doesn't exist, it's created.

LHA assigns the suffix ".LZH" to an archive, unless directed otherwise. If the archive already exists, it's overwritten.

Examples:

```
LHA a program *.exe
```

The above command compresses all .EXE files in the current drive and directory to the archive called "PROGRAM.LZH."

```
LHA a -x texts c:\word5\*.TXT
```

This command also saves the complete path data.

---

d   **delete**

Deletes one or more files from an archive. Wildcards are permitted.

Example:

```
LHA d document info.DOC control.DOC
```

The two files INFO.DOC and CONTROL.DOC are deleted from the DOCUMENT.LZH archive.

---

e   **extract**

Specified files are extracted from an archive to the specified target directory. If the file already exists in the target directory, and if it has the same time stamp or a more recent one than on the archive, the file isn't extracted.

This command is the same as "x", except that path information isn't extracted. To restore the directory structure, use "x."

8. Command Summary And Switches

Example:

```
LHA e archive c:\exefile\*.exe
```

All .EXE files from the ARCHIVE.LZH archive are decompressed to the EXEFILE directory on drive C:.

f   freshen

Updates archived files.

If the date-time of the specified file is more recent than the archived version, the archived version is updated. The "-c" option ignores the time stamp and updates every file.

Example:

```
LHA f texts *.TXT
```

All .TXT files carrying a more recent date-time than the compressed versions in the archive are updated.

l   list

Lists archive contents in table format on the standard output device.

You can bypass the standard output device to create a list file.

Example:

```
LHA l games > List.dat
```

The above command lists the contents of the GAMES archive. Instead of being sent to the screen, the output is sent to a file called "LIST.DAT."

m   move

Moves files to an archive (after compressing them) and deletes the original versions if the operation is successful.

Example:

```
LHA m document *.DOC *.TXT
```

Files ending in ".DOC" and ".TXT" are compressed and placed in an archive called "DOCUMENT.LZH." Then the originals are deleted.

8. Command Summary And Switches

p   **print to standard output**

Prints the contents of one or more archived files on the standard output device.

Examples:

```
LHA p doc info.TXT
```

This command prints the compressed file INFO.TXT to the screen. Unexpected results may occur (beeps, missing characters, etc.) if certain control characters are included.

```
LHA p doc info.TXT >prn
```

Sends the file contents to a connected printer.

---

s   **make SFX-archive**

Converts an existing archive to a self-extracting archive. May be used with the following switches:

-x0	Default: Creates a small SFX module with restricted capabilities.
-x1	Creates a larger SFX module that includes path information.

Example:

```
LHA s texts
```

With this command, an executable archive called "TEXTS.EXE" is created from the normal archive TEXTS.LZH.

---

t   **test archive**

Tests the integrity of normal and executable archives.

The program LHA.EXE itself can also be tested. To do this, change to the directory that contains LHA.EXE, and type the command "LHA t LHA.EXE." If no errors or changes are found, the following message appears:

This file seems to be ORIGINAL distributed from H. Yoshi.

Examples:

```
LHA t archive
```

8. Command Summary And Switches

The ARCHIVE.LZH archive is tested for errors.

`LHA t LHA.EXE`

The above command tests the LHA.EXE program.

---

u   **update**

Updates older files in an archive and adds new ones.

Example:

`LHA u passrc`

This command places new files in the PASSRC.LZH archive, and older versions of archived files are replaced by more current ones.

---

v   **verbose list**

Provides a detailed list of an archive's contents.

Example:

`LHA v -x archive`

This command works exactly the same as the ARJ command ARJ v x archive.

---

x   **extended extract**

Extracts files using complete path information. Existing directories are recreated.

Path information is saved in an archive only if the "-r" and "-x" options are used when compressing.

Example:

`LHA x FUN C:\GAMES\ *.*`

All files from the FUN archive are extracted to the GAMES directory on the hard drive. If the archive includes any subdirectories, these are automatically created under GAMES.

Options

LHA also works with options. Each switch's letter can be followed by a 0, 1, or 2. Sometimes 1 and 2 have the same meaning, in which case 2 isn't listed.

8. Command Summary And Switches

> We'll use the "-" character to designate an option. The "/" character can also be used.

-a   attributes

Designates certain attributes for files to be processed. The default setting "-a0" ignores system and hidden files.

-a0	Files with the system or hidden attributes aren't processed.
-a1	Files with special attributes (hidden and system) are processed.

Examples:

```
LHA a system -a1 *.sys
```

With the above command, all system files are compressed and placed in the SYSTEM.LZH archive.

```
LHA e system -a1 *.sys
```

The above command decompresses system files with the system and hidden attributes.

-c   ignore comparison of time stamp

Suppresses the checking of file time stamps.

Usually the "e", "f", "u", and "x" commands affect only the more current version of a file. The "-c1" option doesn't perform any date-time comparisons.

-c0	Default: Time stamps are compared.
-c1	Time stamps are ignored.

-i   ignore case

Indicates case-sensitivity.

The DOS operating system doesn't recognize the difference between upper and lowercase characters. This option applies only to systems that make this distinction.

8. Command Summary And Switches

-l   long display

Controls type of screen output.

For both compression and decompression, the "-l1" option records paths relative to the current directory. The "-l2" option inserts the directory prefix from the command line.

-l0	Show filenames only.
-l1	Show pathnames relative to working directory.
-l2	Show complete pathnames including working directory from command line.

-m   no message

Automatically answers "yes" to user queries.

With the default setting (-m0), the user must respond to a query when target files with the same name are found. In this case, the following message appears:

> Overwrite? (Y/N)

A query is also displayed for creating directories. The setting "-m1" tells the program to assume a "yes" answer and suppress the query. If you try to overwrite a write-protected file, a "file creation error" still occurs. To solve this problem, use "-m2". When extracting a file that already exists, the program assigns a unique suffix from 000 to 999.

-m0	Default: All queries must be answered manually.
-m1	All queries are automatically answered "yes".
-m2	Extracted file are automatically assigned unique names.

Examples:

```
LHA e -m1 archive
```

All files are extracted from the archive. If a file already exists and is not write-protected, the program overwrites it.

```
LHA e -m2 archive
```

As in the above example, all files are extracted. Duplicate files are assigned unique names by means of ascending numeric suffixes so nothing is overwritten.

8. Command Summary And Switches

-n   no indicator

Limits or suppresses screen output during compression. Normally a moving bar is shown with the compression rate, for example:

```
ooooooooooo 56.5%
```

The bar is suppressed with "-n1".

To suppress all screen output (for example, when using LHA.EXE in a custom program), use "-n2".

-n0	Default: Progress bar is displayed.
-n1	Suppresses progress bar.
-n2	Suppresses progress bar and filenames.

-o   old compatible method

Selects old compression method for compatibility.

The "-o1" option selects the compression method used in LHARC Version 1.13. The file header then appears in LH113c format.

-p   distinguish full path names

Searches precisely for archived files.

If files are extracted without the "-p" option, no effort is made to determine whether duplicate filenames exist under different directories. This means you could end up extracting the wrong file or accidentally overwriting an existing file.

Examples:

```
LHA e DATES imprtant.DOC
```

This command extracts the file called "IMPRTANT.DOC" from the DATES archive. If two such files exist in the archive (suppose they are specified as OLD\IMPRTANT.DOC and IMPRTANT.DOC), both will be extracted. If you want to prevent this, use the "-p" option and specify exactly which one you want.

```
LHA e Dates -p imprtant.DOC
```

With the above command, only IMPRTANT.DOC is extracted.

8. Command Summary And Switches

-r recurse subdirs

Allows subdirectories to be searched recursively. If you archive files from different subdirectories, you should include the "-x" option so that paths are also saved.

Examples:

```
LHA a COMPLETE -r c:\*.TXT
```

This command archives all .TXT files on the C: drive. Paths are not saved. If identical filenames are encountered, LHA displays the following error:

> Same Names in another Path : xxxx.xxx

By including pathnames in the archive, you can save multiple versions of files that have the same names.

```
LHA a COMPLETE -r-x c:\*.TXT
```

-s skip message

Suppresses the message:

> Newer or same file exists

-t time stamp

Matches the time stamp of the archive to that of the archived files. This switch works with the a, d, f, m, and u commands.

-t0	Default: The archive is stamped with the current system time.
-t1	The archive is stamped with the time of the most current file in the archive.

Examples:

```
LHA a Now
```

The program compresses all files from the current directory to the Now archive. The time stamp is the current system time.

```
LHA a -t1 now
```

This command is similar to the previous example, except that the archive takes its time stamp from the most current file saved.

8. Command Summary And Switches

-w   work directory

Defines a work directory where the program temporarily stores information for managing the archiving/extraction process.

The data is assembled first in the work area and then copied to the target medium. After the process is successfully completed, the temporary file space is released. This technique is used for faster processing.

Example:

```
LHA a -we:\ archive *.TXT
```

The .TXT files are temporarily stored on a RAM disk in drive E:, then copied to a diskette in drive A:.

-x   extended names

Archives pathname with file.

This is required, along with the recursion option "-r", if you want to later perform an extended extract ("x" command) to restore the complete directory structure.

Examples:

```
LHA a -x texts c:\word5\book.TXT
```

The BOOK.TXT file is archived along with its complete path.

```
LHA a texts -r-x c:\word5
```

All files in the WORD5 directory and its subdirectories are archived along with complete paths.

-z   zero compression

Saves files without compressing them. Normally all files specified are compressed. This corresponds to the setting "-z0."

-z0	Default: All files are compressed.
-z1	No files are compressed.
-z2	Files ending in ARC, LZH, LZS, PAK, ZIP or ZOO are not compressed.
-zXX	Files ending in XXX are not compressed.

8. Command Summary And Switches

If you don't want to compress files other than the types listed, specify the appropriate endings. Remember that ARJ isn't included among the listed types.

Examples:

```
LHA a -z1 texts *.TXT
```

None of the files selected should be compressed.

```
LHA a -zdbf dbase *.*
```

All dBase (.DBF) files are placed in the DBASE.LZH archive without compression.

```
LHA a D:Backup C:\ -r -x -z2 -zARJ -zGIF
```

All files present on the C: drive are saved to the BACKUP archive on drive D:. Files ending in ARC, LZH, LZS, PAK, ZIP, ZOO, ARJ, and GIF are saved as is, since they already are in compressed form.

/-   **first letter switch**

Considers the first character of a file specification to be part of the normal filename.

LHA sometimes gives a special interpretation to the first character of a filename. The prefix "@" is used to indicate a file that contains instructions for LHA. Such a file is read and interpreted as a sequence of command lines, rather than being archived.

If you want to archive a file whose name begins with "@", use "/-1."

With the "-2" setting, LHA will also recognize "-" as the first character of a filename. The switch is deactivated by typing: "-[0]".

/-1	Treat initial "@" as part of normal filename.
/-2	Treat initial "@" or "-" as part of normal filename.
/-[0]	Deactivate first two options.

ERRORLEVELS

The following table shows the error codes that LHA can return in the ERRORLEVEL variable. You can check the value of ERRORLEVEL in a batch file.

8. Command Summary And Switches

Code	Meaning
0	No error
1	Possible CRC failure in connection with a "t", "x", or "e" command. Other possibilities are insufficient disk space or file already exists.
2	Fatal error, not processed.
3	Temporary archive could not be converted.

On error level 3, the temporary archive remains in the work directory under the name "LHTEMP)2(.LZH". You can salvage your work by renaming this file and saving it as a normal archive.

PKZIP/PKUNZIP

We'll discuss the PKZip and PKUnzip programs in the same section because they use essentially the same commands. If a command applies to only one of these commands, this is indicated in the heading.

PKZIP - Syntax

```
PKZIP [-b[path]] [options] Zipfile [@list] [files...]
```

PKUNZIP - Syntax

```
PKUNZIP [options] Zipfile [drive:path\] [file...]
```

Commands

PKZIP -a add

Adds files to the specified archive. If a file already exists, it is overwritten. If the archive does not exist, it is created.

Examples:

```
PKZIP a archive
```

This command compresses all files from the current drive and directory to the archive called "ARCHIVE.ZIP."

```
PKZIP a e:\pics\graphic c:\windows\*.bmp
```

8. Command Summary And Switches

This command compresses all .BMP files under the WINDOWS directory on drive C: to an archive called "GRAPHIC.ZIP", under the PICS directory on drive E:.

PKZIP -b working directory

Designates a temporary working directory on another drive. This is helpful when you're archiving to diskettes or when you have a large RAM drive available to speed up processing.

Files are archived first to the temporary area and then copied to the target drive and directory. When the process is successfully completed, the temporary archive is released. This usually increases compression speed.

Example:

```
PKZIP a -b e:\ a:\archive *.TXT
```

All .TXT files are temporarily compressed to a RAM disk on drive E: and then copied to a diskette in drive A:. If the process is interrupted, both the temporary and the permanent archive are deleted.

PKZIP -c comment 1

Assigns a comment of up to 60 characters to a compressed file.

> The comment is entered in dialog mode and terminated by pressing [Enter].

Examples:

```
PKZIP a -c texts *.TXT
```

The user is prompted to enter a comment for each file to be compressed.

```
PKZIP -C    comment 2
```

Only updated files receive a comment.

```
PKUNZIP -c   screen extract
```

The contents of a specified compressed file are displayed on the screen. If a file isn't specified, every file on the archive is displayed. The additional use of the "m" option pauses the screen when it is full.

| -cm | Stops after every full screen. |

PKZIP -d delete

Deletes one or more files from an archive.

Example:

PKZIP d archive *.TXT junk.DOC

All files ending in .TXT and the file named "JUNK.DOC" are deleted from the archive.

PKUNZIP -d   create directory

Automatically creates missing directories during decompression.

This command is only useful if the archive was compressed using the "-r" and "-p/P" options.

Example:

PKUNZIP -d complete C:\TEMP\

With the above command, the COMPLETE archive is extracted to C:\TEMP. If COMPLETE contains subdirectories, they are automatically created when necessary.

PKZIP -e extra compression method

Selects the compression method to be used. A second letter identifies the desired method. The following options are available:

-ea	Imploding is used for all ASCII files, and shrinking is used for all binary files.
-eb	Imploding is used for all binary files, and shrinking is used for all ASCII files.
-es	Shrinking is used for all files. This is usually the fastest method.
-ex	Imploding is used for all files. This is the default method.

> Shrinking is slightly faster but less thorough than imploding. Imploding, a slower but more compact compression, is the default setting.

8. Command Summary And Switches

PKUNZIP -e   extract order

Determines the extraction sequence for archived files.

You do not have to extract files in the same sequence in which they were archived. A second letter gives the desired sort criterion (order is always ascending).

-ec	By CRC code.
-ed	By time stamp.
-ee	By file extension.
-en	By filename.
-ep	By compression rate.
-es	By size.

Parameters can be combined.

Example:

```
PKUNZIP -eend BACKUP
```

This command decompresses the file to the current directory. Files are accessed by extension (e), name (n), and date-time (d).

PKZIP, PKUNZIP -f   freshen

Freshens an archive. Archived files are replaced by more current versions.

Example:

```
PKZIP -f -r document *.TXT *.DOC
```

With the above command, the DOCUMENT archive is freshened with all .TXT and .DOC files in the current directory and its underlying subdirectories.

The same command in PKUNZIP extracts only files already present in an older version in the target directory.

PKZIP, PKUNZIP -h   help

Displays the help screen.

8. Command Summary And Switches

PKZIP -i   backup

Archives only files with the archive attribute set.

Once a file has been archived, its bit is cleared. If the same command is immediately repeated, files won't be saved.

Example:

```
PKZIP -i backup c:\*.TXT -r
```

All .TXT files carrying the archive attribute are compressed to the BACKUP.ZIP archive.

PKZIP, PKUNZIP -j   include attributes

Allows attributes to be used for file selection.

-jh	Select hidden files.
-js	Select system files.
-jr	Select write-protected (read-only) files.

Any combination of attributes is also allowed.

Example:

```
PKZIP -a -jhsr MAIN C:\*.* D:\*.*
```

This command archives all files in the root directories of the C: and D: drives. System, hidden, and read-only files like MSDOS.SYS and IO.SYS are included.

-J   exclude attributes

Works like the "-j" switch, but specifies types of files to exclude from an archive. Be sure to observe the proper case to obtain the desired result.

Examples:

```
PKZIP -jhs system *.sys
```

This command compresses all .SYS files, including hidden and system files, to the SYSTEM.ZIP archive.

```
PKZIP -Jr -jsh texts *.TXT
```

All .TXT files that are not write-protected are compressed.

8. Command Summary And Switches

PKZIP -k   keep original date

Keeps the same time stamp when an archive is updated.

Example:

```
PKZIP -f -k archive
```

The date-time on the archive isn't changed when files are rearchived to it.

-l   license

Shows terms of PKZIP license on the screen.

PKZIP -m   move

Places files in the specified archive and deletes the original versions. Deleting doesn't occur until compression and archiving are complete.

Normally Move, like Add, overwrites already-archived files. There are two parameters for changing this, however.

-m	Normal Move.
-mf	Moves only files already in the archive as older versions.
-mu	Same as above, but also includes files not yet present in the archive.

Example:

```
PKZIP -m dbase *.dbf
```

All dBase files are packed to a new archive called "DBASE.ZIP", and their originals are deleted.

PKUNZIP -n   only newer

Extracts only files newer than those on the original disk.

This is a safety feature that prevents accidentally destroying the most current version of a file. Files not present in the target directory are always extracted.

Example:

```
pkunzip -n texts c:\word5\
```

8. Command Summary And Switches

All files in the TEXTS archive are extracted to the WORD5 directory on the C: drive, unless a more current version already exists there.

PKZIP -o time stamp of oldest file

Assigns the time stamp of the oldest archived file to the archive.

The default procedure is to stamp the archive with the current date-time.

Example:

```
PKZIP -a -o Old *.TXT
```

PKUNZIP -o   overwrite

Files with the same names in the target directory are automatically overwritten.

Example:

```
PKUNZIP -o-d GAMES C:\
```

This command overwrites any like-named files in the target directory with the extracted version. This is rather dangerous, especially in the root directory. The "-d" switch creates any missing directories.

PKZIP -p store pathnames

Stores pathnames along with archived files. You must do this if you use the recursion switch to archive multiple directories.

-p	Saves pathnames relative to current directory.
-P	Saves complete path including portion from command line.

Examples:

```
PKZIP -a TEXTS -r -p \WORD\*.TXT
```

Assuming that the current directory is \WORD, this variant will add path information to the archive only for files taken from subdirectories under \WORD.

```
PKZIP -a TEXTS -r -P \WORD\*.TXT
```

This variant stores the complete path information, including the \WORD directory, for every file archived.

8. Command Summary And Switches

PKUNZIP -p   print

Sends file contents to a printer. Available options are:

-p	Contents are sent to printer (default).
-pa	Contents are sent to printer in ASCII format.
-pb	Contents are sent to printer in binary format.
pc	Specifies serial interface as printer port.
pn	Identifies serial interface to be used (for example, COM1). Otherwise assumes standard.

Example:

```
PKUNZIP -pbc2 pics
```

Archived files (presumably graphics) are sent over COM2 to the printer.

PKZIP -r   recurse subdirs

Subdirectories are recursed during processing.

Any commands that access subdirectories should include the "-p/P" switch to distinguish like-named files.

Example:

```
PKZIP -a -r secure c:\*.bak
```

All backup (.BAK) files in the root and underlying directories of the C: drive are packed to the SECURE.ZIP archive.

-s   scramble with password

Applies a password to an archived file.

A password is case-sensitive. It follows the "-s" switch directly, with no space separator. A file archived with a password can only be extracted by entering the same password again.

Example:

```
PKZIP -a secret -sJoshua
```

All new files archived to SECRET.ZIP are given the password "Joshua."

8. Command Summary And Switches

PKUNZIP -t   test zipfile

Checks an archive for data integrity.

Example:

`PKUNZIP -t archive`

With this command, archive is tested for errors.

PKZIP -u update

Adds new files to an archive and updates existing ones that have older time stamps.

Example:

`PKZIP -u passcr`

Adds new files to the PASSCR.ZIP archive. Also updates files already present if a newer version is available.

-v   view archive

Displays archive contents according to certain criteria. A letter may follow the "-v" to indicate criteria desired.

-v	All information.
-vb	Brief format; all information except CRC value and file attributes.
-vt	Technical format; additional information for each file.
-vc	Comments.
-vd	Sort by date.
-ve	Sort by extension.
-vn	Sort by name.
-vo	Sort by order within archive.
-vp	Sort by percent compression.
-vs	Sort by size.
-vr	Reverse sort sequence.

8. Command Summary And Switches

Parameters can be combined.

Example:

```
PKZIP -vbenr COMPLETE
```

This command shows the contents of the COMPLETE archive in brief format, sorted by descending extension/name.

-x   exclude

Excludes specified files from processing.

Examples:

```
PKZIP -a texts *.TXT -xprivate.TXT
```

All .TXT files except PRIVATE.TXT are archived.

```
PKZIP -d texts *.TXT -xsecret.TXT -xprivat.TXT
```

All .TXT files in the TEXTS archive, except for PRIVATE and SECRET, are deleted.

-z   zipfile comment

Queries the user for an archive comment. Entry is in dialog mode. This can also be used to change an existing comment.

ERRORLEVELs in PKZIP

The following table shows the error codes that can be returned by PKZIP.

8. Command Summary And Switches

Code	Error
0	No error.
1	Incorrect filename.
2,3	Error in archive.
4-11	Insufficient memory.
12	No files found to archive or delete.
13	Archive or list file not found.
14	Disk is full.
15	Archive is write-protected.
16	Incorrect parameter in command line.
17	Too many files to process.

ERRORLEVELs in PKUNZIP

The following table shows the error codes that can be returned by PKUNZIP.

Code	Meaning
0	No error.
1	Warning (e.g., CRC failure).
2,3	Error in archive.
4-8	Insufficient memory.
9	File not found.
10	Incorrect parameter in command line.
11	No files found to extract or view.
50	Disk is full.
51	Defective archive, unable to extract.

8. Command Summary And Switches

ZOO

Syntax

ZOO is the only program that has two completely different syntaxes. One is the novice user syntax:

```
ZOO -Cmd archive[.ZOO] file...
```

This syntax contains commands that are abbreviations, which are easily identified.

The other syntax is the expert syntax. We'll describe this in detail, because there are so many combinations and ZOO isn't as widely used as the other programs.

```
ZOO {acfDeghlLPTuUvx}[aAcCdEfImMnNoOpPqu1:/.@n] archive file...
```

Commands

-add

Adds new files to an archive. Overwrites existing files and creates archive if necessary.

Examples:

```
ZOO -add archive
```

This command compresses all files in the current drive and directory to the ARCHIVE.ZOO archive.

```
ZOO -add Games *.exe *.dos *.com
```

The above command compresses all EXE, DOS, and COM files in the current drive and directory to the GAMES archive.

-comment

Adds comments of up to 64K characters to an existing archived file.

To terminate the entry, type "/END" on a separate line. Then the comments for the next file can be entered. Both filenames and wildcards are allowed.

Remember that comments lower the compression rate, especially on small files, because they are not compressed.

Example:

```
ZOO -comment batch autoexec.bat word5.bat
```

8. Command Summary And Switches

With the above command, you'll be asked to enter comments for the two files AUTOEXEC.BAT and WORD5.BAT in the BATCH.ZOO archive.

-delete

Deletes specified files from an archive.

Example:

```
ZOO -delete archive *.TXT
```

All .TXT files are deleted from the archive.

-extract

Extracts one or more files from a specified archive to the current directory or other specified target directory.

If filenames or wildcards aren't specified, all files in the archive are decompressed. Overwriting occurs only for older versions in the target directory, after confirmation from the user.

Example:

```
ZOO -extract archive
```

All files in the ARCHIVE.ZOO archive are decompressed to the current directory.

-freshen

Freshens (updates) an archive by replacing older compressed versions with newer ones. Files not already present aren't added.

-list

Displays the contents of the specified archive on the screen.

Files are listed in the order in which they were compressed (alphabetically). Other sort criteria aren't allowed.

8. Command Summary And Switches

-move

Moves a new file to the specified archive and deletes the original. Deleting takes place only after the file is successfully compressed and archived.

Example:

```
ZOO- move dbase *.dbf
```

All dBASE files in the current directory are compressed to the DBASE.ZOO archive. The original files are then deleted.

-print

Prints the contents of an archive to the standard output device. Normally this is the screen. Output can also be directed to other devices, such as printers (see your DOS manual).

Example:

```
ZOO -print archive >prn
```

The contents of all files compressed in the ARCHIVE.ZOO archive are output to the printer.

-test

Tests the integrity of an archive. If filenames or wildcards aren't specified, every archived file is tested for error-free compression.

Example:

```
ZOO -test imprtant
```

All files in the IMPRTANT.ZOO archive are tested for error-free compression.

-update

Updates older versions of archived files and adds files not present.

Example:

```
ZOO -update passcr
```

New files are added to the PASSCR.ZOO archive, and existing versions are updated if newer versions are found.

8. Command Summary And Switches

ERRORLEVELS

ZOO is very stingy with error codes returned to the operating system. Therefore, you can only determine whether the execution was error-free.

Code	Meaning
0	No error.
1	Error during execution.

Appendix

We've compiled this comprehensive resource list of the compression programs which we discussed in **PKZip, LHArc & Co.** If you're looking for further information on these products, you can contact the manufacturers directly.

Thank you very much for purchasing **PKZip, LHArc & Co.**!

ARJ

Robert and Susan Jung

2606 Village Road West

Norwood, Massachusetts 02062

ICE Version 1.14

Copyright (c) Haruyasu Yoshizaki (Yoshi), 1988-89

Nifty Serve PFF00253

ASCII PCS   pcs02846

LHArc

NIFTY-Serve SDI00506 | PFF00253 Haruyasu Yoshizaki

ASCII-pcs   pcs02846   Yoshi

PC-VAN   FEM12376   Haruyasu Yoshizaki

LZEXE.EXE v0.91

Fabrice BELLARD

451 chemin du mas de Matour

34790 GRABELS (FRANCE)

PKZIP 2.04g

PKWARE, Inc.

9025 N. Deerwood Dr.

Brown Deer, WI 53223-2437

414-354-8699 Voice, 414-354-8559 FAX

414-354-8670 BBS

And:

PC Ware (Australia) Pty. Ltd.

81 1/2 George Street, The Rocks

Sydney, NSW 2000

Australia   Tel: (02) 252 3546

And:

United Kingdom and Ireland:

Shareware Marketing

3a Queen Street

Seaton, Devon. EX12 2NY

England

WinZip(R) 5.0a

Nico Mak Computing, Inc,

P.O. Box 919, Bristol, CT06011

or by email to 70056,241 on CompuServe.

Index

A

Add command 37–38
Algorithms 31
Anchor 13
ANSI 31
Archive bit 31
Archive contents
    Listing 43–45
Archives
    Accessing protected archives 122–123
    Archive files 25–27
    Comments 125–131
    Decompressing 72–84
    Defined 31
    Editing archives 56–65, 58–65
    Identifying SFX archives 111–116
    SFX archives (protecting) 123–124
    Structure of archives 26–27
ARJ mini mini-module 103
ARJ program 35–69
    *See also **ARJ program commands***
    Add command 37–38
    Additional switches 42–43
    ARJSFX features 100–102
    Command reference 182–211
    Comments 128–131
    Compressing directories 48–56, 54–55
    Controlling safety prompts . 79–80, 80–81
    Creating self-extracting archives 99–100
    Data compression methods 139–142
    Decompressing data 79–80, 80–81
    Decompressing directories 90
    Excluding files from archive 47–48
    Extended switches 204-212
    File lists 45–47
    Freshen command 38–40
    Listing archive contents 43–45
    Memory requirements 183
    Mini mini-module 103
    Move command 40
    Restrictions on usage 182
    Syntax 182
    Switches 193-204
    Time stamps 133–134
    Update command 37–38
    Using as a multi-packer 145–155
ARJ program commands
    -! alterntive list symbol 195
    -# file number 195
    -$ volume name 195
    -& critical error handler 194
    -- no more switches 194
    -? help screen 194
    -a file attributes 195–196
    -b backup 196
    -c skip time check 196
    -d delete 196
    -e no pathname 197
    -f freshen 197
    -g garble with password 197–198
    -j shifted switch 198–199
    -jb backup 204–205
    -jc exit after count 205
    -jd disk space 205–206
    -je SFX-archive 205–206
    -jh huffman buffer 206
    -ji index file 206
    -jk keep temp archive 207
    -jl display only filespec 207
    -jm maximum compression 207
    -jn restart at 207
    -jo query/unique 207–208
    -jp pause after screen 208
    -jq set string parameter 208
    -jr recover archive 208
    -js store by suffix 208

Index

-jt test temp archive 209
-jv verbose display 209
-jw extract output name 209
-jx extended position 209–210
-jy assume yes 210
-jz zipfile comment 211
-k backup of archive 198–199
-m method 199
-n new files 199–200
-o on or after 200
-p match pathname 200
-q query on file 200
-r recurse subdirs 200–201
-s archive time-stamp 201–202
-t file type 201–202
-u update 201–202
-v multiple volume 202
-w work directory 203
-x exclude files 203
-y assume yes 204
-z zipfile comment 204
_+ environment 194
A Add 183, 192
B Batch 184
C Comment 184–185
d delete 185
e extract 186
f Freshen 186
g Garble 186–187
i Integrity of ARJ.EXE 187
j join 187
k delete backups 188
l List 188
m Move 188–189
o order archive 189
p print to standard output 190
r remove pathnames 190
r Rename 189
S sample 190
t test 191
u update 191
v verbose list 191
x extract extended 193
y command 198–199
y copy with new options 193
ARJSFX
  Features 100–102
  Mini mini-module 103

ASCII 31
Attributes
  Selecting files with 134–139
Automatic batch files
  LHA program 105–106

B

Batch files
  Using to compress data 66–69
Bit 32

C

Cache program 21-22, 32
Command line 33
Comments 125–131
  ARJ program 128–131
  PKZIP program 126–127
  ZOO program 127–128
Compressing data
  Using batch files 66–69
Compressing directories 48–56
  Recursive search 48–49
  Using ARJ 54–55
  Using LHA 49–51
  Using PKZIP 51–53
Compressing files 35–48
Compression methods
  Comparing 16–22
Compression programs 35–69
  Compressing directories 48–56
  Compressing files 35–48
CRC-Code 32
Critical error messages 33

D

Data compression
  Advantages 2–4
  Archive files 25–27
  Cache programs and compression 21
  Command line structure 23–25
  Comparing methods 16–22
  Components 24–25

Index

Data compression elements 23–34
Data compression shells 29–31
Defined 10–16
Encoding characters 12–14
EXE compression programs 29
How space is saved 14–16
Huffman method 11–12
Methods 139–144
Overview 4–10
Password protection 119–125
Reasons for data compression 2–4
Reducing text files 7–10
Saving space 14–16
Self-extracting archives 27–28
Terminology 31–34
Types of compression 4–7
Uses 1–2
Data compression command line structure ..
.... 23–25
Data compression elements 23–34
Data compression methods 139–144
    ARJ program 139–142
    Compatibility 143–144
    PKZIP program 142–143
Data compression overview 4–10
    Compressing PCX files 4–7
    Compression types 4–7
    Reducing text files 7–10
Data compression shells 29–31
Decompressing archives 72–91
    Creating directories 74–77
    Prompts 79
    Protecting existing files 77–79
    Selecting working directories 74
Decompressing data
    ARJ program 79–80
    Decompressing archives 72–84
    Diversified 71–72
    ICE program 80–81
    Integrated 71–72
    LHA program 80–81
    PAK program 82
    PKUNPAK program 84
    PKUNZIP program 84
    ZOO program 83
Decompressing directories 85–91
    Absolute path 86
    ARJ program 90
    ICE program 88–90
    LHA program 88–90
    PKUNZIP program 87–88
    Relative path 86
    Restoring directory structure 86–87
Decompressing prompts
    Preventing prompts 77
DIET program 166–179
    Compressing files 166–168
    Compressing problem files 170–173
    Deactivating 175–177
    Decompressing files 173–174
    Managing files 169–170
    Memory-resident DIET 174–175
    Temporary directory 175–179
Directories
    Decompressing 85–91
Downwardly compatible 32

E

Editing archives 56
Encoding characters 12–14
EXE compression programs 29
EXE compressors 157–179
    COM file structures 158–159
    DIET program 166–179
    EXE file structures 158
    LZEXE program 159–162
    Operation 157–159
    PKLite program 162

F

File attributes 32
File lists 45–47
    Excluding from an archive 47–48
Files
    Selecting by attributes 134–139
Freshen command 38–40

G

Garble 32
Garbling (passwords) 120

Index

H

Header 32
Hidden 32
High volume archiving
    See **Multi-packer archiving**
Huffman method 11–12

I

IBM graphic character set 33
ICE program
    Decompressing directories 88–90

L

LH-ICE program 59–60
LHA program 59–60, 212–222
    See also **LHA program commands**
    Automatic batch files 105–106
    Commands 212–215
    Compressing directories 49–51
    Creating self-extracting archives .. 103–104
    Decompressing directories 88–90
    ERRORLEVELs 221–222
    LHASFX features 104–105
    LHASFX modules features 105
    Options 215-221
    Syntax 212
LHA program commands
    -a attributes 216
    -c ignore time comparison of time stamp
        216–217
    -i ignore case 216–217
    -m no message 217
    -n no indicator 218
    -o old compatible method 218
    -r recurs subdirs 219
    -s skip message 219
    -t time stamp 219
    -w work directory 220
    -x extended names 220
    -z zero compression 220–221
    /- first letter switch 221–222
    a add 212

d delete 212
d distinguish full path names 218
e extract 212
f freshen 213
l list 213
m move 213
p print to standard output 214
s make SFX-archive 214
t test archive 214
u update 215
v verbose list 215
x extended extract 215
LHASFX
    Functions 105
    Modules 104–105
LZEXE program 159–162
    Compressing COM files 161–162
    Windows programs 161
LZW 33

M

Manual 33
Masking 33
Module 33
Move command 40
Multi-packer archiving 145–155
    Combining commands 150–151
    Creating a multi-volume archive . 145–148
    Extracting multi-volume archives 154–155
    Listing multi-volume archives 155
    Optimizing memory space 148–150
    Using batch files 152–154
Multiple-Volume 33

N

Node 12

O

Options 33

Index

P

PAK program
    Creating self-extracting archives .. 108–109
    Decompressing data 82
    SFX archives 108–109
Password protection 119–125
    Accessing protected archives 122–123
    Entering the password 121–122
    Garbling 120
    Limitations 124–125
    Protecting SFX archives 123–124
    Scrambling 120
PKLite program 162
    Compressing programs 162–164
    Decompressing programs 165
    Options 165
    Overlays 164
PKPAK program 58–59
PKSFX
    Archive options 107–108
PKUNPAK program
    Decompressing programs 84
PKUNZIP program
    See also **PKZIP program**
    Commands 222–232
    Decompressing directories 87–88
    Decompressing programs 84
    Syntax 222
PKZIP program
    Creating self-extracting archives .. 106–107
    -j exclude attributes 226
    -l license 227
    -s scramble with password 229
    -v view archive 230–231
    -x exclude 231
    -z zipfile comment 231–233
    Commands 222
    Comments 126–127
    Compressing directories 51–53
    Data compression methods 142–143
    PKSFX archive options 107–108
    PKUNZIP -d create directory 224
    PKUNZIP -e extract order 225
    PKUNZIP -f freshen 225
    PKUNZIP -f help 225–226
    PKUNZIP -h help 225–226
    PKUNZIP -j include attributes 226
    PKUNZIP -n only newer 227
    PKUNZIP -o overwrite 228
    PKUNZIP -p print 229
    PKUNZIP -t test zipfile 230
    PKZIP -a add 222
    PKZIP -b working directory 223
    PKZIP -c comment 1 223
    PKZIP -d delete 224
    PKZIP -e extra compression method ....
    224–225
    PKZIP -f freshen 225
    PKZIP -i backup 226
    PKZIP -j attributes 226
    PKZIP -k keep original date 227
    PKZIP -m move 227
    PKZIP -o time stamp of oldest file 228
    PKZIP -p store pathnames 228
    PKZIP -r recurse subdirs 229
    PKZIP -u update 230
    SFX archives 106–107
    Syntax 222
Progress bar 34

R

Ratio 34
Recursive search 48–49
Root 13
Root directories
    Self-extracting archives 117

S

Scrambling (passwords) 120
Self-extracting archives 27–28
    ARJ program 99–100
    ARJSFX features 100–102
    Combining programs 109–111
    Identifying SFX archives 111–116
    LHA program 103–104
    LHASFX modules 104–105
    PAK program 108–109
    PKZIP program 106–107
    Root directories 117
    SFX archive structure 28

Index

SFX archives 97–117
    Tips on using 117
    Using 98–111
SFX archives
    See also **Self-extracting archives**
    Combining programs 109–111
    File structure 97–98
    Identifying 111–116
    Password protection 123–124
    SFX defined 34
    Structure 28
    Tips on using 117
System file 34

T

Terminology 31–34
Text files
    Defined 34
    Reducing 7–10
Time Stamps 131–134
    ARJ program 133–134
    Defined 34
    Displaying 131

U

Update command 37–38

V

Verbose list 34
Volume 34
Volume label 34

Z

ZOO program
    Comments 127–128
    Decompressing data 83
    ERRORLEVELs 236
Zoo program commands
    -add 233
    -comment 233
    -delete 234
    -extract 234
    -freshen 234–235
    -list 234–235
    -move 235
    -print 235
    -test 235
    -update 235
    Syntax 233

PC catalog

Order Toll Free 1-800-451-4319
Books and Software

Abacus

 To order direct call Toll Free 1-800-451-4319

In US and Canada add $5.00 shipping and handling. Foreign orders add $13.00 per item.
Michigan residents add 6% sales tax.

Multimedia Presentation

The Photo CD Book

The Photo CD opens up new and fascinating possibilities in the area of photography. Thanks to this technology, regular photos can be stored on CD and can be viewed, edited and used in multimedia presentations on the PC.

The Photo CD Book is a hands-on guide to Photo CD technology. It concentrates on everyday, practical use. After a "quick start" introduction, including technical basics and hardware and software configurations, the author introduces the use of various applications including image processing, printer output and image presentation programs. This book also covers how to convert your PC into a photo lab, including how to edit pictures and produce edited photos on the printer or in an exposure studio.

The Photo CD Book comes complete with a companion CD-ROM that will help you to understand the capabilities of the Kodak Photo CD and how to get the most from it, without having to become an expert. Included on the CD-ROM are Toshiba's Photo/ Graphic Viewer; real PCD photo examples used in the book; a collection of the most popular shareware graphics utilities including PaintShop Pro and Graphics WorkShop; and several industry standard Phillips CD-I software drivers. Also on disc is an extensive practice session including picture editing, printing and picture presentations.

Author: Heinz von Bulow
Order Item: #B195
ISBN: 1-55755-195-2
Suggested retail price: $29.95 US/ $39.95 CAN with companiom CD-ROM

To order direct call Toll Free 1-800-451-4319

In US and Canada add $5.00 shipping and handling. Foreign orders add $13.00 per item.
Michigan residents add 6% sales tax.

Multimedia Presentation

CD-ROM! The Naked Truth & Killer Animations

The multimedia explosion has been fueled by the drastic price reduction of CD-ROM drives. For the US, analysts predict that almost 15 million new CD-ROM drives will be sold this year! This book guides today's you through a better understanding of your CD-ROM drive and then lets you explore over 500 meg of programs and animations. CD-ROM The Naked Truth and Killer Animations is a valuable, "all-in-one" product for the CD-ROM, multimedia enthusiast. It's a book about CD-ROM technology with a ton of multimedia software to titillate your imagination.

CD-ROM! The Naked Truth and Killer Animations walks you through the nitty gritty and into the wild side of multimedia. The newcomer will learn all about installation, hardware configuration, and how he can optimize, configure and tune his computer system for the best performance. Complete with software utilities, you'll be able to check and test the performance of the CD-ROM drive. Not only that, there's a special "caching" program, HyperDisk, that helps you juice the speed of your drive with read-forward technology. The book also includes:

* CD-ROM Formats
* How CDs Work
* Drive Technology
* Speeding Up CD Access
* Video, Animation and Sound
* Producing Customized CDs
* CD-ROM Programming
* Kodak Photo CD's

Author: Harald Hahn
Order Item: #B266
ISBN: 1-55755-266-5
Suggested retail price: $34.95 US / $44.95 CAN includes CD-ROM

To order direct call Toll Free 1-800-451-4319

In US and Canada add $5.00 shipping and handling. Foreign orders add $13.00 per item.
Michigan residents add 6% sales tax.

**Productivity Series books are for users who want
to become more productive with their PC.**

Upgrading & Maintaining Your PC

Upgrading & Maintaining Your PC provides an overview of the fundamental and most important components of a personal computer. It describes PC and compatible computers from the outside to the inside. **Upgrading & Maintaining Your PC** also introduces you to the relationship between individual components to help you get to know your computer better.

PCs are a major investment. **Upgrading & Maintaining Your PC** will show you how to turn your PC into a high perfomance computing machine. This book describes what you will see when you open the "hood" and how all the parts work together. You'll learn how to add a hard drive, increase your computer's memory, upgrade to a higher resolution monitor or turn an XT into a fast AT or 386 screamer. **Upgrading & Maintaining Your PC** shows you how to do so, easy and economically, without having to be an electronics wizard.

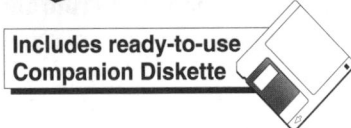

System Sleuth Analyzer from Dariana Technology Group, Inc. is on the companion disk bundled with this guide. *System Sleuth Analyzer* is a $99.95 toolbox of valuable PC diagnostic aids rolled into a single, easy to use software utility. System Sleuth lets you explore exacting details of your PC without the fear of accidental, unrecoverable modifications to a particular subsystem. The menu-driven interface displays all aspects of machine information for easy recognition.

Authors: Ulrich Schuller & Hans-Georg Veddeler
Order Item: #B167
ISBN: 1-55755-167-7
Suggested retail price: $34.95 US/ $44.95 CAN with companion disk

To order direct call Toll Free 1-800-451-4319

In US and Canada add $5.00 shipping and handling. Foreign orders add $13.00 per item.
Michigan residents add 6% sales tax.

Developers Series books are for professional software developers who require in-depth technical information and programming techniques.

PC Intern: *System Programming*

PC Intern is a completely revised edition of our bestselling *PC System Programming* book for which sales exceeded 100,000 copies. **PC Intern** is a literal encyclopedia for the DOS programmer. Whether you program in assembly language, C, Pascal or BASIC, you'll find dozens of practical, parallel working examples in each of these languages. **PC Intern** clearly describes the technical aspects of programming under DOS. More than 1000 pages are devoted to making DOS programming easier.

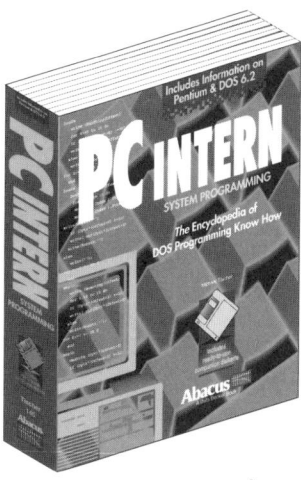

Some of the topics covered include:

- PC memory organization
- Using extended and expanded memory
- Hardware and software interrupts
- COM and EXE programs
- Handling program interrupts in BASIC, Turbo Pascal, C and Assembly Language
- DOS structures and functions
- BIOS fundamentals
- Programming video cards
- TSR programs
- Writing device drivers
- Multitasking

The clearly documented examples make it easy for the reader to adapt the programs for his own requirements.

Author: Michael Tischer
Order Item: #B145
ISBN: 1-55755-145-6
Suggested retail price: $59.95 US/ $75.95 with 3½" companion diskette

To order direct call Toll Free 1-800-451-4319

In US and Canada add $5.00 shipping and handling. Foreign orders add $13.00 per item. Michigan residents add 6% sales tax.

Productivity Series books are for users who want to become more productive with their PC.

Electronic Alphabet

Art, science, or both? **The Electronic Alphabet** illustrates that the effective use of fonts is both an art and a science. Studied and applied, effective typography puts power in the word and the work. The right font can convey an attitude, an emotion, the significance of a subject. It can persuade.

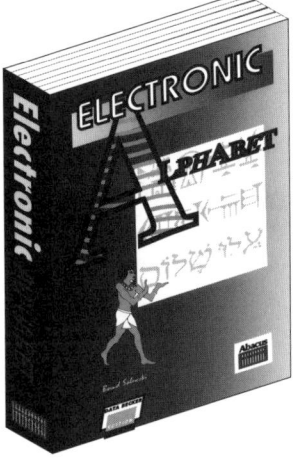

The computer industry gave birth to TrueType fonts, in fact, whole families of fonts. Each as different as fingerprints. Each with its own special font quality. This book helps every communicator understand the history of fonts, their lineage, the "font families", character sets and how they can be used most effectively.

The Electronic Alphabet also explains how to design and create your own fonts by using various programs, such as Fontographer, TypeDesigner, and Corel*Draw!* And if you don't want to design your own, there are numerous sources for fonts, including shareware, which are reviewed in the book.

On the technical side, not scientific, but technical, Windows users will learn how to install and configure fonts in the TrueType, PostScript Type 1, and PCL-V formats. Users will also find tips on solving problems and errors that occur while printing, installing fonts, and deinstalling fonts - some of the realities of working with fonts on computers and with software.

As a special bonus, Electronic Alphabet comes with a companion CD-ROM with over 100 TrueType fonts, a font manager and a font editor. The font manager has several font viewers, a font archiver, and even lets you print out hard copy of all your fonts. Over 300 MB of font software!

Authors: Bernd Salewski
Order Item: #B259
ISBN: 1-55755-259-2
SRP: $29.95 US/ $39.95 CAN with CD-ROM

To order direct call Toll Free 1-800-451-4319

In US and Canada add $5.00 shipping and handling. Foreign orders add $13.00 per item. Michigan residents add 6% sales tax.

Entertainment for All Ages

Stereograms
Create Hidden 3D Illusions

Stereogram is a worldwide phenomena that combines computer technology with cleverness to create spellbinding 3D art and illusions. This book begins with the real story and history behind 3D stereograms which dates back to the 1960's, but only became popular in the '90s. You'll even discover who developed this phenomena as it is seen everywhere today. The book will coach you through the viewing techniques needed to see this special art in your "minds eye".

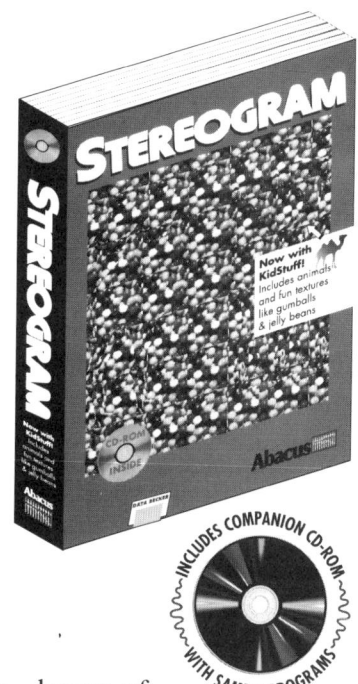

The CD-ROM with this book contains dozens of KidStuff images which can be used to create fun stereograms. Background images of animals like the kangaroo, cheetah and elephant, and foreground textures like gumballs, jelly beans and macaroni & cheese can be combined to create over 100 different stereograms. These completed stereograms can be printed with any Windows-based PC and a printer. Using Windows Paintbrush, the ready-made images can be combined with 48 different templates for calendars, greeting cards, etc. Watch the hidden images "pop out".

Author: UP Vision Computergraphik
Order Item: #B273
ISBN: 1-55755-273-8
Suggested retail price: $29.95 US / $39.95 CAN includes CD-ROM

To order direct call Toll Free 1-800-451-4319

In US and Canada add $5.00 shipping and handling. Foreign orders add $13.00 per item. Michigan residents add 6% sales tax.

**Productivity Series books are for users who want
to become more productive with their PC.**

Excel 5 Complete, Special Edition

Excel 5 Complete is the latest release in our "Complete" user guide series. Our "Complete" books have earned a reputation among end-users as being thorough, informative, and easy to learn from—for beginners through advanced level computer users — and this book is no exception.

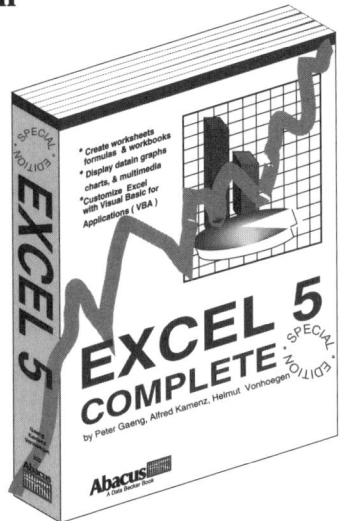

The new version of Microsoft's Excel, version 5, sets new standards in functionality and user-friendliness. **Excel 5 Complete** covers the full functional spectrum of this widely used spreadsheet program, with special emphasis on the new features in version 5.

Beginners and users upgrading from previous versions of Excel will learn from the introductory chapter in which new features, fundamentals, and special aspects of Excel 5 are introduced in an easy-to-understand manner. From there, the user is led, step-by-step, into creating a spreadsheet, the use of the new pivot views, working with formulas, and the diverse opportunities for using data exchange.

A special concentration is on the graphical representation of values in the form of tables or complete presentations (including multimedia). The new database functions are also introduced, as are the fantastic options available with object-oriented data exchange through OLE 2.0 (object linking and embedding).

Other subjects covered include:
- Using macros
- Introduction to VBA programming language (Visual Basic for Applications)
- Example oriented function reference.
- Companion diskettes with all of the example applications from the book

Authors: Peter Gaeng, Alfred Kamenz & Helmut Vonhoegen
Order Item: #B252
ISBN: 1-55755-252-5
Suggested retail price: $34.95 US / $44.95 CAN with companion diskettes

To order direct call Toll Free 1-800-451-4319

In US and Canada add $5.00 shipping and handling. Foreign orders add $13.00 per item. Michigan residents add 6% sales tax.

**Productivity Series books are for users who want
to become more productive with their PC.**

Excel for Science and Technology

transcends all other Excel for Windows books on the market. Microsoft Excel is the premier Windows-based spread-sheets and this book/disk combination focuses on the power of Excel beyond the spreadsheet. This book starts where most leave off. **Excel for Science and Technology** concentrates on the Analysis ToolPak in Excel and the special capabilities built into it for the professional working in science and technology related fields. Whether you need to manipulate data and present the facts for your business, department, or research, **Excel for Science and Technology** will become an invaluable resource.

After a brief overview of Excel 4 spreadsheets, graphics and databases, this book explores these areas:

- Excel Solver and Scenario Manager
- Chemistry-Stoichimetry and the Rule of Alligation Technology-Conversion. Logical Construction Set, Illumination
- Mathematics Functions such as Graphs, Curves, Numerical Integration Drawing and Tables
- Physics and Excel- the collection of formulas, Oscillations and Waves, Animated Diagrams and Circular Paths
- Statistics and Social Sciences-Gathering Empirical Data, Deductive Statistics, Database Statistics, Correlation and Linear Regression
- Ecology-Growth and decline, Population Dynamics, meaningfulness of Ecological Models

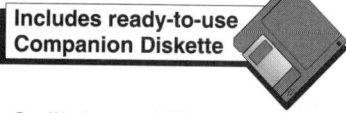

Includes ready-to-use Companion Diskette

Like the book, the companion disk with **Excel for Science and Technology** is practical. You'll be able to immediatley apply what you learn with the macros and worksheets on the disk, which is related to the special powers of Excel covered in the book. This makes **Excel for Science and Technology** more than a book; now it's an indispensable professional work tool.

Author: Peter Gaeng
Order Item: #B196
ISBN 1-55755-196-0
Suggested retail price: $34.95 US/ $44.95 with companion diskette

To order direct call Toll Free 1-800-451-4319

In US and Canada add $5.00 shipping and handling. Foreign orders add $13.00 per item.
Michigan residents add 6% sales tax.

Readme File for PKZip, LHArc & Co.

Companion Disk

Readme File for **PKZip, LHArc & Co.** Companion Disk from Abacus (C) 1995

Congratulations on your purchase of **PKZip, LHArc & Co**. The INSTALL.EXE program will create a directory titled PACKDISK. This is the main directory for the contents of this companion disk.

To install this companion diskette, place it into your 3 1/2" drive A.

Type a:INSTALL press <ENTER>

The install program will ask you for a source drive and a destination drive. Follow the instructions on the screen. The INSTALL program creates a PACKDISK directory, then creates subdirectories, into which the programs are inserted.

The following directories will be created in the PACKDISK directory:
ARJ241, BAT, LH-ICE, LHA213, LZ-EXE, PKLIT103, PKZ204G, and WINZIP55.

Please, before you attempt to use any of these shareware products read the documentation files that accompany them.

Shareware is copyrighted and the author asks for payment if you use it. You may try out the program for a limited time, typically 10 to 30 days, and then decide whether you want to keep it. If you continue to use it, you are requested to send the author a nominal fee. Shareware benefits both the user and the author as it allows prices to remain low by avoiding distribution, packaging, and advertising costs. You may contact Abacus Technical Staff on CompuServe Information Service by typing 'Go Abacus' at any prompt.

We have also included WINZIP55.EXE on this companion disk. This is courtesy NICO MAK COMPUTING INC. Copyright 1991-1994. You MUST install WINZIP 5.5 from WINDOWS with the **Run... File** command from your Program Manager. PLEASE, read the instructions provided by NICO MAK COMPUTING, INC.

Abacus
5370 52nd Street SE
Grand Rapids, MI. 49512
Fax: 1-616-698-0325